D1247229

DANTE GABRIEL ROSSETTI

GARLAND REFERENCE LIBRARY
OF THE HUMANITIES
(VOL. 286)

DANTE GABRIEL ROSSETTI
An Annotated Bibliography

Francis L. Fennell

GARLAND PUBLISHING, INC. • NEW YORK & LONDON
1982

Library of Congress Cataloging in Publication Data

Fennell, Francis L.
  Dante Gabriel Rossetti, an annotated bibliography.

  (Garland reference library of the humanities ;
v. 286)
  Includes index.
  1. Rossetti, Dante Gabriel, 1828–1882—Bibliography.
I. Title. II. Series.
Z8759.8.F45 [PR5246]   016.7592   80-9034
ISBN 0-8240-9327-5   AACR2

Printed on acid-free, 250-year-life paper
Manufactured in the United States of America

In Memoriam Charles W. Hart

CONTENTS

PREFACE

The past two decades have seen a remarkable revival of interest in the Pre-Raphaelites and their work. Rossetti, as the leading figure among them, has been the chief beneficiary of this renewed interest. The publication of both primary and secondary material has grown steadily, to the point where someone first exploring Rossetti's work may be overwhelmed at the task of deciding where even to begin.

This book, an annotated bibliography of Rossetti, aims at making that task easier. The most important earlier Rossetti bibliography is contained in various sections of William E. Fredeman's *Pre-Raphaelitism: A Bibliocritical Study* (Cambridge, Mass.: Harvard University Press, 1965). Although *Pre-Raphaelitism* is an excellent resource, it is now almost twenty years old (its cutoff date is 1962), has substantive annotations for only about a third of its entries, and usually restricts what annotations it does have to a descriptive phrase or a very brief quotation. The sections on the Pre-Raphaelites in the two editions of Frederic Faverty's *The Victorian Poets: A Guide to Research* (Cambridge, Mass.: Harvard University Press, 1956, 1968), later updated in the pages of *Victorian Poetry*, offer cogent discussions of the material but are selective and emphasize Rossetti's literary work. The need now is for a single work which is current, which covers both literature and art, and which tells the prospective student what he or she can expect to find in each relevant item.

The goal of this book is to offer a bibliographical tool useful to as wide an audience as possible: undergraduates, graduate students, doctoral candidates, scholars in both literature and the fine arts, and the interested general public. Some will need it only for quick reference. For example, the undergraduate student who has been assigned a term paper on "Jenny" can use the Table of Contents and turn immediately to pp. 124–126, finding there summaries of the articles which discuss that poem together with cross-references to other important sources of information. The annotations allow the student to decide which works must be consulted and which ones are likely to be peripheral to his or her special focus. Others, doctoral candidates for example, may need to use the whole book to get an overview of Rossetti scholarship. Such a student might find the topical index (pp. 279–282) and the list of dissertations (pp. 253–260) particularly useful in compiling a reading list appropriate for his or her research interest.

The present work includes an annotated bibliography of material published from the time of Rossetti's death in April of 1882 up to January 1, 1980. The reader should note what has and what has not been included.

Excluded from this bibliography are comments published on Rossetti during his lifetime, because such material has been fully documented in Fredeman's *Pre-Raphaelitism*, a widely available reference, and in S.N. Ghose's *Dante Gabriel Rossetti and Contemporary Criticism (1849–1882)* (Dijon: Imprimerie Darantiere, 1929), recently reprinted. Also excluded are casual references, routine obituary notices, encyclopedia entries, exhibition listings, and reviews of secondary sources except for important review essays such as item 472. Very short (one-or-two paragraph) discussions have also been eliminated unless they offer interesting material not easily available elsewhere (e.g., item 296).

Some selectivity has been desirable in the sections on the source materials. The principles for selection are explained in the prefatory comments to the appropriate sections—see, for example, p. 9 or p. 10. It should be added that it was not feasible to include in the "Biographical Studies" section all of the many biographical works published about Rossetti's friends and associates, even when those works commented on Rossetti. Nevertheless, a generous sampling of those works is provided, and no work was excluded whose relevant contents are not available in other, cited sources.

Within these limits I have made every effort to identify and describe all items which make a significant comment on Rossetti as poet, artist, or personality. I have tried to bear in mind the needs of the typical users described above: what does the user need to know about what has been said about Rossetti?

All items in the bibliography are annotated, with the following exceptions: items in languages other than English, French, German, Italian, or Spanish; items which the compiler was unable to consult; dissertations, which are given a separate listing. Entries falling into either of the first two categories are clearly labelled and amount to less than 5% of the whole. The annotations are descriptive rather than critical, although occasionally it has been necessary to enter a short *caveat* about spurious works or dubious claims (see, for example, item 250). In framing these annotations I have tried to keep in mind that not all readers are Rossetti specialists. Nevertheless, certain names and biographical facts—e.g., Lizzie Siddal, Janey Morris, Rossetti's attempted suicide—recur so often that they cannot be explained afresh each time. The beginning student of Rossetti should therefore consult first the brief Rossetti chronology which follows this preface, because the annotations will presume a familiarity with these names and events. If necessary the reader can then obtain further information on these people and events by consulting such sources as the *Dictionary of National Biography*. This beginning reader will also be aided by the fact that all journal titles are given in full.

The principal research tools in compiling this work include *Art Index*, *Dissertation Abstracts [International]*, the annual bibliographies in *PMLA*, and the annual Victorian bibliographies published first by *Modern Philology* and then by *Victorian Studies*. For the earlier periods I am indebted to the *New Cambridge Bibliography of English Literature*, Ehrsam, Deily, and Smith's *Bibliographies of Twelve Victorian Authors* (New York: Wilson, 1936), and Fredeman's *Pre-Raphaelitism*. Computer checks on dissertations and accessed journal articles have been helpful. I have also added new items not included in other sources.

The bibliography is organized into nine major sections, as follows: Bibliographies; Source Materials for Literary Works; Source Materials for Artistic Works; Letters; Biographical Studies; Studies of Rossetti as a Writer; Studies of Rossetti as an Artist; Studies of Rossetti as a Poet-Painter; Dissertations. The second, third, sixth, and seventh sections contain subdivisions as shown in the Table of Contents. As noted earlier, readers should consult the appropriate headnotes to each section or subdivision in order to determine what they can expect to find in that section or subdivision.

Within each section or subdivision the arrangement is chronological, from April 1882 to January 1980, although within a given year the arrangement is alphabetical. This chronological arrangement has the advantage of giving readers some sense of the trends in Rossetti scholarship during the last century. Those readers who require alphabetical access can use the index.

Many items in this bibliography would of course be eligible for inclusion in two or more sections. Benson's *Rossetti* (item 357), for example: it is partly biographical, partly critical, and has claim on both the fifth and sixth sections. In these cases I have chosen what seems to be the most appropriate category and then cross-referenced the item at the end of the other possible category or categories. Source studies of individual works, for example, are included in the sections on those works, but they are also cross-referenced at the end of the sections on relationships with other poets or painters. Additional cross-references within the annotations themselves try to tie together those items which comment on each other or which deal with the same topic.

Three preferences deserve mention here: (1) when an article appeared in a journal and then later as a monograph or book, I have entered the monograph or book, but the annotation will list the journal of origin and date; (2) when two editions of the same work have been published, I have generally listed the later edition unless it was notably less substantial than the first; (3) when a doctoral dissertation was later published, I have given it two separate entries, once as a monograph or book and again as a separate publication among the dissertations. This last step deserves a word of explanation. On the one hand it seems desirable to preserve the principle of no work being cited more than once. Sometimes the difference between dissertation and published work is negligible, especially in the case of some European dissertations, and it seems forced to treat them as separate works. On the other hand, many dissertations are revised quite substantially before they are published, and for them the "non-repetition" principle makes little sense. The deciding factor was the immense convenience for the reader of having all dissertations listed together. In this case it seems that convenience for the user ought to take precedence over consistency.

A word about the index. The listing includes all names in both the citations and the annotations. Individual works by Rossetti are not listed because the user will note from the Table of Contents that he or she can proceed directly to either the "Criticism of Individual Literary Works," divided into six parts, or the "Criticism of Individual Artistic Works." The cross-references at the ends of these sections will point to more general works which contain substantial comments on particular works. (These cross-references are based on mention of the work in an annotation, and the annotation in turn tries to refer to all works discussed extensively in the cited item.) Readers should note that index references are to item numbers rather than to page numbers.

I must add a word of thanks to the many people who have been so generous in helping me bring this project to completion. Arthur Livingston gave valuable research assistance at an early stage. Dr. Thomas Bennett, Director of Research Services for Loyola University of Chicago, provided travel money, a typing grant, and other material help. Sister Bonaventure of the Loyola University Library was diligent in securing interlibrary loans. Mr. Robert Neagle compiled a major part of the index. Ms. Linda Condon typed the manuscript with care and dispatch. The staffs of the libraries at the following institutions also gave their assistance: Art Institute of Chicago; Chicago Public Library; Delaware Art Museum; Duke University; Field Museum; Indiana University; Library of Congress; Mundelein College; Newberry Library; Northwestern University; Southern Illinois University; University of Chicago; University of Wisconsin, Madison. Special thanks to the Committee on Faculty Appointments of Loyola University of Chicago, which granted me a semester's leave of absence in the spring of 1980 so that I could finish the research on this book.

And for Kay, Monica, Claire, and Mark I can only offer—as always—much much more than thanks.

Evanston, Illinois
December 1980

A ROSSETTI CHRONOLOGY

1828   Born Gabriel Charles Dante Rossetti, 12 May 1828. Second child and first son of Gabriele Rossetti, an exiled Italian patriot and Dante scholar, and Frances Polidori Rossetti, a former governess. Siblings were: Maria, b. 1827; William Michael, b. 1829; Christina, b. 1830.

ca. 1836–41   Attendance at "Mr. Paul's" school and King's College School.

ca. 1841–45   Attendance at Sass's School for young artists.

ca. 1845–48   Attendance at Antique School of the Royal Academy; by 1847 poetry was at least a very large avocation—first versions of "The Blessed Damozel" and "My Sister's Sleep," for example.

1848   Apprenticeship in the studio of Ford Madox Brown, exposure to the German Nazarean painters. Formation of the Pre-Raphaelite Brotherhood, with William Holman Hunt, John Everett Millais, James Collinson, Frederick G. Stephens, Thomas Woolner, and his brother.

1849   Continental tour; founding of *The Germ*, literary organ of the Pre-Raphaelite Brotherhood.

ca. 1850–52   Attacks on the P.R.B. and a successful defense of it by John Ruskin and others; first meeting with Elizabeth Siddal.

1857   "Jovial Campaign" at Oxford, decorating the Union murals, with new acquaintances William Morris and Edward Burne-Jones—thus beginning the "second generation" of Pre-Raphaelites. Publication of the Moxon Tennyson.

1860   Marriage to Elizabeth (Lizzie) Siddal, 23 May. Increasing

	friendship with Algernon Charles Swinburne, fellow poet.
1861	Publication of *The Early Italian Poets*, translations.
1862	Death of Lizzie Siddal Rossetti, 10 February—accident or suicide? Manuscript of poems buried in her coffin.
ca. 1863	Residence at 16 Cheyne Walk, Chelsea (Tudor House). Fanny Cornforth installed as "housekeeper," Swinburne and George Meredith are co-tenants.
ca. 1865	Increasing fame and affluence from oil paintings.
ca. 1868	Resumption of interest in Janey Morris, whom Rossetti first met at Oxford a decade before and who had married William Morris. Serious affair begins? Also friendships with William Allingham, Charles Augustus Howell, Henry Treffry Dunn (Rossetti's art assistant), Thomas Gordon Hake, Frederic Shields, Frederick Sandys, William Stillman, James McNeill Whistler, and Theodore Watts[-Dunton]. Resumes writing poetry.
1869	Health begins to decline; stays at Penkill Castle with Alice Boyd and William Bell Scott, during which time his poetry manuscripts are exhumed.
1870	Publication of *Poems*, April.
1871	Joint tenancy (with William Morris) of Kelmscott Manor. Attack by Robert Buchanan in *Contemporary Review*, "The Fleshly School of Poetry: Mr. D.G. Rossetti," October.
1872	Attempted suicide and general nervous collapse, June; recovery is gradual and only partial.
1874	Leaves Kelmscott—permanent return (except for vacations) to 16 Cheyne Walk.
ca. 1875–80	Decline in physical and artistic strength. Addiction to chloral hydrate increases. Friendships with Philip Bourke Marston, Arthur O'Shaughnessy, and others.
1881	Publication of *Ballads and Sonnets* and a new edition of *Poems*; friendship with Hall Caine.
1882	Removal, for health reasons, to Westcliff Bungalow, Birchington-on-Sea, in February; death on Easter Sunday, 9 April.

Bibliographies

1. Rossetti, William Michael. *Bibliography of the Works of Dante Gabriel Rossetti*. London: Ellis, 1905. 53 pp.

   Contains mostly a listing of primary materials, with full descriptions of fifty-four items plus notes on letters, illustrations, and translations. First published serially in *The Bibliographer* (1902), supplemented in the same journal by W.F. Prideaux's "Additions to the Bibliography of the Works of Dante Gabriel Rossetti" (1902). Reprinted 1979.

2. Rossetti, William Michael. *Dante Gabriel Rossetti: Classified Lists of His Writings with Dates*. London: privately printed, 1906. 48 pp.

   Offers four useful lists: one of the works published in the 1886 edition of the *Collected Works*; one of the published work not included in the 1886 edition; one of the works listed alphabetically; and one of the works listed chronologically.

3. [Boyle, J.R.] *A Brief Account of the English Pre-Raphaelites*. New York: Dodd, Mead, 1906. 10 pp.

   A five-page summary of the history of Pre-Raphaelitism is used to introduce an annotated list of books on Pre-Raphaelitism and on early Italian art available from the publisher.

4. Vaughan, Charles E. *Bibliographies of Swinburne, Morris, and Rossetti*. [Oxford: Clarendon Press], 1914. 12 pp.

   The small section on Rossetti (pp. 11-12) lists nineteen books, either works by Rossetti or translations of his work. Reprinted 1979.

5. Ghose, S.N. *Dante Gabriel Rossetti and Contemporary Criticism (1849-1882)*. Dijon: Imprimerie Darantiere, 1929. 244 pp.

   Contains a bibliography of and excerpts from Victorian criticisms of Rossetti's poetry and painting. Divided into four parts: the early P.R.B. years (1849-1852), the public acceptance of Pre-Raphaelitism (1853-1862), the period of indifference (1863-1871), and the years of controversy and acclaim (1872-1882). Some French criticism is also included. Each item begins with an introductory comment by the author, and some criticisms are only summarized and not excerpted. Reprinted 1978.

6. Ehrsam, Theodore, Robert Deily, and Robert Smith. "Dante Gabriel Rossetti." *Bibliographies of Twelve Victorian Authors*. New York: Wilson, 1936, pp. 202-225.

   Offers two sections: one bibliographical, emphasizing primary materials, and one biographical-critical. Each section is arranged alphabetically by author or editor. This compilation is the most comprehensive one available up to its cut-off date (July 1934). Added to by item 7.

7. Fucilla, Joseph G. "Bibliographies of Twelve Victorian Authors: A Supplement." *Modern Philology* 37 (1939): 89-96.

   Adds items, including some on Rossetti, omitted from Ehrsam, Deily, and Smith (see item 6).

8. Templeman, William D., ed. *Bibliographies of Studies in Victorian Literature for the Thirteen Years, 1932-1944*. Urbana: University of Illinois Press, 1945. 450 pp.

   Reprints in convenient hardcover form the annual bibliographies which had appeared in the May issues of *Modern Philology* for the years indicated.

9. Jones, Howard Mumford. "The Pre-Raphaelites." *The Victorian Poets: A Guide to Research*. Edited by F. Faverty. Cambridge, Mass.: Harvard University Press, 1956, pp. 161-195.

   Surveys scholarship on Rossetti and his associates up to the mid-1950's. The scholarship is evaluated and *desiderata* are listed. Jones emphasizes the need to see Rossetti as a craftsman, the poet who insisted on "fundamental brainwork."

10. Wright, Austin, ed. *Bibliographies of Studies in Victorian Literature for the Ten Years 1945-1954*. Urbana: University of Illinois Press, 1956. 310 pp.

    Reprints in convenient hardcover form the annual Victorian bibliographies of *Modern Philology*; a continuation of item 8.

11. Fredeman, William E. *Pre-Raphaelitism: A Biblio-critical Study*. Cambridge, Mass.: Harvard University Press, 1965. 327 pp.

    Intends to be "a critical reference guide to the whole

subject of Pre-Raphaelitism." This is the most complete
catalog of Pre-Raphaelite materials yet assembled. It
includes both primary and secondary sources related to
Rossetti and his circle. The largest section (pp. 90-
132) is devoted to Rossetti; this section is in turn
divided into thirteen subsections dealing with such topics
as "Works," "Letters," and "Selected Reviews." Other
sections are concerned with Pre-Raphaelitism in general,
with the publication of *The Germ*, and with other matters
of interest to students of Rossetti. The arrangement
within each section is chronological, and the cut-off
date is 1962.

12. Slack, Robert C., ed. *Bibliographies of Studies in Vic-
    torian Literature for the Ten Years 1955-1964*. Urbana:
    University of Illinois Press, 1967. 461 pp.

    Reprints in convenient hardcover form the annual Vic-
    torian bibliographies which appeared in *Modern Philology*
    and then, from 1958 on, in *Victorian Studies*. A contin-
    uation of items 8 and 10.

13. Fredeman, William E. "The Pre-Raphaelites." *The Vic-
    torian Poets: A Guide to Research*. Second Edition.
    Edited by F. Faverty. Cambridge, Mass.: Harvard Uni-
    versity Press, 1968, pp. 251-316.

    Surveys recent scholarship, with emphasis on the decade
    since Howard Mumford Jones first essayed the task (see
    item 9). The author suggests general trends in the
    scholarship, such as the fact that Rossetti's ideas get
    more treatment than his technique, and points out *desider-
    ata*, such as a critical edition of the poetry.

14. Fredeman, William E. "Dante Gabriel Rossetti." *New
    Cambridge Bibliography of English Literature*. Vol. 3.
    Edited by G. Watson. Cambridge University Press,
    1969, pp. 490, 494.

    Contains lists of primary and secondary material, in
    handy reference-book form. This list supersedes the one
    by G.A. Brown in the old *CBEL*.

15. Fredeman, William E. "The Pre-Raphaelites." *Victorian
    Poetry* 12 (Spring Supplement 1974): 77-99.

    Continues the work of item 13 by surveying and evaluat-
    ing the scholarship up to the conclusion of 1972.

16.   Life, Allan R. "The Pre-Raphaelites." *Victorian Poetry*
      15 (1977): 265-273.

      Updates the survey of recent scholarship undertaken by
      Fredeman (item 15).

17.   Life, Allan R. "The Pre-Raphaelites." *Victorian Poetry*
      16 (1978): 246-252.

      Surveys selected items on Rossetti and his associates,
      mostly from the year 1977. A continuation of item 17.

18.   Life, Allan R. "The Pre-Raphaelites." *Victorian Poetry*
      17 (1979): 238-245.

      Surveys selected items on Rossetti and his associates,
      mostly from the year 1978. A continuation of items 16
      and 17.

See also items 65, 157, and 341.

Source Material
for Literary Works

This section lists only the four books published during Rossetti's lifetime. It excludes trial books, privately printed works, and items published in magazines or journals. For a complete listing of these other materials, see item 11 (section 23).

19. *The Early Italian Poets from Ciullo d' Alcamo to Dante Alighieri: (1100-1200-1300) in the Original Metres, Together with Dante's Vita Nuova.* London: Smith, Elder, 1861. 464 pp.

 Divided into two parts: poets chiefly before Dante, and Dante and his circle. In his preface Rossetti announces that "literality of rendering is altogether secondary" --the purpose is to transmit beauty, and if the translator accomplishes this task he has succeeded. Rossetti also alludes to the limited subject matter and the obscurity of these Italian poets; both charges were later to be placed against his own poetry. The translations themselves are of forty-four separate poets in Part One, each being represented by an average of two or three poems, and thirteen poets in Part Two, with Dante, Guido Cavalcanti, and Cecco Angiolieri having the largest share at fifteen or more poems each. Revised and retitled 1874.

20. *Poems.* London: Ellis, 1870. 282 pp.

 Rossetti's first major appearance as a poet in his own right, an appearance made possible by the exhumation of his manuscripts from Lizzie Siddal's coffin (see item 256). The volume contains fifty sonnets for the proposed *House of Life* sequence, including "Nuptial Sleep," the poem which was to figure so largely in the "Fleshly School" controversy and to be suppressed in the 1881 edition. *Poems* was followed quickly by American (Roberts) and German (Tauchnitz) editions.

21. *Ballads and Sonnets.* London: Ellis, 1881. 335 pp.

 Contains three new ballads ("Rose Mary," "The White Ship," "The King's Tragedy"), fourteen lyrics, twenty-five sonnets, and the complete text of *The House of Life.* See item 1 for a complete history of the compilation of this volume.

22. *Poems. A New Edition.* London: Ellis, 1881. 294 pp.

   This volume contains most of the poems first seen in
   item 20, except that the *House of Life* has been removed
   (see item 21) and a few sonnets have been eliminated.
   Four new poems and three new translations are added; of
   these, only "The Bride's Prelude" is significant.

SECTION B: IMPORTANT LATER EDITIONS

Included in this section are the most complete edition of
Rossetti's literary works (item 26), special scholarly editions
of selected poems, editions of unpublished works, editions for
the general market, and anthologies which contain large and
representative selections from Rossetti's works. Editions and
collections of lesser importance can be found listed in item
11 (section 23).

23. *Lenore by Gottfried August Bürger.* Translated from the
       German by Dante Gabriel Rossetti. London: Ellis and
       Elevey, 1900. 35pp.

   Rossetti's translation, done at age sixteen, emphasizes
   the romantic side of this grisly tale. The circumstances
   surrounding the translation are described by William
   Michael Rossetti in a preface.

24. Rossetti, William Michael, ed. *The Germ ... Being a*
       Facsimile Reprint of the Literary Organ of the Pre-
       Raphaelite Brotherhood, Published in 1850. London:
       Stock, 1901. 192 pp.

   Contains, besides the facsimile, a thirty-page introduction by the editor in which *The Germ* is seen as "a
   most decided failure." Some reviews from 1850 are reprinted and the editor comments on individual contributions, including Dante Gabriel's.

25. *Hartmann von Aue. Henry the Leper (Der Arme Heinrich).*
       Paraphrased by Dante Gabriel Rossetti. With an intro-
       duction by William P. Trent. 2 vols. Boston: The
       Bibliophile Society, 1905. 65 pp.

   Volume One contains a facsimile of Rossetti's translation, done at age sixteen or seventeen and improved upon
   later. Volume Two offers a typescript plus notes.

26. *The Works of Dante Gabriel Rossetti*. Edited with Preface
    and Notes by William Michael Rossetti. Revised and
    Enlarged Edition. London: Ellis, 1911. 684 pp.

    Still the most complete edition of Rossetti's poetry
    and prose. Includes some works, especially juvenilia,
    not printed in the editor's earlier editions (1886,
    1891, 1899-1901, 1904), as well as the editor's chronol-
    ogy of Rossetti's writings and extensive notes. There
    are still lacunae--see items 32, 46, 47, 53, 57, 59, 60,
    511, 517, 640.

27. *Rossetti: Poems and Translations 1850-1870*. London:
    Oxford University Press, 1913. 482 pp.

    This volume forms part of the Oxford Standard Authors
    series and is therefore probably the most widely avail-
    able edition of Rossetti's poetry. The obvious limitation
    is the absence of any poetry written after 1870. The
    text of items 19 and 20 is accompanied by "Hand and Soul"
    and three poems from *The Germ*, but no critical apparatus
    is included.

28. *The House of Life: A Sonnet-Sequence by Dante Gabriel
    Rossetti*. With an Introduction and Notes by Paull F.
    Baum. Cambridge, Mass.: Harvard University Press,
    1928. 242 pp.

    Contains extensive notes, a full introduction, and ac-
    curate texts, but no variant readings. The editor pro-
    poses a thematic order for the sequence: first Love in
    opposition to Insomnia and Remorse, then Change turning
    into Fate. He also discusses the autobiographical con-
    text and the poet's strengths and weaknesses ("His gift
    is music, not brains.").

29. *Dante Gabriel Rossetti: The Blessed Damozel. The
    Unpublished Manuscript, Texts and Collation*. With an
    Introduction by Paull F. Baum. Chapel Hill: Univer-
    sity of North Carolina Press, 1937. 30 pp.

    Reprints four versions of the poem: the final rendering
    of 1881, and earlier versions from the 1847 manuscript,
    The Germ, and *The Oxford and Cambridge Magazine*. In his
    introduction the editor discusses the history of the poem
    and its variant readings--but see items 493, 500, and 501.
    Information on sources, characteristics, and critical
    reception is also provided.

30. *Dante Gabriel Rossetti: Poems, Ballads, and Sonnets.*
     Selections from the Posthumous Poems and from His
     Translations. Hand and Soul. Edited by Paull F. Baum.
     New York: Doubleday Doran, 1937. 399 pp.

     The best Rossetti anthology, although avowedly "not an
     edition for scholars." *Poems* and *Ballads and Sonnets* are
     reprinted as they were published by Rossetti in 1881, i.e.
     without the rearrangements made later by William Michael
     Rossetti. The notes are both factual and interpretive.
     The introduction sees Rossetti's poetry as subtle, orig-
     inal, lyrical; Rossetti's ornateness, however, can verge
     on the grotesque and his intensity can cloy.

31. *Rossetti's "Sister Helen."* Edited by Janet C. Troxell.
     New Haven: Yale University Press, 1939. 95 pp.

     Traces the ballad from its first appearance in the
     Düsseldorf Artists' Album (1854) to the final *Poems*
     (1881). The editor collates all versions of the poem,
     both published and unpublished, thus establishing a
     definitive text and showing Rossetti's constant and
     careful revision of the work.

32. *Dante Gabriel Rossetti: Jan Van Hunks.* Edited from the
     Original Manuscripts by John Robert Wahl. New York:
     New York Public Library, 1952. 97 pp.

     Offers a definitive text, with variants, of the poem
     about a Dutchman's smoking contest with the devil. The
     ballad was begun in 1847 and finished during Rossetti's
     final illness at Birchington-on-Sea. See items 508 and
     509, plus a note by William E. Fredeman in *TLS*, 19 May
     1961, p. 309.

33. *The Kelmscott Love Sonnets of Dante Gabriel Rossetti.*
     Edited with an Introductory Essay by John Robert Wahl.
     Camptown: A.H. Balkema, 1954. 40 pp.

     Publishes thirty-one sonnets plus textual notes. These
     sonnets were written by Rossetti at Kelmscott, mostly
     during the summer of 1871, when he was alone with Jane
     Morris. The editor believes many of these sonnets were
     altered before publication in 1881 in order to make them
     seem to be about Lizzie Siddal rather than about their
     true subject.

34. *Dante Gabriel Rossetti: Poems*. Edited with an Intro-
      duction and Notes by Oswald Doughty. London: Dent,
      1957. 328 pp.

      Offers the best accessible modern collection of Ros-
      setti's poetry. The entries are arranged so as "to show
      the method and sequence of their [original] publication."
      The edition is fairly comprehensive but contains no
      variant readings and no critical or textual notes.

35. Buckley, Jerome H., and George B. Woods, eds. "Dante
      Gabriel Rossetti." *Poetry of the Victorian Period*.
      3rd edition. Chicago: Scott Foresman, 1965, pp. 505-
      561.

      This volume contains the most extensive selection from
      Rossetti of any of the standard Victorian period anthol-
      ogies: forty-two poems plus *The House of Life* complete.

36. Marshall, William H., ed. "Dante Gabriel Rossetti (1828-
      1882)." *The Major Victorian Poets*. New York: Washing-
      ton Square Press, 1966, pp. 495-622.

      The next most comprehensive period anthology after item
      35: sixteen poems plus *The House of Life* complete.

37. Merritt, James D., ed. "Dante Gabriel Rossetti." *The
      Pre-Raphaelite Poem*. New York: Dutton, 1966, pp. 33-70.

      Among the seventeen poets represented in this anthology,
      Rossetti occupies the leading place with twenty-five
      selections from his work. No annotation. The intro-
      duction defines Pre-Raphaelite poetry as works marked by
      descriptive detail, sensuous imagery, obscure symbolism,
      morbid subject matter, medievalism, and a ballad-like
      tone.

38. Buckley, Jerome H., ed. "Dante Gabriel Rossetti." *The
      Pre-Raphaelites*. New York: Modern Library, 1968,
      pp. 3-196.

      Contains the most generous sampling of Rossetti's work
      among the three anthologies devoted to the Pre-Raphaelites
      (see items 37 and 39): *The House of Life* complete, forty-
      three other poems, and "Hand and Soul." Rossetti's
      interest is said to be the "psychology of moods."

39. Lang, C.Y., ed. "Dante Gabriel Rossetti." *The Pre-Raphaelites and Their Circle*. Boston: Houghton Mifflin, 1968, pp. 1-129.

     Contains eighteen poems by Rossetti plus *The House of Life* complete. The editor includes some notes, and in his introduction he praises Rossetti for "intellectual subtlety" and the creation of "symbolic atmosphere."

40. Milano, Paolo, ed. *The Portable Dante*. New York: Viking, 1969. 662 pp.

     This volume offers the most accessible text of Rossetti's translation of the *Vita Nuova*, which is reprinted here on pp. 547-618.

41. Hosmon, Robert S., ed. *The Germ: A Pre-Raphaelite Little Magazine*. Miami: University of Miami Press, 1970. 278 pp.

     A reprint of the literary organ of the P.R.B. as printed in four numbers, January-April 1850. [Note: reviewers pointed out deficiencies in this volume; it does not entirely replace item 24, which it largely reprints.]

42. Stanford, Derek, ed. *Pre-Raphaelite Writing: An Anthology* London: Dent, 1973. 207 pp.

     Collects numerous items written by and about the P.R.B., including Rossetti. Both phases of the movement are represented by articles, diaries, letters, stories, newspaper and journal reviews, parodies, selections from *The Germ* and *The Oxford and Cambridge Magazine*. In addition to his contributions in these categories, Rossetti is also represented in a short anthology of Pre-Raphaelite poetry.

See also items 61, 354, 455, 1063.

SECTION C: DESCRIPTIONS OF MANUSCRIPTS AND ADDITIONS TO CANON

This section includes articles and books which describe the manuscript holdings either of individuals or of institutions. Studies of the manuscripts themselves, e.g. textual studies, will be found in the section dealing with individual works. Also included here are books and articles which propose additions to the canon of Rossetti's literary works.

43. Rossetti, William Michael. "Some Scraps of Verse and
    Prose by Dante Gabriel Rossetti." *Pall Mall Magazine*
    16 (1898): 480-496.

    Prints some little pieces which William Michael had
    deliberately omitted from the collected works but which
    now can appear. Although minor, they are not judged to
    be inferior work. Included are an earlier version of
    "Ave," "Sacrament Hymn," "The English Revolution of 1848,"
    poems on Shakespeare and Blake, poems derived from travel
    abroad, some *bout-rimes* sonnets, and an unfinished tale
    entitled "Deuced Odd." Included later in item 26.

44. Smith, Harry Bache. "Dante Gabriel Rossetti." *A Senti-
    mental Library*. [London]: privately printed, 1914,
    pp. 157-163.

    Describes seventeen items from Smith's private collec-
    tion of rare material associated with Rossetti. Included
    are the original manuscript of "William and Mary" and
    Rossetti's copy of Main's *Treasury of English Sonnets* in
    which the poet had marked his favorites.

45. Wise, Thomas James. "Rossetti (Charles Dante Gabriel)."
    The Ashley Library: A Catalogue. Vol. 4. London:
    privately printed, 1923, pp. 108-160.

    Contains a summary of the materials relating to Rossetti
    which had been collected by the eminent bibliographer--
    and forger--T.J. Wise; the text is accompanied by good
    reproductions of manuscripts, proofs, and title pages.
    As with all Wise matters, this book must be used in con-
    junction with Carter and Pollard's exposé (item 49).

46. Wallerstein, Ruth C. "The Bancroft Manuscripts of Ros-
    setti's Sonnets." *Modern Language Notes* 44 (1929):
    279-284.

    Describes the manuscripts of fifteen sonnets in the
    Bancroft Collection at the Delaware Art Museum and gives
    variant readings. The texts of two hitherto unpublished
    sonnets are also provided. But see item 50.

47. Baum, Paull Franklin, ed. *Dante Gabriel Rossetti: An
    Analytical List of Manuscripts in the Duke University
    Library, with Hitherto Unpublished Verse and Prose*.
    Durham, N.C.: Duke University Press, 1931. 122 pp.

    Contains exactly what the lengthy title promises: an

analytical list of material in the Duke collections and
reproductions of selected items from that material. Principal among the latter are twelve unpublished sonnets, a
variant of "To Mary in Summer," and notes for "God's Graal"
and other poems. See also items 48 and 509. Reprinted
1979.

48. Winwar, Frances. "Dante Gabriel's or William Michael's?
     An Attempt to Establish the Authorship of Some of
     Rossetti's Sonnets." *Publications of the Modern Lang-
     uage Association* 48 (1933): 312-315.

     Contends that two poems described by Baum as "unpub-
     lished" (item 47) had in fact appeared before, and that
     nine others were really by William Michael and should
     therefore be deleted from Rossetti's canon.

49. Carter, John, and Graham Pollard. "Dante Gabriel Rossetti.
     *An Enquiry into the Nature of Certain Nineteenth Century
     Pamphlets*. London: Constable, 1934, pp. 213-221.

     Indicts two forgeries perpetrated by T.J. Wise: an edi-
     tion of *Sister Helen* supposedly printed in 1857, and an
     edition of *Verses* supposedly printed in 1881.

50. Baum, Paull F. "The Bancroft Manuscripts of Dante Gabriel
     Rossetti." *Modern Philology* 39 (1941): 47-68.

     Describes in greater detail than Wallerstein (item 46)
     the Rossetti manuscripts in the Bancroft Collection of
     the Delaware Art Museum. Variant readings are given for
     thirty-two poems and several fragments, all but two of
     which were written after the publication of *Poems* 1870.

51. Metzdorf, Robert, compiler. "Rossetti, Dante Gabriel."
     *The Tinker Library: A Bibliographical Catalogue of the
     Books and Manuscripts Collected by Chauncey Brewster
     Tinker*. New Haven: Yale University Press, 1959, pp.
     364-369.

     Lists thirty items in Tinker's possession which relate
     to Rossetti, including five manuscripts, four letters,
     and several first editions.

52. Todd, William B. "D.G. Rossetti's *Early Italian Poets,
     1861*." *Book Collector* 9 (1960): 329-331.

     Traces the way in which T.J. Wise secured credentials
     from William Michael Rossetti for a copy of this book,
     now in the Wrenn Collection at the University of Texas.
     See also follow-up note by Simon Nowell Smith, vol. 10.

53. LeBourgeois, John Y. "D.G. Rossetti in the Private Books of Frederick Locker-Lampson and Lady Mount-Temple." *Notes & Queries* 216 (1971): 254-255.

    Prints two short poems not found in Rosseti's collected works from Locker-Lampson's privately printed *Autobiography,* and one selection from "The Blessed Damozel" found in Lady Mount-Temple's *Memorials* of her husband.

54. [Anonymous]. "Recent Acquisitions--Rossetti Manuscripts and Books." *Princeton University Library Chronicle* 33 (1972): 251-252.

    Describes materials added to the Troxell Collection through the donations of Robert Taylor. These include manuscripts, seventeen letters, thirty printed volumes, and other miscellaneous material.

55. Fraser, Robert S. "The Rossetti Collection of Janet Camp Troxell: A Survey with Some Sidelights." *Princeton University Library Chronicle* 33 (1972): 146-175.

    The Curator of Rare Books surveys the Troxell material, which consists of thirteen archival boxes of manuscripts and 227 printed titles. Sixteen proofs and trial books for *Poems* (1870) are described briefly. Letters by Rossetti--257 in all--also form part of the collection and include letters to William Bell Scott, Robert Browning (see item 639), and Charles Augustus Howell; another part consists of ninety-two letters *to* Rossetti. Other items of importance include Rossetti's death mask, two sketches, typescripts, and materials from other Pre-Raphaelites.

56. Troxell, Janet Camp. "Collecting the Rossettis." *Princeton University Library Chronicle* 33 (1972): 142-145.

    Summarizes the author's interest in collecting items from Rossetti's personal history, such as letters to Miss Losh and Howell and letters from Jane Morris, and also items from his career as a poet, such as manuscripts and proof sheets. These acquisitions covered a period of thirty-five years, 1930-1965.

57. Fennell, Francis L. "The Rossetti Collection at the Library of Congress: A Checklist." *Bulletin of Bibliography* 30 (1973): 132-136.

Describes the library's holdings of Rossetti material,
including some unpublished letters and manuscripts.
Variant readings for some of the unpublished poetry are
also included, as well as one new poem complete and portions of a second.

58. Keane, Robert N. "The Rossettis at Princeton." *Manuscripts* 25 (1973): 113-118.

Describes the Troxell gift to Princeton (see items 55
and 56), with special emphasis on Rossetti's trial books
and on his friendship with William Bell Scott.

59. Lindsay, Jack, and William E. Fredeman, eds. "D.G. Rossetti's 'The Death of Topsy.'" *Victorian Poetry* 13
(1975): 177-179.

Prints a hiterto-unpublished one-act playlet by Rossetti.

60. Allentuck, Marcia. "A New Rossetti Prose Critique of
Deverell?" *Papers of the Bibliographical Society of
America* 72 (1978): 235-237.

Argues that the 1851 *Spectator* critique of Deverell was
by D.G. Rossetti, not William Michael as has been supposed.

See also items 11 (sections 2-7, 22, 23), 126, 132, 142, 316,
517, 570.

Source Material
for Artistic Works

SECTION A: COLLECTIONS OF REPRODUCTIONS

This section includes works whose primary purpose is to offer
reproductions of Rossetti's paintings and drawings. In some
cases, such as item 62 or item 64, a work also contains biographical or reference material and could therefore be included
in other sections. It is included here first because one of
its primary purposes is to illustrate Rossetti's achievement
as an artist; it is also cross-referenced in the other appropriate sections.

61. Carrington, FitzRoy, arranger. *Pictures and Poems by
    Dante Gabriel Rossetti*. New York: Russell, 1899. 54 pp.

    Juxtaposes twenty-three paintings and the poems which
    accompany or illustrate them. The book shows the skillful
    interpenetration of the two arts, an achievement which the
    arranger says is Rossetti's chief claim on our interest.

62. Marillier, H[enry] C. *Dante Gabriel Rossetti: An Illus-
    strated Memorial of His Art and Life*. London: Bell,
    1899. 270 pp.

    Combines a summary of Rossetti's life and artistic career
    with analysis and criticism of selected works. Rossetti
    emerges as an attractive, almost lovable genius. Included
    are numerous reproductions of both paintings and sketches,
    accompanied by a chronological listing of all of Rossetti's
    artistic works and their history. A very important early
    reference--but superseded now by item 76. Reprinted 1979.

63. Rossetti, William Michael. *Permanent Photographs after
    the Works of Dante Gabriel Rossetti: With an Explana-
    tory Text*. London: Mansell, 1900. 21 pp.

    An illustrated catalogue of the photographic reproduc-
    tions done by W.A. Mansell & Co., the leading English art
    photographers of the time. Nine oils, three watercolors,
    and seventy-four drawings are included. William Michael
    supplied a one-page introduction and an informational
    descriptive paragraph for each photograph.

64. [Angeli], Helen Rossetti. *The Life and Work of Dante
    Gabriel Rossetti*. London: Virtue, 1902. 32 pp.+

    Contains fifty-five two-color illustrations, mostly by
    Rossetti, many full-page. The accompanying text offers
    a six-part chronological survey of Rossetti's career

as a painter. The works of the final years are judged to
be the richest period in his art, one in which he blended
physical and spiritual beauty. Rossetti's strengths were
simplicity, color, and mysticism; his defect was exagger-
ation. Originally the Easter number of the *Art Journal*;
reprinted 1979.

65. [Woodberry, George E.] "The Works of Rossetti." *Masters
    in Art* 4 (1903): 465-483.

    Has ten full-page plates. Each picture is described in
    detail, and the text is accompanied by large extracts from
    published criticism plus a biographical summary, a list
    of principal paintings, and a bibliography.

66. *Dante Gabriel Rossetti*. London: Newnes, [1905]. 32 pp.+

    Includes fifty-seven plates plus a short biographical
    sketch by Ernest Radford; accompanies item 67.

67. *Drawings of Rossetti*. London: Newnes, [1905]. 27 pp.+

    Includes fifty-six plates which reproduce some of the
    best of Rossetti's drawings. An introductory essay, "The
    Drawings of D.G. Rossetti" by T. Martin Wood, downplays
    the influence of Pre-Raphaelitism. Rossetti is instead
    the potential genius betrayed by weaknesses of insight
    and technique. Dramatic illustration was his forte--the
    simpler the better.

68. *A Few Masterpieces of the Pre-Raphaelite School*. New York:
    Berlin Photographic Company, [1905].

    Not examined.

69. [Phythian, John Ernest]. *The Pre-Raphaelite Brotherhood*.
    London: Newnes, [1905]. 20 pp.+

    Offers a visual survey of works by the entire P.R.B.,
    including several by Rossetti. With items 66 and 67 forms
    a series on Rossetti's artistic achievement.

70. Angeli, [Helen] Rossetti. *Dante Gabriele Rossetti*. Ber-
    gamo: Instituto Italiano d' Arti Grafiche, 1906. 143 pp.

    Contains over eighty black-and-white illustrations. The
    introduction, which is drawn from item 64, contests the idea
    of Rossetti as a painter who repeated himself *ad nauseam*,

although it can be admitted that the art falls into two
distinct periods (the early Pre-Raphaelite work and the
later period, when Dante was the predominant inspiration).

71. Marillier, Henry C. *Rossetti*. London: Bell, 1906.
    112 pp.

    A smaller and cheaper version of item 62.

72. *Masterpieces of Dante Gabriel Rossetti (1828-1882):
    Sixty Reproductions from the Original Oil Paintings.*
    London: Gowans and Gray, 1912. 68 pp.

    Arranges chronologically sixty black-and-white photo-
    graphs of Rossetti's works, accompanied by a list of
    current owners.

73. Victoria and Albert Museum. *A Picture Book of the Pre-
    Raphaelites and Their School.* London: H.M.S.O., 1926.
    2 pp.+

    Illustrates the museum's Pre-Raphaelite paintings;
    three full-page black-and-white plates, including one of
    The Day Dream, are devoted to Rossetti.

74. Ironside, Robin. *Pre-Raphaelite Painters.* London:
    Phaidon, 1948. 49 pp.+

    Offers a general introduction to the visual aspects of
    the Pre-Raphaelite movement. Rossetti is represented by
    nineteen black-and-white plates, each with a commentary.
    His early work (1852-1860) is judged the best for beauty
    and intensity. In an introductory essay the author views
    Rossetti as a mystic with an impossibly romantic ideal
    of love.

75. *A Picture Book of the Pre-Raphaelite Paintings in the
    Manchester City Art Galleries.* Manchester: Art Galler-
    ies Committee, 1952.

    Not examined.

76. Surtees, Virginia. *The Paintings and Drawings of Dante
    Gabriel Rossetti: A Catalogue Raisonné.* 2 vols.
    London: Oxford University Press, 1971. 267 pp.+

    The major reference work on Rossetti as an artist. The
    entries are arranged chronologically within categories (e.g.

paintings, drawings, portraits, etc.). One volume contains 225 plates of almost all of Rossetti's artistic
works: oils, watercolors, chalk drawings, sketches. The
other volume contains full annotations for each work,
with information on history, provenance, alternate versions, replicas, reproductions, and critical commentary
(including Rossetti's own as evidenced in letters and
biographical material).

77. Harrison, Martin, revised by Susan Miller. *Pre-Raphaelite
     Paintings and Graphics*. London: Academy Editions, 1973.
     84 pp.

     Shows the evolution of Pre-Raphaelite art by a chrono-
     logical arrangement of paintings and graphic designs.
     Rossetti is represented by fifteen black-and-white repro-
     ductions.

78. Henderson, Marina. *D.G. Rossetti*. Introduction by Susan
     Miller. New York: St. Martin's Press, 1973. 102 pp.

     Reproduces over 100 of Rossetti's drawings and paintings.
     Accompanying them are excerpts from published criticism of
     the works in question. The introduction establishes the
     biographical context.

79. Birmingham City Museums and Andrea Rose. *Pre-Raphaelite
     Drawings: Dante Gabriel Rossetti*. Chicago: University
     of Chicago Press, 1977. 72 pp.

     Reproduces the Rossetti drawings in the collection of
     the Birmingham City Museums, including several drawings
     not catalogued in Surtees (item 76). Also serves as a
     guide to three 10.5 x 15 cm. microfiche sheets which ac-
     company the printed volume and contain the reproductions.

80. Harding, James. *The Pre-Raphaelites*. New York: Rizzoli,
     1977. 96 pp.

     Reproduces thirty-two full-color plates and dozens of
     black-and-white plates of Pre-Raphaelite work by twenty
     artists. Rossetti is represented by thirteen paintings.
     The earlier phase of the movement, especially the first
     decade, is stressed.

81. Rose, Andrea. *The Pre-Raphaelites*. Oxford: Phaidon
     Press, 1977. 64 pp.

     Contains forty-eight full-color reproductions of Pre-
     Raphaelite paintings, including five by Rossetti. The

sixteen-page introduction tries to set out the historical
context within which these artists must be viewed.

See also items 91, 96-98, 101-105, 107-114, 376, 684-687, 700,
706, 708, 721, 724, 731, 737, 744, 765, 827, 834, 861, 862,
901, 906, 972, 999, 1006, 1054, 1056, 1063, 1099.

SECTION B: LOCATION LISTS, COLLECTIONS, CANON, CATALOGS

Included in this section are location lists, descriptions of
public and private collections of paintings, studies of Rossetti's artistic canon, and catalogs of recent exhibitions.
For exhibitions earlier than 1962 see item 11 (section 14),
although the most informative of those catalogs are also included here.

82. Burlington Fine Arts Club. *Pictures, Drawings, Designs,
    and Studies by the Late Dante Gabriel Rossetti.* London:
    Burlington Fine Arts Club, 1883. 56 pp.

    Catalogs the 153 items in the posthumous exhibition
    which began at the club in January of 1883. Included
    is a short biographical sketch by H. Virtue Tebbs.

83. Rossetti, William Michael. "Notes on Rossetti and His
    Works." *Art Journal* 46 (1884): 148-152, 165-168,
    204-208.

    Offers "details of fact, corrections of errors, per-
    sonal reminiscences and the like" bearing on the works
    exhibited at the Burlington Fine Arts Club and the Royal
    Academy; arranged into a year-by-year progression.

84. Rossetti, William Michael. "A Pre-Raphaelite Collection."
    Art Journal 58 (1896): 129-134.

    Discusses the Pre-Raphaelite paintings, many of them by
    Dante Gabriel Rossetti, which had been collected by James
    Leathart.

85. Temple, A[lfred] G[eorge]. "Collection of William Coltart,
    Esq., of Woodleigh, Birkenhead." *Art Journal* 58 (1896):
    97-101.

    Includes descriptions and information on the positioning
    of three Rossetti works owned by Coltart: *Lady Lilith*,
    The Borgia Family, and *Lucrezia* (all watercolors).

86. Koch, Theodore W. "Modern Art Inspired by Dante." *Hand-list of Framed Reproductions of Pictures and Portraits Belonging to the Dante Collection.* Ithaca: Cornell University Press, 1900, pp. 6-20.

    Contains descriptions of nine items by Rossetti related to Dante; these items form part of the Cornell Dante Collection.

87. Toynbee, Paget. *Chronological List, with Notes, of Paintings and Drawings from Dante by Dante Gabriel Rossetti.* Turin: Fratelli Bocca, 1912. 32 pp.

    Contains exactly what its title indicates.

88. Birmingham City Museum and Art Gallery. "Drawings and Studies by Dante Gabriel Rossetti." *Catalogue of the Collection of Drawings and Studies by Sir Edward Burne-Jones, Dante Gabriel Rossetti, ... and others.* Birmingham: City Museum and Gallery, 1913, pp. 23-49.

    Lists and describes 149 items, including drawings for *Found* and *Mary Magdalene at the Door of Simon the Pharisee* as well as designs for title pages and stained glass windows. Superseded in some ways by item 94.

89. [Victoria and Albert Museum]. "Rossetti, Gabriel Charles Dante." *Catalogue of Water Colour Paintings by British Artists and Foreigners Working in Great Britain.* London: Board of Education, 1927, pp. 459-461.

    Gives details on eleven works by Rossetti which are owned by the museum, plus a short biographical summary.

90. [Walker Art Gallery]. *Walker Art Gallery: Illustrated Catalogue of the Permanent Collection.* Liverpool: City Corporation, 1927. 227 pp.

    Offers information on the holdings of a museum which houses one of the most important Pre-Raphaelite collections; the Rossetti items include his largest canvas, *Dante's Dream*, bought by the Corporation in 1881 for 1500 guineas.

91. Tatlock, R.R., et al. "Dante Gabriel Rossetti." *Record of the Collections in the Lady Lever Art Gallery.* London: Batsford, 1928, pp. 110-111.

    Describes three major works in the collection: *Blessed*

Damozel (Leyland's version), *Pandora*, and *Sibylla Palmi-fera*, the last of which is reproduced.

92. Birmingham City Museum and Art Gallery. *Catalogue of the Permanent Collection of Paintings*. Birmingham: City Museum and Art Gallery, 1930. 228 pp.

    Provides information on paintings only--for drawings, see items 79 and 94.

93. Hamill, Alfred E. "Dante Gabriel Rossetti in America." *Notes & Queries* 165 (1933): 358-359.

    Lists seventeen paintings by Rossetti which were known to be in American hands in 1933; supplements two works mentioned on page 229 of the same volume.

94. Birmingham City Museum and Art Gallery. "Rossetti (Gabriel Charles Dante), 1828-1882." *Catalogue of the Permanent Collection of Drawings*. Derby: Bemrose, 1939, pp. 310-369.

    Contains information on the size and provenance of over 150 drawings in the museum's collection, most of which came from the Charles Fairfax Murray bequest. See item 79, and for paintings see item 92; in terms of drawings, this book supersedes item 88.

95. Davies, Randall. "Rossetti's Earliest Drawings." *Burlington Magazine* 76 (1940): 22, 26.

    Assigns four drawings, two on the Faust legend, to Rossetti. Three of the drawings have Rossetti's monogram, and all were completed during or about 1846.

96. [Fogg Museum, Harvard University]. "Introduction" and "Dante Gabriel Rossetti." *Paintings and Drawings of the Pre-Raphaelites and Their Circle*. Cambridge, Mass.: Fogg Museum, 1946, pp. 7-13, 71-98.

    Catalog for the spring 1946 exhibition, most of which was based on the Grenville Winthrop bequest. Rossetti is represented by twenty-six works, each of which is described in detail together with information on provenance and exhibitions plus a bibliography. The introduction by Agnes Mangan pays tribute to Rossetti's generosity, enthusiasm, and magic, although even his best work is betrayed by his lack of patience. See also item 795.

97. Birmingham City Museum and Art Gallery. "Rossetti,
     Gabriel Charles Dante." *The Pre-Raphaelite Brother-
     hood (1848-1862).* Birmingham: City Museum and Art
     Gallery, 1947, pp. 24-28.

     Lists and offers information on the twenty-two works
     by Rossetti which appeared in the summer exhibition
     staged by the gallery. The introductory note sees
     Rossetti as combining symbolism, literalism, and imagi-
     native intensity.

98. Whitechapel Gallery. "Dante Gabriel Rossetti." *The
     Pre-Raphaelites.* London: Whitechapel Gallery, 1948,
     pp. 24-32.

     Lists sixty items by Rossetti which formed part of the
     spring exhibition at the gallery and gives brief ex-
     planations of each.

99. Chamot, Mary. *The Tate Gallery. British School. A
     Concise Catalogue.* London: Tate Gallery, 1953. 306 pp.

     Not examined.

100. Bennett, Mary. "A Check-list of Pre-Raphaelite Pictures
     Exhibited at Liverpool 1846-1867, and Some of Their
     Northern Collectors." *Burlington Magazine* 105 (1963):
     486-495.

     Discusses pictures exhibited at the Liverpool Academy
     and the men who bought them, including such important
     early Rossetti patrons as John Miller, Thomas Plint,
     James Leathart, and George Rae. Locations for these im-
     portant works are also specified.

101. Art Association of Indianapolis, Indiana. *The Pre-
     Raphaelites.* Indianapolis: Art Association, 1964.
     103 pp.

     Catalog of the 1964 spring exhibition at the Herron
     Museum of Art. Twenty-five works by Rossetti are re-
     produced in black and white and accompanied by notes.

102. Cummer Art Gallery. "Dante Gabriel Rossetti." *Artists
     of Victoria's England.* Jacksonville, Florida: Cummer
     Art Gallery, 1965, pp. 10-11.

     Describes four drawings which formed part of the
     winter exhibition.

103. Parris, Leslie. *The Pre-Raphaelites*. London: Tate
     Gallery, 1966. 16 pp.

     Catalog of the 1966 Tate Gallery exhibition. Includes
     thirty-two plates, seven (the largest number) being works
     by Rossetti.

104. Cummings, Frederick, and Allen Staley, compilers. "Dante
     Gabriel Rossetti." *Romantic Art in Britain: Paintings
     and Drawings 1760-1860*. Philadelphia: Museum of Art,
     1968, pp. 309-315.

     Offers extensive notes on five Rossetti works which
     formed part of a spring exhibition at the Philadelphia
     Museum of Art. Rossetti's watercolors of the late 1850s
     are his best work and "draw attention to the extraordi-
     narily abstract qualities of surface design in these
     works."

105. Laing Art Gallery. "Dante Gabriel Rossetti (1828-1882)."
     Paintings and Drawings from the Leathart Collection.
     Newcastle-upon-Tyne: Laing Art Gallery, 1968, pp. 28-32.

     Provides detailed information on nine less frequently
     exhibited works by Rossetti, all of which had appeared
     in the fall exhibition.

106. Allentuck, Marcia. "The Authenticity of Dante Gabriel
     Rossetti's 'Burd-Alane': An Unpublished Document."
     Burlington Magazine 112 (1970): 818.

     Excerpts an 1896 letter from Charles Fairfax Murray
     to Samuel R. Bancroft which echoes the doubts raised by
     Marillier (item 62) regarding this picture's authenticity.

107. Lakeview Center for the Arts and Sciences. "Dante
     Gabriel Rossetti." *The Victorian Rebellion: The Pre-
     Raphaelite Brotherhood and Their Contemporaries*.
     Peoria, Illinois: Lakeview Center for the Arts and
     Sciences, 1971, pp. 68-71.

     Describes the sixteen works by Rossetti that formed a
     section in the fall exhibition.

108. Lowe Art Museum. *The Revolt of the Pre-Raphaelites*.
     Coral Gables: University of Miami, 1972. 54 pp.

     The spring exhibition included seven works by Rossetti,

and an introduction to the catalog (by Nicholas Salerno)
sees Rossetti as an artist who fails when he overloads
the symbolism but who succeeds when he avoids "ideas."

109. Royal Academy (London). *Dante Gabriel Rossetti, Painter
      and Poet*. London: Royal Academy, 1973. 112 pp.

      Catalog for the winter exhibition. Includes 379 en-
      tries with commentary, divided into fourteen sections,
      plus twenty-four black-and-white plates. The intro-
      duction by John Gere sees Rossetti's best work as
      deliberately clumsy: the effect is heraldic, the im-
      portant matters are tone, color, and atmosphere. (See
      items 844, 846, 848, 851-853.)

110. [Staatliche Kunsthalle]. "Dante Gabriel Rossetti."
      Präraffaeliten. Baden-Baden: State Art Museum, 1973,
      pp. 173-219.

      Catalog for the winter exhibition, prepared by Günther
      Metken. Rossetti is fully represented: fifty-four paint-
      ings and drawings, all reproduced here, six in color.

111. Surtees, Virginia. "'Beauty and the Bird': A New Ros-
      setti Drawing." *Burlington Magazine* 115 (1973): 84-87.

      Describes Rossetti's friendship with Ruth Herbert, his
      use of her as a model, and the hitherto-unpublished
      sketch which accompanied the sonnet of the same title.

112. Surtees, Virginia. "A Conversation Piece at Blackfriars."
      Apollo 97 (1973): 146-147.

      Identifies a drawing long thought to be Val Prinsep's
      as really a sketch of Fanny Cornforth and G.P. Boyce done
      by Rossetti in his Blackfriars studio in December 1858.

113. Manchester Art Gallery. *Pre-Raphaelite Paintings*. Man-
      chester: City Art Gallery, 1974. 135 pp.

      Describes and illustrates the museum's excellent Pre-
      Raphaelite holdings. Rossetti is represented by eleven
      works, all described and reproduced in black and white.
      Chief among them are *Astarte Syriaca*, *Joli Coeur*, and
      The Bower Meadow.

114. Elzea, Rowland and Betty. *The Pre-Raphaelite Era, 1848-
      1914*. Wilmington: Delaware Art Museum, 1976. 233 pp.

Catalog of the 1976 spring exhibition, one which traced Pre-Raphaelitism from 1848 through Aestheticism, the Arts and Crafts movement, and Art Nouveau. Especially noteworthy is the inclusion of continental figures like DeGlehn, Levy-Dhurmer, and Schwabe.

115. Agosta, Lucien. "The Rossettis at Texas." *Pre-Raphaelite Review* 1 (May 1978): 111-112.

Records five studies by Rossetti now at the Humanities Research Center and not cataloged in Surtees (item 76).

116. Brown, David. "Pre-Raphaelite Drawings in the Bryson Bequest to the Ashmolean Museum." *Master Drawings* 16 (1978): 287-293.

Observes that Rossetti is "the presiding genius" of the collection. In addition to the drawings already listed in Surtees (item 76), note should be made of a Sir Galahad design for the Oxford Union and a group of four virtues (Love, Generosity, Hope, and Wisdom). Copies of Rossetti works executed by Stephens, Murray, and others are also included, as is a checklist of eighteen other items.

117. Parkinson, Ronald. "Victorian Paintings and Drawings." *The Connoisseur* 200 (1979): 146.

Notes that the drawing "My Lady Greensleeves," attributed to Rossetti when sold recently by Sotheby's, was cataloged inaccurately. It may not be genuine-- "it seemed too gentle and affectionate for Rossetti."

See also items 11, 65, 72, 76, 151, 716, 743, 822, 872, 879, 891, 893, 894, 903, 906, 908, 959, 966, 968, 976-978, 989, 993, 1046, 1077.

Letters

118. Ingram, John. *Oliver Madox Brown: A Biographical Sketch*. London: Stock, 1883. 238 pp.

Contains five letters from Rossetti to young "Nolly" Brown, son of Ford Madox Brown and a doomed boy-genius. Subjects include Nolly's novel *Gabriel Denver* and his father's painting *The Last of England*.

119. Prideaux, W.F. "D.G. Rossetti." *Notes & Queries*, 6th series, 8 (1883): 364.

Notes to potential biographers that a letter in *The Athenaeum* on 21 August 1852 was by Rossetti.

120. Rossetti, William Michael, ed. *Dante Gabriel Rossetti: His Family Letters, with a Memoir*. 2 vols. London: Ellis, 1895. 876 pp.

The first volume is given over to a lengthy memoir--really a full though discreet biography--by the poet's brother. Rossetti emerges as a no-nonsense, sane, practical man, at least until the last decade. He "prized rectitude," "shunned meanness," and was a leader whose strong will occasionally led to wilfulness. The biographical details are particularly rich for the earlier years. In the second volume the editor reprints 317 letters from Rossetti to members of his family: his aunt Charlotte, his grandfather, his uncle, his sister-in-law, as well of course as his mother, father, sisters, and brother. Reprinted 1970.

121. Hill, George Birkbeck, ed. *Letters of Dante Gabriel Rossetti to William Allingham, 1854-1870*. London: Unwin, 1897. 307 pp.

Prints sixty-five Rossetti letters, some of which were first published in four *Atlantic Monthly* articles (May-August 1896). All letters are annotated and a few are expurgated "lest they give pain." Allingham was a close friend and a fellow poet. These letters cover several important topics, both biographical (e.g. Rossetti's marriage and his wife's death) and artistic (e.g. Rossetti's poems and his opinions on books). The letters also show Rossetti's mercantile sense and his knowledge of London low life.

122. Rossetti, William Michael, ed. *Ruskin: Rossetti: Pre-Raphaelitism. Papers 1854-1862*. London: Allen, 1899. 327 pp.

Contains forty letters from Rossetti to his wife, his brother, Madox Brown, and others. Also included are seventy letters from Ruskin to Rossetti, letters from Browning, William Bell Scott, and others, and items related to such matters as Morris and Company or the Hogarth Club. Ruskin is shown to be less influential than some think.

123. Rossetti, William Michael, ed. *Praeraphaelite Diaries and Letters*. London: Hurst and Blackett, 1900. 328 pp.

Contains twenty-four early letters by Rossetti (1835-1854), six letters by Ford Madox Brown plus his diary for the years 1847-1856, and the editor's P.R.B. journal kept from 1849 to 1853. For an unexpurgated version of this last, see item 306.

124. Rossetti, William Michael, ed. *Rossetti Papers 1862 to 1870*. London: Sands, 1903. 559 pp.

More letters (sixty by Rossetti), journals, and papers, continuing items 120, 122, and 123. The arrangement is chronological; the editor has omitted some material, but includes explanatory notes for what he has retained. The chief topics are seances, "blue china," the break with Ruskin, Christina Rossetti's poetry, and the revival of Rossetti's own interest in poetry.

125. Mills, Ernestine. *The Life and Letters of Frederic Shields*. London: Longmans, 1912. 368 pp.

Has numerous references to Rossetti and the Pre-Raphaelites and sections of Shields's diary. The most important feature for students of Rossetti is the collection of over fifty letters from Rossetti to Shields.

126. Arnold, William Harris. "Victorian Books and Letters." *Ventures in Book Collecting*. London: Scribner, 1923, pp. 188-226.

Included are four Rossetti presentation copies and two letters, one from Robert Browning and one to Leigh Hunt.

127. Doughty, Oswald, ed. *The Letters of Dante Gabriel Rossetti to His Publisher F.S. Ellis*. London: Scholartis Press, 1928. 150 pp.

Prints ninety-six letters, covering the years 1870-

1881 and concerned primarily with the publication of
Poems and of the two 1881 volumes. Rossetti shows ex-
treme sensitivity to hostile criticism and excessive
concern about arranging a friendly reception for his
poetry. These letters also document the poet's care
in supervising every detail connected with the publication of his books, including his passion for revision.

128. Purves, John. "Dante Gabriel Rossetti: Letters to Miss
     Alice Boyd." *Fortnightly Review* 129 (1928): 577-594.

     Offers sixteen letters chosen from those Rossetti
     wrote to Alice Boyd, interspersed with descriptive com-
     ments by the author. The subjects include Rossetti's
     renewed interest in poetry, the progress of his pic-
     tures, and the "doings" of the London Pre-Raphaelites.

129. Compton-Rickett, Arthur. "Rossetti-Swinburne Letters."
     Portraits and Personalities. London: Selwyn and
     Blount, 1937, pp. 311-320.

     Reprints seven letters from Rossetti to Swinburne,
     plus extracts from Swinburne's replies and critical
     commentary by the author. The topic usually is poetry.
     Published first in the *Times Literary Supplement* (1919).

130. Troxell, Janet C., ed. *Three Rossettis: Unpublished
     Letters to and from Dante Gabriel, Christina, William.*
     Cambridge, Mass.: Harvard University Press, 1937.
     216 pp.

     Includes approximately sixty letters by Rossetti to
     such correspondents as Frederick Sandys, Theodore Watts-
     Dunton, Edmund Gosse, C.A. Howell, and his mother; all
     are linked by the editor's extensive biographical com-
     mentary. Of special interest are Rossetti's letters
     relating to the exhumation of his wife's body (see item
     256). The book also contains several letters to Rossetti
     from Ruskin, Brown, Charles Wells, and others.

131. Baum, Paull F., ed. *Dante Gabriel Rossetti's Letters to
     Fanny Cornforth*. Baltimore: Johns Hopkins University
     Press, 1940. 142 pp.

     Prints the extant letters written by Rossetti to Fanny
     Cornforth, his mistress, model, and housekeeper, during
     the years 1870-1882. The letters themselves reveal
     little except details of Rossetti's domestic life, his

sense of humor, and the greed of his "Good Elephant."
The editor summarizes the history of their affectionate
and mutually useful relationship.

132. Marchand, Leslie A. "The Symington Collection." *Journal
      of the Rutgers University Library* 12 (1948): 1-15.

      Notes that the Symington Collection contains, among
      other items, several Rossetti family letters, transcripts
      of Rossetti's letters to Watts-Dunton, notes collected
      for a biography of Lizzie Siddal, and other miscellanies.

133. Packer, Lona Mosk, ed. *The Rossetti-Macmillan Letters:
      Some 133 Unpublished Letters Written to Alexander
      Macmillan, F.S. Ellis, and Others, by Dante Gabriel,
      Christina, and William Michael Rossetti 1861-1889.*
      Berkeley: University of California Press, 1963. 166 pp.

      Includes thirty annotated letters from Rossetti to
      Alexander Macmillan. Of particular interest are the
      letters connected with Rossetti's attempt to get Mac-
      millan to publish Swinburne's *Poems and Ballads* and
      with Rossetti's own illustrations for Christina's *Goblin
      Market* volume. Rossetti also seems to have handled some
      of the business arrangements for Christina.

134. Briggs, R.C.H. "Letters to Janey." *Journal of the
      William Morris Society* 1, no. 4 (1964): 3-22.

      Offers an early account of the somewhat disappointing
      contents of Rossetti's letters to Jane Morris (see item
      144). The author is able to conclude only that Janey
      was a stimulus for Rossetti--the nature of that stimulus
      remains undetermined.

135. Grylls, R. Glynn. "The Reserved Rossetti Letters."
      Times Literary Supplement, 30 January 1964, p. 96.

      Describes the 117 letters from Rossetti to Jane Morris
      which had been reserved by the British Museum until this
      year. The letters are "inconclusive" on the nature of
      their relationship. See item 144.

136. Doughty, Oswald, and John R. Wahl, eds. *The Letters of
      Dante Gabriel Rossetti*. 4 vols. Oxford: Clarendon
      Press, 1965-1967. 1,953 pp.

      The most complete edition of the correspondence so far,

with thousands of letters to scores of correspondents,
all accompanied by copious notes. The letters offer a
panorama of Rossetti's life and his activities as poet,
painter, and designer. The editors' notes are useful
and illuminating. But the edition is marred by some
faults of commission, such as an inadequate introduction
and the failure to produce a promised index volume. It
is also marred--and this is even more important--by very
large faults of omission (see item 137 for specifics).
Consequently the Clarendon Press has announced a revised
edition of the complete correspondence, this time under
the editorship of W.E. Fredeman; it is scheduled for
publication sometime in the mid-1980s.

137. Fredeman, William E. "Rossetti's Letters." *Malahat
Review* 1 (1967), 6 (1968): 134-141, 115-126, resp.

A review of the Doughty-Wahl edition of the correspondence (item 136), noteworthy as the most comprehensive listing of that edition's lacunae. Special emphasis
is also given to editorial confusions, inconsistencies,
and errors.

138. Pagès, Mireille. "This Divided Mind: Essai de revue
critique des Lettres de Dante Gabriel Rossetti."
Études Anglaises 23 (1970): 311-320.

A review-essay based on item 136. Sees the correspondence as significant because it gives us the literary
and artistic scene of Victorian England as well as the
inner history of a fascinating personality, a man torn
by many dualisms. The author makes great claims for
Rossetti's skill as a letter writer.

139. LeBourgeois, John Y. "A Rossetti-Morris Letter." *Notes
& Queries* 216 (1971): 255.

Prints a short unpublished 1874 letter from Rossetti
to Morris which shows Rossetti's active interest in "the
Firm" and his continued regard for Morris.

140. Minnick, Thomas L. "A New Rossetti Letter." *Blake
Newsletter* 5 (1972): 181-182.

Prints an 1862 letter from Rossetti to W. Ireland
concerning a dinner with Mrs. Gilchrist to discuss the
projected *Life of Blake*.

141. Maurin, Mario. "Dante Gabriel Rossetti and Ernest
     Chesneau." *Victorian Newsletter* 44 (1973): 24-26.

     Offers the entire text of a long letter from Rossetti
     to the French art critic in which the painter disclaims
     the leadership role in the P.R.B. which Chesneau had
     assigned to him. See also items 143 and 667.

142. Burnett, Alfred D. "The Rossettis and Pre-Raphaelites."
     The Abbott Collection of Literary Manuscripts.
     Durham: University Library, 1975, pp. 18-23.

     Describes materials collected by Prof. Claude Abbott,
     including many Rossetti letters to Shields, Brown, Watts-
     Dunton, and his brother, along with letters to Rossetti
     from Brown and Ruskin.

143. Cline, C.L. "Dante Gabriel Rossetti's 'Last' Letter."
     Library Chronicle of the University of Texas 9 (1975?):
     74-77.

     Prints and comments on a deathbed letter from Rossetti
     to Ernest Chesneau in which Rossetti complains about
     the influence of market forces on his painting. See
     also items 141 and 667.

144. Bryson, John, and Janet C. Troxell, eds. *Dante Gabriel
     Rossetti and Jane Morris: Their Correspondence.*
     Oxford: Clarendon Press, 1976. 219 pp.

     Chronicles the long, tortured relationship of Rossetti
     and his beloved Janey. Disappoints those who expected
     torrid declarations of love or the revelation of in-
     timate details, but does establish the strength and
     durability of Rossetti's devotion to his friend's wife.
     Included are 150 letters covering the years 1868-1881,
     plus appendices and numerous plates and illustrations.

145. Berg, Margaret. "Ruskin: An Allusion in a Rossetti
     Letter." *Notes & Queries* 24 (1977): 24-25.

     Corrects a footnote in Hill's edition of Rossetti's
     letters to Allingham (see item 121)--Rossetti is alluding
     to Ruskin.

146. Cline, C.L., ed. *The Owl and the Rossettis: Letters of
     Charles A. Howell and Dante Gabriel, Christina, and*

William Michael Rossetti. State College: Pennsylvania
State University Press, 1978. 261 pp.

Prints 438 letters between Howell (or his wife) and
the Rossettis. Howell was Rossetti's friend and picture
agent in the early 1870s; the letters therefore give
valuable information about Rossetti's social and financial affairs during this period, when he spent much of
his time at Kelmscott. Howell emerges as a man of few
scruples, and Rossetti is often indictable as a co-
conspirator. A long introduction chronicles Howell's
activities from 1857 to 1890.

147. Fennell, Francis L., ed. *The Rossetti-Leyland Letters:
The Correspondence of an Artist and His Patron.* Athens:
Ohio University Press, 1978. 111 pp.

Contains the correspondence (137 letters) exchanged
by Rossetti and his most important art patron, Frederick
R. Leyland. Rossetti seems not to have been as skillful
a bargainer as others have assumed, at least when matched
with Leyland. Besides financial arrangements, these
letters also discuss personal affairs and offer valuable
comments by the artist on his later paintings.

See also items 170, 186, 198, 222, 246, 256, 268, 270, 288,
297, 309, 311, 320, 624, and 639.

Biographical Studies

148. Caine, T. Hall. *Recollections of Dante Gabriel Rossetti.*
London: Stock, 1882. 297 pp.

Narrates the late years, from the author's first acquaintance with Rossetti in the summer of 1879 until
the poet's death in April 1882. Caine emphasizes Rossetti's character traits: his secrecy, isolation, drug
addiction, and also his generosity and wit. This book
begins the tradition of viewing Rossetti as a morbid
recluse, largely because the author did not know his
subject during the subject's youth. It also concentrates
on literary matters, since Caine was an aspiring writer.
Revised versions appeared in *My Story* (London: Heinemann,
1908, pp. 75-247) and again as *Recollections of Rossetti*
(London: Cassell, 1928). Reprinted 1972.

149. Hancock, Thomas. "Dante G. Rossetti." *Academy* 21 (1882):
323.

Recounts the friendship between the author's cousin,
the sculptor John Hancock, and the young Rossetti, a
fellow student at the Sass school. [This letter is
followed by a short one from "W. Wilkins" about locating
"Hand and Soul," a query answered in the next issue by
G.B. Smith.]

150. Robinson, Mary. "Dante Gabriel Rossetti." *Harper's
Magazine* 65 (1882): 691-701.

Summarizes Rossetti's career for an American audience.
The second phase of Pre-Raphaelitism is the more important one and Rossetti is an artist whose works are
a "perpetual pleasure." The author includes a first-
hand description of 16 Cheyne Walk and its interior as
it appeared during Rossetti's tenancy.

151. Sharp, William. *Dante Gabriel Rossetti: A Record and
a Study.* London: Macmillan, 1882. 432 pp.

A sympathetic biography by a friend. Much of it is
given over to recording details of Rossetti's artistic
output. There are poetic descriptions of many of
Rossetti's better-known works, such as *La Ghirlandata*,
Dante's Dream, and *The Blessed Damozel*, and the author
concludes that Rossetti was better at oils than at
watercolors. The chapters summarizing Rossetti's
career as a poet arrive at the summary judgment that
his was "the largest and noblest-minded philosophy of

our age." An appendix lists 395 Rossetti paintings and
gives their history and provenance. Reprinted 1970.

152. [Anonymous.] "Memorials of Rossetti." *Atlantic Monthly*
      51 (1883): 549-555.

      Reviews the Caine and Sharp books (items 148 and 151)
      and concludes that Rossetti's intensity caused his
      physical, emotional, and artistic breakdown. This
      intensity and its resultant suffering accounts for the
      oppressive atmosphere of the painting and the poetry--
      "Beauty becomes his disease." Rossetti will rank higher
      as a painter than as a poet.

153. Watts[-Dunton], Theodore. "The Truth about Rossetti."
      Nineteenth Century 13 (1883): 404-423.

      Tries to break down misconceptions about Rossetti. He
      was a painter first, not a poet. His goal was to unite
      poetic emotions and realistic methods, to achieve a
      sensuous mysticism, an optimistic supernaturalism.
      Personally, Rossetti was a man easily loved: his later
      seclusion came from a lack of sympathy, from ennui, and
      from chloral-induced melancholy, not from grief at
      Buchanan's ill-tempered attacks.

154. Lee, Vernon [=Violet Paget]. *Miss Brown: A Novel*.
      3 vols. London: Blackwoods, 1884. 685 pp.

      Roman à clef about Rossetti, the Pre-Raphaelites, and
      other current figures. The novel begins in Florence,
      ends in London, and concerns itself with Miss Brown's
      "education" at the hands of characters like "Cosmo
      Clough" (O'Shaughnessy), "Walter Hamlin" (Rossetti), and
      others.

155. Linton W[illiam] J[ames]. *Memories*. London: Lawrence,
      1895. 236 pp.

      Contains a brief account of the author's visit to
      Rossetti at 16 Cheyne Walk.

156. Fox-Bourne, H.R. "Dante Gabriel Rossetti." *Gentleman's
      Magazine* 262 (1887): 596-610.

      Summarizes Rossetti's life and finds him a gifted man
      weakened by unhappy circumstance. He mingled strength
      and weakness, sympathy and prejudice, both as an artist
      and as a human being.

157. Knight, Joseph. *Life of Dante Gabriel Rossetti*. London:
      Walter Scott, 1887. 186 pp.

      Another biography by a friend. Focuses more on Rossetti
      as a poet than as a painter, and describes the subject's
      life with more sympathy and more authorial reticence
      than either Caine or Sharp (see items 148 and 151). An
      appendix offers an early bibliography by John P. Anderson.
      Reprinted 1971.

158. Wotton, Mabel E. "Dante Gabriel Rossetti." *Word Portraits
      of Famous Writers*. London: Bentley, 1887, pp. 256-
      262.

      Quotes descriptions by William Sharp and Hall Caine
      in order to define Rossetti's physical appearance.

159. Rossetti, William Michael. "The Portraits of Dante
      Gabriel Rossetti." *Magazine of Art* 12 (1889): 21-26,
      57-61, 138-140.

      Gives an account of the known portraits of Rossetti,
      from a miniature painted by Filippo Pistrucci in 1834
      (age 6) to the pencil portrait done by Frederic Shields
      after Rossetti's death. The author comments on the
      qualities of the works themselves, on the circumstances
      of their composition, and on their likeness to the
      subject; anecdotes are included throughout.

160. Weigand, Wilhelm. "Dante Gabriel Rossetti." *Die
      Gegenwart* 35 (1889): 38-40.

      Introduces Rossetti, his career, and his achievements
      to a German audience presumed unfamiliar with him.

161. Hardinge, William. "A Reminiscence of Rossetti."
      Universal Review 6 (1890): 398-411.

      Prints the notes made by the author on the occasion of
      a visit to Rossetti in June of 1878. The contents of
      the rooms at Cheyne Walk, Rossetti's works in progress,
      and the poet-painter's appearance and remarks are all
      noted. The chief impression was of brightness, vivacity.

162. Hunt, William Holman. "Memories of Rossetti." *Musical
      World* 70 (1890): 526-528.

      Wants to dispell the view of Rossetti as a gloomy

psychotic. In his younger days, at least, the author's
friend was buoyant, cheerful, and fun-loving; his art
was neither mannered nor slovenly. Memories of P.R.B.
days are shared: dinners thrown for Buchanan Read, the
first acquaintance with Madox Brown, rowing on the dark
Thames, renting bachelor quarters together. [Note:
this was intended for the unveiling of the Chelsea
memorial to Rossetti; for a later view, see item 194.]

163.   Hake, T. Gordon. *Memories of Eighty Years*. London:
        Bentley, 1892. 304 pp.

        Refers to Rossetti throughout, but especially in
        Chapters 55-57. Dr. Hake was a long-time friend, and
        he chronicles his association in everything from festive
        dinners at Cheyne Walk to the nervous breakdown in 1872.
        Rossetti's collapse and resultant mental illness, upon
        which the author gives valuable medical testimony, will
        explain his artistic decline. Hake's information on the
        stays at Bognor and Roehampton is also important.

164.   Prinsep, Valentine C. "The Private Art Collections of
        London.... Rossetti and His Friend." *Art Journal*
        54 (1892): 129-134.

        Describes the Frederick R. Leyland mansion at 47
        Prince's Gate, with special reference to Leyland's
        friendship with Rossetti and the many Rossetti paintings
        on Leyland's walls. Also emphasizes the "cockney" side
        of Rossetti's personality--his love of slang, of boxing
        booths. [Note: a companion article entitled "A Collec-
        tor's Correspondence" discusses the exchange of letters
        between Leyland and Rossetti--see item 147.]

165.   Scott, William Bell. *Autobiographical Notes*. Edited by
        W. Minto. 2 vols. New York: Harper, 1892. 676 pp.

        Contains numerous references to Rossetti. Scott, al-
        though a close friend, shows Rossetti's warts: his
        domineering nature, his evasiveness, his shabby treat-
        ment of others, his "cowardice" in the face of Buchanan's
        attacks. Important events in Rossetti's life, including
        the death of his wife, his stays with Scott at Penkill,
        his nervous breakdown, his life at Cheyne Walk, and his
        fatal illness, are also chronicled. [Scott's account,
        while prejudiced, remains indispensable because of his
        unique access to certain key moments, especially during
        the sojourns at Penkill.] Reprinted 1970.

166. Hinkson, Katherine T. "Dante Gabriel Rossetti--A Strayed
Catholic." *Ave Maria* 37 (1893): 281-286.

Contends that Rossetti was Catholic in spirit, as shown
both by his art and his deathbed wish for a priest--this
last recorded in the diary of the "odious" William Bell
Scott (see item 165).

167. Caine, Lily Hall. "A Child's Recollection of Rossetti."
New Review 11 (1894): 246-255.

Recounts her brief acquaintance with Rossetti when she
came to live with her older brother (Hall Caine) at
Cheyne Walk in January of 1882. The dark, decayed,
somber interior of the house is described, as well as
the ghost that supposedly inhabited it. Rossetti was
unfailingly kind, even during his sojourn at Birchington-
on-Sea, which the child also shared until almost the end.

168. Noble, James Ashcroft. "At the Grave of Rossetti."
Bookman [New York] 1 (1895): 170-173.

Describes what a visitor to Birchington-on-Sea would
find: the white "Rossetti" bungalow, the grave, the
memorial window, the squalid town itself.

169. Hueffer, Ford Madox. *Ford Madox Brown: A Record of His
Life and Work*. London: Longmans, 1896. 459 pp.

Contains numerous references to Rossetti. Brown was
first Rossetti's teacher, then his fellow artist and
life-long friend. He was also a very important confidant.

170. Skelton, John. "Mainly about Rossetti." *The Table-
Talk of Shirley*. Edinburgh: Blackwood, 1896, pp.
79-94.

Protests against William Bell Scott's view (see item
165) that Rossetti was ungenerous, moody, and self-
congratulatory. Recalls the author's friendship with
Rossetti in the early 1860s, when Rossetti could still
declaim the poems buried in his wife's coffin. Ten
letters from the poet illustrate his generosity toward
other poets and his concern over adverse reaction to
the 1870 *Poems*. [This review-essay first appeared in
Blackwood's Magazine in 1893; "Shirley" was the author's
customary pseudonym.]

171. Watts[-Dunton], Theodore. "The Life of D.G. Rossetti."
      Spectator 76 (1896): 596-597.

      Explains that the author has not yet abandoned his in-
      tention to write a biography of Rossetti [but see items
      206 and 219]. Such a biography would offer a more cheer-
      ful view of Rossetti's character: the poet's gloom, even
      during the last decade, was often only a pose.

172. Sulman, Thomas. "A Memorable Art Class." *Good Words*
      38 (1897): 547-551.

      Recounts the author's enrollment in an art class at
      the Working Men's College, 1854. Rossetti taught water-
      color and figure. He was quiet, kind, sincere, but not
      attentive to routine. [Reprinted in the same year in
      Living Age; see also item 189.]

173. Gregg, Frederick J. "Reminiscences of the Rossettis."
      Book Buyer n.s. 16 (1898): 315-318.

      Surveys recent scholarship on the family and concludes
      that Dante Gabriel was "utterly wanting" in any vanity;
      furthermore, in relationship to his wife, Rossetti was
      always "an ideal lover."

174. Stillman, William J. "Dante Rossetti and Chloral."
      Academy, 19 March 1898, p. 333.

      Corrects the view that the author induced Rossetti to
      begin the use of chloral. While Rossetti did take one
      triple dose at his advice in 1870, the experiment was
      judged a failure. Repeated use of chloral did not
      commence until later.

175. Watts-Dunton, Theodore. *Aylwin: A Novel*. London:
      Hurst and Blackett, 1898. 460 pp.

      A *roman à clef*, with Rossetti portrayed under the guise
      of the painter D'Arcy. Other characters from Rossetti's
      life also appear: "DeCastro" (Howell), "Symonds" (Ley-
      land), "Tupper" (Watts-Dunton himself). Offers des-
      criptions of Rossetti's character, his life at Cheyne
      Walk, his passion for out-of-the-way curio shops, his
      mysticism, and other topics. Note: later editions of
      the novel also contain an appendix "In Defense of a
      Great and Beloved Poet Whose Character is Delineated
      in This Story."

176. Livingston, L.S. "First Books of Some English Authors
        III. Dante Gabriel and Christina G. Rossetti."
        Bookman [New York] 10 (1899): 245-247.

        Describes the childhood verses of the two Rossetti
        children and their two privately printed books (Dante's
        is *Sir Hugh the Heron*).

177. Mackail, John William. *Life of William Morris*. 2 vols.
        London: Longmans, Green, 1899. 739 pp.

        Comments on Rossetti's friendship with Morris in the
        years 1857-1862, with some discreet remarks also about
        the later years. Topics include Rossetti's joint
        tenancy of Kelmscott, his disinterest in politics, his
        generosity, and his role in Morris & Company.

178. Millais, John Guille. "PreRaphaelitism: Its Meaning
        and Its History." *Life and Letters of Sir John
        Everett Millais*. Vol. 1. London: Stokes, 1899,
        pp. 43-68.

        Describes the early friendship of Millais and Rossetti,
        with naturally a greater emphasis on the role of the
        former rather than the latter in founding the P.R.B.

179. [Anonymous]. "Buchanan and Rossetti." *Bookman* [New
        York] 12 (1901): 524-526.

        Points out Buchanan's harshness, especially towards
        Rossetti; yet he himself was treated with forebearance,
        and thus coals are heaped upon his head.

180. Barbiera, Raffaello. "La strana vita di Dante Gabriele
        Rossetti." *Immortali e dimenticati*. Milan: Cogliati,
        1901. 486 pp.

        Not examined.

181. [Dalziel, George and Edward]. "Chapter III: Millais,
        Hunt, Rossetti...." *The Brothers Dalziel: A Record
        of Fifty Years' Work in Conjunction with Many of the
        Most Distinguished Artists of the Period, 1840-1890*.
        London: Methuen, 1901, pp. 81-137.

        Recalls among other ventures work on the Moxon Tennyson,
        for which the Dalziel brothers served as wood engravers
        on such works as Rossetti's *St. Cecillia*. See item 960.

182.   Gilchrist, Herbert H. "Recollections of Rossetti."
       Lippincott's Magazine 68 (1901): 571-576.

       Describes meeting Rossetti in the winter of 1879 and
       several times thereafter. Rossetti was a genial host
       and offered opinions on several topics, including Blake's
       watercolors, Whitman's poetry, and his own paintings.

183.   Robinson, Mary [=Agnes Duclaux]. "Rossetti." *Grands
       ecrivains d' outre-manche*. Paris: Lévy, 1901,
       pp. 271-334.

       Chronicles Rossetti's life and analyzes his personality,
       finding him engaging, joyous, persuasive, idealistic,
       dominating, and impulsive. His tragedy stems from his
       unfortunate marriage. A review-essay on item 120;
       reprinted from *Revue de Paris* (1896).

184.   Stillman, William J. "Rossetti and His Friends." *The
       Autobiography of a Journalist*. Vol. 2. Boston:
       Houghton Mifflin, 1901, pp. 467-484.

       Describes his acquaintance with Rossetti during the
       1870s. Topics receiving special attention include the
       poet's stay with Stillman at Robertsbridge, his intro-
       duction to chloral, his collapse in 1872, his volubility,
       and his insatiable need for company.

185.   Seddon, John P. "The Works of the P.R.B. in Llandaff
       Cathedral." *Public Library Journal* [Cardiff] 4 (1903):
       28-30, 49-51, 66-70.

       Contains details on Rossetti's execution of the trip-
       tych in the cathedral. Work was begun in 1856 and fin-
       ished in 1864. Other topics include Rossetti's shrewd
       bargaining, his habits in London, and his skill in
       ecclesiastical art.

186.   Wyzewa, Teodor de. "Dante-Gabriel Rossetti." *Peintres
       de jadis et d' aujourd'hui*. Paris: Perrin, 1903,
       pp. 275-312.

       Reviews recent editions of Rossetti's letters and finds
       him a poor correspondent. But from these volumes one
       can nonetheless glean both the fascination and the re-
       pulsion exercised by Rossetti's personality. One can
       also see why Rossetti was "the Robin Hood of art"--he
       was skillful at prying money out of the rich. Reprinted
       from *Revue des Beaux-arts* (1898).

187. [Burne-Jones, Georgiana]. *Memorials of Edward Burne-Jones*. 2 vols. London: Macmillan, 1904. 681 pp.

    Has numerous references to Rossetti, most of them sympathetic. Important topics include Lizzie Siddal's death, the burial of the manuscripts, and Rossetti's dislike of exhibitions. Burne-Jones was one of the few early acquaintances whose friendship continued on into the later years; his admiration remained largely undiminished.

188. Dunn, Henry Treffry. *Recollections of Dante Gabriel Rossetti and His Circle*. Edited by G. Pedrick. London: Elkin Matthews, 1904. 96 pp.

    Contains Dunn's memories of life at Cheyne Walk, where he resided for about fifteen years as Rossetti's art assistant and general factotum. There are many anecdotes, mostly about Rossetti's friends, personal habits, pets, and manias (especially spiritualism and the occult). Although Dunn was in a position to know every secret of Rossetti's, the book maintains its discretion on such matters as the Jane Morris affair and contents itself with amusing tid-bits. See also item 288.

189. Emslie, J.P. "Art Teaching in the Early Days." *The Working Men's College, 1854-1904*. Edited by J. Davies. London: Macmillan, 1904, pp. 34-53.

    Recalls Rossetti's classes in color techniques given at the college in the late 1850s. Memories include Rossetti's disagreements with Ruskin, his teaching techniques, his genial personality, and his lack of professional jealousy. See also item 172.

190. Prinsep, Valentine C. "A Chapter from a Painter's Reminiscence. The Oxford Circle: Rossetti, Burne-Jones, and William Morris." *Magazine of Art* 27 (1904): 167-172.

    Recounts how Rossetti recruited the author for the Oxford Union project despite his inexperience. Also included are details of the "chaffing" during the day's work and a typical evening's entertainment at the lodgings on George Street. The author manages to fit in other anecdotes of his friendship with Rossetti too. For a continuation of the account beyond 1858, see item 191.

191.   Prinsep, Valentine C. "A Chapter from a Painter's
        Reminiscence. II. Dante Gabriel Rossetti." *Maga-
        zine of Art* 27 (1904): 281-286.

        Continues the narrative of item 190, with the scene
        now shifted to London, where the author dined with
        Rossetti almost daily. Rossetti hated music, hard work,
        exercise of any kind. He loved "stunners," curios,
        badinage, the night life. His wife's tragic death must
        not be blamed on Rossetti, because his conduct was exem-
        plary and his grief genuine. Life at Cheyne Walk,
        amidst wombats and ravens, is also described.

192.   Rutledge, Guy. "Some Notes on the Life and Work of
        Dante Gabriel Rossetti." *Liverpool Philomathic
        Society Proceedings* 58 (1904-1905): 111-139.

        Not examined.

193.   Caine, T. Hall. "Dante Gabriel Rossetti." *The Poets
        and Poetry of the Nineteenth Century*. Edited by A.H.
        Miles. Vol. 5. London: Routledge, 1905.

        Sketches Rossetti's life, with chief emphasis on his
        character: "a vivid personality, irresistible in his
        fascination, powerful even in his weakness," a man who
        was both complex and contradictory. First issued 1891-
        1897.

194.   Hunt, William Holman. *Pre-Raphaelitism and the Pre-
        Raphaelite Brotherhood*. 2 vols. London: Macmillan
        1905-1906. 1,005 pp.

        Offers Hunt's own detailed version of the founding of
        the P.R.B., one which emphasizes his own role at the ex-
        pense of Rossetti's. There are numerous allusions to
        Rossetti throughout. Rossetti is portrayed as a de-
        lightful, witty companion and as an artistic genius.
        But he was not a true Pre-Raphaelite, he was not an
        easy man to get along with, and he was not (this by
        implication) as good a painter as the author.

195.   [Anonymous]. "Pre-Raphaelitism in Outline." *Book
        News Monthly* 24 (1906): 696-698.

        Gives brief biographical sketches of the chief figures
        in the group, including Rossetti, its "acknowledged
        leader," whose English surroundings saved him from the
        "excesses" of his Italian temperament.

196. Bright, Norma K. "Social Intercourse among the Pre-
     Raphaelites." *Book News* 24 (1906): 691-695.

     Summarizes the personal relationships among the Pre-
     Raphaelites, especially Rossetti's relationships with
     Lizzie Siddal, with Burne-Jones, and with Morris. Ros-
     setti is said to have needed a stable family life to
     settle him down.

197. Hubbard, Elbert. *Little Journeys to the Homes of
     Famous Lovers: Dante Gabriel Rossetti and Elizabeth
     Eleanor Siddal.* East Aurora, N.Y.: Roycrofters,
     1906. 84 pp.

     Romanticizes the Rossetti family, so much so that
     Rossetti's mother even becomes the inspiration (via
     Carlyle) of Emerson. Gives a novelistic account of
     the lovers' marriage, attributing its delay to Ros-
     setti's fear of losing her.

198. Rossetti, William Michael. *Some Reminiscences.* 2 vols.
     New York: Scribners, 1906. 576 pp.

     Offers memories of the author's childhood, including
     visits to the Polidori home at Holmer Green. These
     scenes were shared by Dante Gabriel. Other relevant
     topics include the Pre-Raphaelite Brotherhood, the
     circle of friends at Cheyne Walk, William Michael's
     weekly visits to his recluse brother, Dante Gabriel's
     death, and William Michael's scholarly work on his
     brother and the rest of the family. For William Michael's
     views of his brother see item 120 plus his "Dante Ros-
     setti and Elizabeth Siddal," *Burlington Magazine* 1 (1903):
     273-295, which offers a charitable interpretation of
     Rossetti's courtship and marriage.

199. Allingham, William. *William Allingham: A Diary.* Edited
     by H. Allingham and D. Radford. London: Macmillan,
     1907. 404 pp.

     Contains valuable records by the author of his friend-
     ship with Rossetti, their joint vacations, and Rossetti's
     opinions on everyone from Shakespeare to Charles Wells
     and George Eliot. The portrait of Rossetti is favorable.

200. Douglas, James. *Theodore Watts-Dunton: Poet, Novelist,
     Critic.* London: Hodder and Stoughton, 1904. 483 pp.

Considers Watts-Dunton's deep affection for Rossetti,
their mutual interest in poetry, and the former's influence on the latter. This influence stemmed in part
from Watts-Dunton's immense usefulness, first as a
solicitor and later as a friend and general factotum.

201. Terry, Ellen. "Rossetti, Bernhardt, Irving, 1865-1867."
      The Story of My Life. London: Hutchinson, 1907,
      pp. 68-82.

Sketches Rossetti's fascination with animals--the bull,
the peacock, the formice, the armadillo--and his negli-
gence of them.

202. Carr, J[oseph] Comyns. "Dante Gabriel Rossetti." *Some
      Eminent Victorians: Personal Recollections in the World
      of Art and Letters*. London: Duckworth, 1908, pp. 59-70.

Recalls his early acquaintance with Rossetti's paintings and his visits to Cheyne Walk. Also recorded are
several of Rossetti's *obiter dicta* on artists such as
Turner, Moore, Burne-Jones, Leighton, and others.

203. Rutter, Frank. *Dante Gabriel Rossetti: Painter and Man
      of Letters*. London: Richards, 1908. 157 pp.

Surveys Rossetti's life under five headings: early
years, the P.R.B., Lizzie Siddal, the late 1850s, and
the later years. A final chapter evaluates Rossetti
as a memorable artist because of his contributions to
symbolism and to "ascetic mysticism." Rossetti has intensity, but he lacks craftsmanship and is a great
artist only in certain inspired moments. Extensive
quotation from the family letters, plus twenty-four
black-and-white illustrations. Reprinted 1975.

204. Watts-Dunton, Theodore. "Rossetti and Charles Wells:
      A Reminiscence of Kelmscott Manor." *Joseph and His
      Brethren*, by Charles Wells. London: Oxford Univer-
      sity Press, 1908, pp. xix-lviii.

Retells the history of Rossetti's enthusiasm for Wells'
play and his promotion of it during the 1870s. Watts-
Dunton was first indoctrinated into the Wells cult when
he visited Rossetti at Kelmscott. Life at the manor and
its exquisite appointments during Rossetti's stay,
especially the "Tapestry Room" and the studio, are also
described.

205. Meredith, George. "Dante Gabriel Rossetti." *English Review* 2 (1909): 631.

   Rebuts the view that the author left Cheyne Walk because of some ham-and-eggs incident. Any remonstrance he ever made was offered solely out of concern for Rossetti's health.

206. Watts-Dunton, Theodore. "Rossettiana: A Glimpse of Rossetti and Morris at Kelmscott." *English Review* 1 (1909): 323-332.

   Explains his failure to undertake the projected biography and describes the circumstances surrounding the writing of two hitherto-unpublished sonnets by Rossetti. The author adds reminiscences of life with Rossetti at Kelmscott, Herne Bay, Bognor, and Birchington-on-Sea. Other subjects include the founding of Morris & Company and Rossetti's hydrocele operation. See also item 219.

207. Hueffer, Ford Madox. "An Old Circle" and "Some Pre-Raphaelite Reminiscences." *Harper's Magazine* 120 (1910): 364-372, 762-768.

   Recalls visiting Rossetti and seeing him lolling on his sofa, two women dropping grapes into his mouth. On other topics, the author also remembers the backbiting and quarreling that went on in the Brown-Rossetti-Morris-Jones circle, and he attempts to set right the story of Meredith's joint tenancy of Cheyne Walk. Later revised for inclusion in *Ancient Lights and New Reflections* (1911).

208. Sharp, Elizabeth Amy. "The Death of Rossetti." *William Sharp (Fiona Macleod): A Memoir.* New York: Duffield, 1910, pp. 58-77.

   Describes Sharp's friendship with Rossetti during the last years, his attendance at Rossetti's bedside at Birchington-on-Sea, and the circumstances surrounding his 1882 *Life* (item 151).

209. Swinburne, Algernon C. *A Record of a Friendship.* London: privately printed, 1910. 9 pp.

   Preserves an autobiographical fragment, written on the occasion of Rossetti's death in 1882, in which Swinburne recalls his early friendship with Rossetti and Lizzie Siddal and his affection for them.

210. Bensusan, Samuel Levy. *The Charm of Rossetti*. London:
      Jack, [1911]. 47 pp.

      Not examined.

211. Byron, Mary C. *A Day with Dante Gabriel Rossetti*.
      London: Hodder and Stoughton, 1911. 48 pp.

      Pictures an archetypal but fictitious day in July of
      1871, with an impressionistic portrait of Rossetti at
      Cheyne Walk: reading, painting, composing poems, all
      the while dwelling on his dead wife. [Note: this nar-
      rative contains many inaccuracies and anachronisms.]

212. Hueffer, Ford Madox. "D.G.R." *Bookman* 40 (1911): 113-120

      Reminds readers that Rossetti in the 1870s was a conun-
      drum. The treatment accorded Rossetti by his subsequent
      biographers is summarized and the author concludes that
      most of them mislead and bore. Yet Rossetti was a great
      figure, if only because of his influence on others and
      the breadth of his appeal. He saved England from Prus-
      sianization and Americanization. In fact anyone who
      does not recognize his greatness "will be a dirty, un-
      grateful little pork butcher."

213. LaGallienne, Richard. "Dante Gabriel Rossetti and Eliza-
      beth Siddal." *The Loves of the Poets*. New York:
      Baker and Taylor, 1911, pp. 145-180.

      Narrates the history of Rossetti's courtship and mar-
      riage, finding in the famous lovers an example of the
      process by which personal history becomes a universal
      symbol. Reprinted in *Old Love Stories Retold* (1924).

214. Rowley, Charles. "The Rossettis." *Fifty Years of Work
      without Wages*. London: Hodder and Stoughton, [1911],
      pp. 111-126.

      Recounts his activities in making frames for Rossetti,
      his efforts to secure a Rossetti painting for the city
      of Manchester, and his attendance at Cheyne Walk dinners
      where Rossetti ate "with all the gusto of a ploughboy."

215. Salomon, Solomon J. "Rossetti's Tomb." *Academy* 84
      (1913): 63.

      Responds to a letter of Algernon Ashton (p. 31) about
      the erection of a railing around Rossetti's gravesite.

216. Carr, J[oseph] Comyns. "With Rossetti in Cheyne Walk."
      Coasting Bohemia. London: Macmillan, 1914, pp. 42-55.

      Recalls days and evening spent with Rossetti in his
      studio. The dominant qualities of Rossetti were his
      strength, eloquence, impatience, and generosity. But
      Rossetti broke with the author when Carr published some
      criticisms extolling Burne-Jones.

217. Francillon, R[obert] E. "Chapter XII ... Dante Gabriel
      Rossetti...." *Mid-Victorian Memories*. London: Hodder
      and Stoughton, 1914.

      Recalls evenings at Dr. Westland Marston's, with Ros-
      setti sitting silently beside Jane Morris, both clearly
      unenlivened guests.

218. Taglialatela, Eduardo. *Dante Gabriele Rossetti*. Rome:
      Vallardi, 1914.

      Not examined.

219. Watts-Dunton, Theodore. "Dante Gabriel Rossetti." *Old
      Familiar Faces*. New York: Dutton, 1916, pp. 69-119.

      Judges recent biographies in the light of his old and
      deep friendship with Rossetti. As a poet imagination
      was Rossetti's blessing and also his bane. Yet his
      personality exceeded even his poetry. The author apolo-
      gizes indirectly for not undertaking a memoir himself,
      but the task is too daunting. He will, however, publish
      "Jan Van Hunks" and the "Sphinx" sonnets.

220. Gosse, Edmund. "Early Life in London." *The Life of
      Algernon Charles Swinburne*. New York: Macmillan,
      1917, pp. 65-106.

      Reports on Swinburne's friendship with Rossetti, their
      mutual criticism of poetry, Rossetti's protectiveness,
      and their joint tenancy of Cheyne Walk, which came at
      Rossetti's behest after the death of Lizzie Siddal.

221. Schücking, Levin Ludwig. "Rossetti's Persönlichkeit."
      Englische Studien 51 (1917): 189-225.

      Traces the evolution of Rossetti's personality through
      five stages: early development, the years dominated by
      Lizzie Siddal, the fortunate period, the beginning of

the decline, and the last years. A sixth section considers Rossetti's artistic creed; he is typical of
Romantic decadence. Reprinted in the author's *Essays*
(1948).

222. Woolner, Amy. *Thomas Woolner, R.A., Sculptor and Poet.*
      London: Chapman and Hall, 1917. 352 pp.

      Contains several references to Rossetti and six letters
      from him to Woolner. Woolner was one of the original
      members of the P.R.B., although he had little contact
      with Rossetti after the early 1850s.

223. Williamson, G[eorge] C[harles]. "Dante Gabriel Rossetti."
      Murray Marks and His Friends: A Tribute of Regard.
      London: Lane, 1919, pp. 51-83.

      Chronicles the friendship between Rossetti and Marks,
      his dealer in porcelein, blue china, and other *objets
      d' art*. Marks was of great material service to Rossetti:
      discounting his bills, finding buyers for paintings,
      seeking out Blue Nankin, arranging for everything from
      mats to protect Rossetti's garden tent against the wombat
      to a plumber who could plug up a Tudor House leak. Also
      discussed are the negotiations for *La Bello Mano*.

224. Ellis, Stewart Marsh. ["Meredith at Chelsea."] *George
      Meredith: His Life and Friends in Relation to His
      Work*. New York: Dodd, Mead, 1920, pp. 148-157.

      Describes Meredith's share in the tenancy of 16 Cheyne
      Walk (Tudor House). Meredith undertook it because of
      the difficulty of commuting to Copham while reading for
      Chapman and Hall. He left because he found he was un-
      suited for life with Rossetti and--especially--Swinburne.

225. Miller, Joaquin [=C.H. Miller]. "Recollections of the
      Rossetti Dinner." *Overland Monthly* 75 (1920): 138-141.

      Reports on an 1871 dinner at Rossetti's house, when the
      conversation turned to such topics as Italian winemaking,
      poetry, religion, Homer, and love of the beautiful. Ros-
      setti is "the master," the others his beloved disciples.

226. Colvin, Sir Sidney. "Dante Gabriel Rossetti." *Memories
      and Notes of Persons and Places, 1852-1912*. London:
      Arnold, 1921, pp. 60-75.

      Describes his youthful hero-worship of Rossetti in the

years 1868-1872, when the author was a frequent visitor
to Cheyne Walk. Colvin was not enthralled by the paintings, which he found exaggerated and unpleasantly streaky,
but the poetry enchanted him by its imagery and color.
Other subjects include Rossetti's reading techniques
and the author's role in aiding the revision of the manuscripts for *Poems* 1870. Originally printed in *Scribner's
Magazine* (1920).

227. Beerbohm, Max. *Rossetti and His Circle*. London:
  Heinemann, 1922. 35 pp.

  Contains twenty-three color plates, fourteen of which
  offer caricatures of the man whom the artist-author calls
  one of the three most interesting Englishmen of the
  nineteenth century (the other two are Byron and Disraeli).
  Reprinted 1974.

228. Duryea, Minga Pope. "Cobden-Sanderson's Garden at Ham-
  mersmith, with Glimpses of the Gardens of William
  Morris and Rossetti." *Scribner's Magazine* 74 (1923):
  25-34.

  Describes the garden at Tudor House: its ivy-covered
  wall, its inlaid mosaic fountain, its mulberry trees.
  Rossetti's studio fronted on this garden.

229. Morrah, Herbert A. "Art at the Union." *The Oxford
  Union, 1823-1923*. London: Cassell, 1923, pp. 166-191.

  Recounts the commissioning of the Oxford Union murals,
  the "Jovial Campaign" of 1857, the nature and subject
  matter of the completed murals, the degeneration of the
  works in later years, and finally the ill-fated attempts
  to restore them. Some of these restoration efforts were
  frustrated by Rossetti because of his resentment of
  William Riviere's contributions.

230. Symons, Arthur. "The Rossettis." *Dramatis Personae*.
  Indianapolis: Bobbs-Merrill, 1923, pp. 118-131.

  Impressionistic view of the three siblings. Dante
  Gabriel is brooding, voluptuous, imaginative, a victim
  of "lust of the eyes."

231. Stirling, A[nna] M.W. "Tales of the Pre-Raphaelites and
  Others." *Life's Little Day: Some Tales and Other Reminiscences*. London: Butterworth, 1924, pp. 209-237.

Gives some family anecdotes about Rossetti (R.S.
Stanhope, the Pre-Raphaelite, was the author's uncle).
Stories including the dousing of Rossetti during the
Jovial Campaign, Rossetti's painting of Virtue Tebbs's
wife, and the wombat eating Rossetti's hat.

232. Forbes-Robertson, Johnston. "The Theatre Royal Drawing
      Room." *A Player Under Three Reigns*. London: Unwin,
      1925, pp. 35-48.

      Describes visits to Cheyne Walk in the late 1860s and
      his own role as the model for Eros in *Dante's Dream*.
      See also item 235.

233. Withers, Percy. "Blake, Shields, and Rossetti." *Times
      Literary Supplement*, 18 August 1927, p. 561.

      Confirms the fact that a drawing of Blake's bedroom
      by Shields evoked Rossetti's sonnet. The drawings were
      done at Rossetti's behest, the sonnet was his return
      gift to Shields.

234. Ardagh, J. "Dante Gabriel Rossetti." *Notes & Queries*
      154 (1928): 280, 431.

      Lists memorial tablets to Rossetti erected as of the
      year of his centennial.

235. Forbes-Robertson, Sir Johnston. "D.G. Rossetti, 1828-
      1928. The Tribute of a Friend." *Times* [London],
      11 May 1928, pp. 17-18.

      A centenary tribute which makes great claims for
      Rossetti as poet and painter. Included also is a re-
      collection of posing at age sixteen for the head of
      Cupid in *Dante's Dream* (see item 232).

236. Giartosio de Courten, Maria. *I. Rossetti, storia di
      una famiglia*. Milan: Alpes, 1928. 362 pp.

      Not examined.

237. Hall, S. Elizabeth. "Dante Gabriel Rossetti." *Quest*
      19 (1928): 367-384.

      Summarizes statements made by others about Rossetti's
      character. He was a genius, gifted with a vision of the
      ideal but betrayed by fatal weaknesses.

238. Lucas, E[dward] V[errall]. "Edward Burne-Jones and D.G. Rossetti--1857 and on." *The Colvins and Their Friends*. London: Methuen, 1928, pp. 32-46.

    Describes the young Colvins' hero-worship of Rossetti during the early 1870s, mostly by quoting extracts from item 226.

239. Smith, Harry Bache. "Dante Gabriel Rossetti, 1828-1928." *Century Magazine* 117 (1928): 245-253.

    Summarizes the painter-poet's career. Although he was not great in either field, Rossetti had a very creative imagination and a genius for finding a technique to suit his needs.

240. Taylor, Rachel A. "A King in Exile." *Spectator* 140 (1928): 719-721.

    A review-essay on item 241. Defines Rossetti's temperament as "romantic, hybrid, difficult, aristocratic, and melancholy." His life's goal was the presently unfashionable love-ideal.

241. Waugh, Evelyn. *Rossetti: His Life and Works*. London: Duckworth, 1928. 232 pp.

    Chronicles Rossetti's life and ends up judging him a "mediocrity" because he lacked the "essential rectitude" characteristic of all great artists. Still Rossetti deserves to be treated at length because he occasionally and unknowingly soared into great art. The author [writing with charm and good humor, and soon to be better known as a novelist] focuses more on the painting than on the poetry, and offers some new information on the Fanny Cornforth relationship. Reprinted 1975; see also item 1082.

242. "Stet" [=Thomas Earle Welby]. "Rossetti and His Publisher." *Back Numbers*. London: Constable, 1929, pp. 94-97.

    Observes that the Rossetti preserved in the letters to his publisher Ellis (item 127) was genuinely fearful of losing his eyesight and thus his income. He also alternated between the Rabelaisian Rossetti of the 1860s and the overwrought creature of the 1870s--we can see the transition taking place.

243. Wiegler, Paul. "Guggum." *Genius in Love and Death*.
      Translated by C. Rauschenbush. London: Boni, 1929,
      pp. 226-236.

      Offers a short novella focusing on Rossetti's infat-
      uation with Lizzie Siddal, their marriage, and her sub-
      sequent death.

244. Doughty, Oswald. "Rossetti: Samuel Butler." *Times
      Literary Supplement*, 27 November 1930, p. 1014.

      Announces the author's intention to undertake the
      biography of Rossetti (see item 281), and asks if anyone
      knows why Samuel Butler claimed to have met Rossetti two
      years after the latter's death. [The query was answered
      in the next issue, p. 1042, by Hugh Baker, who noted
      that Butler only claimed to have talked *about*, not *with*,
      Rossetti.]

245. Hunt, Violet. "The Beginning of the Pre-Raphaelites."
      Saturday Review 152 (1931): 144, 177-178, 208-209,
      232-233, 261.

      Offers a novelistic treatment of the early days of
      the P.R.B., including some inspired guesses about the
      thinking of the "poor dears." King Rossetti emerges
      as the chief figure, a skillful raconteur who led this
      exodus out of artistic sloppiness.

246. Purves, John. "Dante Gabriel Rossetti and His Godfather,
      Charles Lyell of Kinnordy." *University of Edinburgh
      Journal* 4 (1931): 110-118.

      Discusses Gabriele Rossetti's friendship with Lyell
      and the circumstances surrounding Rossetti's baptism,
      for which Lyell stood as sponsor. Also included is an
      1848 letter from the painter to his godfather and a
      summary of the extensive correspondence between Gabriele
      and Lyell, with numerous references to "il picciolo
      Dantino."

247. Rothenstein, William. *Men and Memories*. Vol. 1. London:
      Faber, [1931]. 390 pp.

      Contains references to Rossetti and his circle through-
      out (Rothenstein married the daughter of William Knewstub,
      Rossetti's art assistant).

248. Number deleted.

249. Bickley, Francis L. *The Pre-Raphaelite Comedy*. London: Constable, 1932. 276 pp.

   Narrates in detail the history of the P.R.B. up to its dissolution, which the author places in 1857. The schoolmasterish Hunt gave the Brotherhood its techniques, Rossetti its leadership. Rossetti's torn loyalties to Lizzie Siddal and Fanny Cornforth resulted in tension among the brethren and contributed to the foundering of the movement, although its influence was to be immense.

250. Hunt, Violet. *The Wife of Rossetti, Her Life and Death*. London: John Lane, 1932. 339 pp.

   Fictionalizes the life of Lizzie Siddal--we are made privy to the thoughts of the chief characters. Offers an unfavorable view of Rossetti's personality (he is weak, cruel, selfish, and inconsiderate) and attributes Lizzie's suicide to his relationship with Fanny Cornforth. [Note: this biography is unreliable on many factual matters, from small--Rossetti is said to begin his chloral habit in 1861--to large, e.g. the charge that the inquest testimony was all fabricated by Brown and others.]

251. Nothwang, Irene. *Die Frau, die Liebe, und der Tod bei Dante Gabriel Rossetti*. Stuttgart: Felbach, 1932. 49 pp.

   Offers a summary of Rossetti's friendship with and then marriage to Elizabeth Siddal, as well as the tragic effect of her death on him as reflected in his life and his art (both painting and poetry).

252. MacCarthy, Desmond. "Rossetti and Hall Caine." *Portraits I*. New York: Macmillan, 1932, pp. 226-233.

   Summarizes the relationship of the Cheyne Walk recluse and his earnest young biographer (see item 148). Rossetti's poetry is deliberately obscure, but its quaint charm soon palls.

253. Waller, Ross D. "The Young Rossettis." *The Rossetti Family, 1824-1854*. Manchester: Manchester University Press, 1932, pp. 164-242.

   The book as a whole concentrates on Gabriele Rossetti; this chapter deals with the upbringing of the children

and with Gabriele's personal and intellectual influence
on them. Other topics include Gabriele's concern about
his son's wayward habits, his love for "that dearest
little Gabriel, the very core of my heart," and his absorption in the mystical interpretation of Dante.

254. Chesson, W.H. "Rossetti's Marriage." *Quarterly Review*
      260 (1933): 84-93.

      A review-essay based on item 250. Finds Hunt's book
      a "psychological masterpiece" and Rossetti therefore is
      a malign genius. Uses evidence such as private notes
      and inquest testimony to buttress Miss Hunt's claims.
      Lizzie's suicide was caused by Rossetti's adultery and
      by money woes.

255. Larg, David. *Trial by Virgins: Fragment of a Biography*.
      London: Davies, 1933. 330 pp.

      Describes Rossetti's life up until the death of Lizzie
      Siddal in 1862. Scenes and dialog are invented, the
      treatment is novelistic [and factually unreliable].
      Rossetti emerges as an inconsiderate, self-centered,
      Italianate boor, and Lizzie as a queer, distant piece
      of statuary who was incapable of love. Although per-
      sonally blameless, Lizzie proves the futility of a life
      devoted solely to beauty.

256. [Troxell], Janet Buck. "Charles Augustus Howell and the
      Exhumation of Rossetti's Poems." *The Colophon*, no. 15
      (1933): [33-47].

      Retells briefly Howell's life: his birth in Portugal,
      his rise in prosperity, his connection with Ruskin,
      Burne-Jones, Swinburne, Whistler, and of course Rossetti.
      Eight letters connected with the exhumation of Rossetti's
      manuscripts, an affair handled by Howell, are printed.

257. Winwar, Frances [=Frances Grebanier]. *Poor Splendid
      Wings: The Rossettis and Their Circle*. Boston:
      Little, Brown, 1933. 413 pp.

      Provides fictionalized biographies of the major Pre-
      Raphaelites. Rossetti dominates the book, especially
      his worship of the dead Lizzie through his devotion to
      the living Jane Morris. [Note: despite the author's
      claim to have warranted every scene by outside sources,
      the treatment is inaccurate and sometimes sensational.]

258. Bragman, Louis J. "The Case of Dante Gabriel Rossetti:
     A Psychological Study of a Chloral Addict." *American
     Journal of Psychiatry* 92 (1936): 1111-1112.

     Calls Rossetti "the greatest poet *and* painter since
     Michaelangelo," but one whose life was darkened by drug
     addiction. Contemporary accounts establish a clinical
     analysis of the origin and nature of this addiction.

259. Angeli, Helen Rossetti. "Dante Gabriel Rossetti."
     Dublin Review 201 (1937): 364-367.

     Challenges that part of Dom T.V. Moore's article (item
     1051) which accuses Rossetti of failure and negligence
     as a husband. The existing evidence shows that Rossetti
     loved his wife and that her death was an accident, not
     a vengeful suicide.

260. Praz, Mario. "La famiglia Rossetti." *Studi e svaghi
     inglesi*. Florence: Sansoni, 1937, pp. 95-108.

     Describes the members of the Rossetti family, including
     the morbidly erotic Dante Gabriel. His tragic love for
     Lizzie Siddal and his lugubrious sensualism determined
     the course of his life.

261. Macht, David, and N.L. Gessford. "The Unfortunate Drug
     Experiences of Dante Gabriel Rossetti." *Bulletin of
     the History of Medicine* 6 (1938): 34-61.

     Views Rossetti as a clinical case study of "synergism":
     the combined effect of chloral hydrate and alcohol ex-
     ceeded the sum of the effects attributable to either
     drug alone, and the result was a mental and physical
     breakdown. See also item 258.

262. Ray, S.N. *Rossettiana--First Series*. Dacca: privately
     printed, 1941. 55 pp. [*Second Series* not examined.]

     Contains two essays: "Browning and the Rossetti Circle,"
     which describes the relationship of the two poets and the
     influence of Browning's dramatism on Rossetti's painting;
     and "Towards the Identification of the New Beloved of
     The House of Life," which proposes Jane Morris as the
     beloved (this in the days when such a conclusion was not
     a commonplace, although hinted at by works such as item
     257 and others).

263. Gaunt, William. *The Pre-Raphaelite Tragedy*. London:
      Cape, 1942. 256 pp.

      Plays its title off against Bickley's book (item 249),
      creating a morality play in which Rossetti's psycho-
      pathology and an uncongenial age both contribute to the
      destruction of a movement which held immense promise.
      Uses a novelistic style to recount the adventures of
      the P.R.B. from 1843 to 1896, with special concentration
      on Hunt, Millais, Rossetti, and Morris. Rossetti, in-
      dolent and sensuous, distorts and destroys his own
      artistic faculties by overindulgence in chloral and
      alcohol. See also item 264.

264. Gaunt, William. *The Aesthetic Adventure*. New York:
      Harcourt Brace, 1945. 224 pp.

      A follow-up volume to item 263. Traces the history
      of aestheticism in England, with Rossetti figuring
      largely as a foil to the more cosmopolitan and *avant-
      garde* Whistler and as the high priest of the religion
      of beauty.

265. Angeli, Helen Rossetti. *Dante Gabriel Rossetti: His
      Friends and Enemies*. London: Hamish Hamilton, 1949.
      291 pp.

      Attempts to locate Rossetti in the context of his
      friends--many of whom, alas, had occasion later to join
      the second group, his enemies. There are chapters on
      Rossetti's relationships with each of the following:
      Ruskin, Brown, Swinburne, the P.R.B. members, Morris,
      Jane Morris, Burne-Jones, Whistler, Meredith, Howell,
      Scott, Browning, and later sycophants like Hall Caine.

266. Burton, Hester. "Friends." *Barbara Bodichon, 1827-
      1891*. London: Murray, 1949, pp. 181-205.

      Summarizes the friendship of Mme. Bodichon and Rossetti,
      which resulted in Rossetti using her estate at Scalands
      for his recovery in 1870 from eye disease.

267. Leon, Derrick. *Ruskin: The Great Victorian*. London:
      Routledge and Kegan Paul, 1949. 595 pp.

      Contains numerous references to Rossetti, as well as
      several letters to him from the art critic who came to
      the timely defense of the fledgling P.R.B.

268. Wright, T[homas]. *The Life of John Payne*. London: Unwin, 1949. 283 pp.

Describes Payne's friendship with Rossetti during the 1870s, when the young poet was part of Ford Madox Brown's circle, receiving encouragement from Rossetti (three such letters are quoted). In later years Payne viewed his mentor as lacking in spontaneity, a poet who succeeded only through "puffery."

269. Altick, Richard D. "Post Mortems." *The Scholar Adventurers*. New York: Macmillan, 1950, pp. 249-269.

Summarizes the fatal illnesses and addictions of famous English poets, including Rossetti's addiction to chloral hydrate and whiskey.

270. Doughty, Oswald. "Rossetti and Mrs. Morris." *Times Literary Supplement*, 8 June 1951, p. 357.

Prints two letters from Rossetti to Dr. Hake which the author believes will support his conjectures about Rossetti's passion for Mrs. Morris (see item 281, the first edition of which had appeared in 1949). Further *TLS* correspondence and replies in issue numbers 2579, 2585, 2586, and 2588.

271. Cassiday, John A. "Robert Buchanan and the Fleshly Controversy." *Publications of the Modern Language Association* 67, no. 2 (March 1952): 65-93.

Chronicles Buchanan's career, from his early promise through the "Fleshly School" controversy to his later obscurity. The antipathy for Rossetti's poetry stemmed from earlier literary quarrels with Swinburne and William Michael Rossetti, from ill health, and from morbid religiosity. His later apology was genuine, but his career was destroyed nonetheless.

272. Preston, Kerrison, ed. *Letters from Graham Robertson*. London: Hamish Hamilton, 1953. 542 pp.

Contains numerous references to Rossetti by one who knew him (see item 235). The Violet Hunt biography (item 250) is disparaged as being especially unfair to Rossetti; it is the product of a writer with a real animus against her subject's husband.

273.   Stevenson, Lionel. "The House at Chelsea." *The Ordeal
       of George Meredith*. New York: Scribners, 1953, pp.
       108-125.

       Notes that Meredith was drawn to Rossetti because of
       the Pre-Raphaelite doctrine of frankness in art. But
       his fastidiousness and his sense of irony--including his
       ridicule of Rossetti's taste in women--led to the break
       both in their friendship and their joint tenancy of 16
       Cheyne Walk.

274.   Shute, Nerina. *Victorian Love Story: A Study of the Vic-
       torian Romantics Based on the Life of Dante Gabriel
       Rossetti: A Novel*. London: Jarrolds, 1954. 296 pp.

       Treats the familiar cast: Rossetti, "Johnny" Millais,
       "Sid" Siddal, Fanny Cornforth, "Topsy" Morris, Janey
       Morris, and the rest. The emphasis in this novel is on
       Rossetti's many love affairs.

275.   Batchelor, Paula. *Angel with Bright Hair*. London:
       Methuen, 1957. 254 pp.

       Another novelistic treatment of the life of Rossetti,
       this time with the emphasis on his relationship with
       Lizzie Siddal and his fascination with her beauty, which
       became for him the archetype of all feminine beauty.

276.   Ray, S.N. "The First Literary Friendship of D.G. Ros-
       setti." *Notes & Queries* 202 (1957): 435-454.

       Discusses the minor poet Major Robert Calder Campbell,
       who promoted such poets as Keats and Ebenezer Jones to
       the youthful Rossetti.

277.   Henderson, Philip. "La Belle Iseult." *The Saturday Book*.
       Edited by John Hadfield. Vol. 18. London: Hutchinson,
       1958, pp. 139-153.

       Retells the story of the love triangle of Rossetti,
       Morris, and Morris' "picturesque but dumb" wife. The
       conclusion is that the Rossetti-Jane Morris affair was
       long-lasting and physically intimate, the source both of
       Rossetti's poetry and Morris' misery. That misery also
       owed much to Morris' disillusion with himself for trying
       to make Jane his "Belle Iseult" while she was only a
       "mournful Pre-Raphaelite pinup."

278. Ferriday, Peter. "Peacock Room." *Architectural Review* 125 (1959): 407-414.

Contains thumbnail sketches of all the principals connected with the Peacock Room, including Rossetti, who introduced Leyland and Whistler. Rossetti "founded and funded the aesthetic movement in England"; he was an immensely attractive man for all of his seediness and decay.

279. Lang, C.Y., ed. *The Swinburne Letters*. 6 vols. New Haven: Yale University Press, 1959-1962.

Contains numerous references to Rossetti, especially in the earlier volumes. The relationship between the two poets was obviously a close one, as these letters show.

280. Williamson, Hugh Ross. "The Lost Letter." *Time and Tide* 40 (1959): 305-307.

Uses a letter from Hall Caine to speculate that Alice Boyd was Rossetti's secret love. [But see the numerous challenges to this thesis, especially the one by W.D. Paden in the 4 April number of the same journal.]

281. Doughty, Oswald. *A Victorian Romantic: Dante Gabriel Rossetti*. Second Edition. London: Oxford University Press, 1960. 712 pp.

The most complete biography. Provides "a study of the development of the personality," thus eschewing a critical approach to the painting or the poetry. Tries to avoid the sensational and arrives at some rather unsympathetic judgments about the subject. Rossetti's guilt over his wife's presumed suicide and a renewed passion for Jane Morris are the two determining factors in explaining Rossetti's later years. Most of the sonnets in "The House of Life" have a basis in biography: they are not about abstractions or a beatified Lizzie but rather about a very real and very physical affair with Mrs. Morris.

282. Rosenbaum, Robert A. "Dante Gabriel Rossetti, 1828-1882." *Earnest Victorians*. New York: Hawthorn, 1961, pp. 203-255.

A pastiche of comments on Rossetti and Pre-Raphaelitism by such contemporaries as Hunt, Millais, Ruskin, Scott, Dickens, Caine, Brown, and Patmore, interspersed with connecting material and commentary by the author. The emphasis is on Rossetti's magnetic personality.

283. Bennett, Mary. "The Pre-Raphaelites and the Liverpool
      Prize." *Apollo* 76 (1962): 748-753.

      Describes the often successful attempts of the Pre-
      Raphaelites to win the annual Liverpool Prize. Although
      Rossetti felt his subjects and style were too recondite
      for the competition, the Pre-Raphaelite ties with Liver-
      pool brought him patrons like Rae, Leathart, McCracken,
      and Miller.

284. Weber, Carl J. "The 'Discovery' of FitzGerald's *Rubaiyat*.
      Library Chronicle of the University of Texas 7, no. 3
      (Summer 1963): 3-11.

      Proves that FitzGerald's poem was first trumpeted by
      Whitley Stokes, not Rossetti or Swinburne, and in 1861,
      not 1862. But in 1862 Rossetti finally read the pamphlet
      given to him by Stokes a year earlier and then enthused
      about it to Swinburne, who in turn bought the copy now
      in the University of Texas Library.

285. Franklin, Colin. "'The Blessed Damozel' at Penkill."
      Essays in Criticism 14 (1964): 331-335.

      Relates the unusual events which marked Rossetti's stay
      at Penkill in 1868 to the bird-and-bell lines from the
      1856 version of "The Blessed Damozel," showing how art
      thus prefigured life.

286. Grylls, Rosalie Glynn. *Portrait of Rossetti*. London:
      Macdonald, 1964. 255 pp.

      Tries to offer a corrective to the strictures of Doughty
      (item 281) regarding Rossetti's motives and his relation-
      ship with Jane Morris, and often ends up verging on a
      panegyric. This is the first biography to draw extensivel
      upon Rossetti's letters to Mrs. Morris. The sympathetic
      treatment of its subject is extended even to his dismissal
      of old friends during the 1870s.

287. Packer, Lona Mosk. "Maria Francesca to Dante Gabriel
      Rossetti: Some Unpublished Letters." *Publications of
      the Modern Language Association* 79, no. 5 (December
      1964): 613-169.

      Reprints the full text of seven letters to Rossetti from
      his older sister. Written between 1872 and 1875, these
      affectionate letters show how much Maria had to supplement
      her brother's meagre knowledge of Italian.

288. Pedrick, Gale. *Life with Rossetti; or, No Peacocks Allowed*. London: Macdonald, 1964. 237 pp.

   Retells the old story of Rossetti's domestic life at Cheyne Walk, this time from the point of view of Henry Treffry Dunn, Rossetti's art assistant and general factotum. Pedrick, as Dunn's nephew, draws on unpublished correspondence between Dunn and Rossetti. See item 188.

289. Archer, Michael. "Rossetti and the Wombat." *Apollo* 81 (1965): 178-185.

   Notes Rossetti's fascination with animals, especially wombats. Wombats enticed Rossetti as early as 1857, and in 1869 he purchased one from Jamrach, thus furnishing the basis for several drawings and stories.

290. Henderson, Phillip. *William Morris: His Life, Work and Friends*. London: Thames and Hudson, 1967. 388 pp.

   Describes--particularly in chapters 2, 5, and 6--Morris' relations with Rossetti and his bitter reaction to the estrangement from Jane and the liaison between her and his old friend.

291. Dufty, A.R. "Kelmscott, William Morris's Holiday Home." *Connoisseur* 169 (1968): 205-212.

   Summarizes and illustrates Morris' tenancy of Kelmscott, with inevitably a discussion of Rossetti's co-tenancy and his relationship with Jane Morris.

292. Johnson, Fridolf. "William Morris." *American Artist* 32, no. 10 (December 1968): 43-49.

   Views Rossetti's unfortunate passion for Jane Morris as the explanation for both his own poetic obsessions and Morris'. The publication of *Poems* in 1870 must have enlightened Morris about how far the affair had gone.

293. Stanley, Fred L. "Christina Georgina to Dante Gabriel: An Unpublished Letter." *English Language Notes* 5 (1968): 283-285.

   Prints the text of an unpublished [and relatively unimportant] letter, probably dating from the mid-1870s; the letter shows the affectionate ties between the two poets.

294. Burd, Van Akin. "Ruskin, Rossetti, and William Bell
        Scott: A Second Arrangement." *Philological Quarterly*
        48 (1969): 102-107.

        Describes the circumstances surrounding the photographs
        taken of Rossetti, Ruskin, and Scott at Chelsea during
        the summer of 1863.

295. Vinciguerra, Mario. *John Ruskin ed i preraffaeliti*.
        Milan: Quaderni dell' Osservatore, 1969. 113 pp.

        Attributes Ruskin's involvement with the Pre-Raphaelites
        not so much to common principles--although they did exist
        --as to his fascination with the personality of Rossetti.
        The "two Rossettis" theory, i.e. he is half English, half
        Italian, must be rejected. It was popularized by English
        and French critics who did not know what to make of the
        poet's mercurial temperament, but the Italian element in
        Rossetti's personality was really very small and he was
        ignorant of almost all Italian art and literature beyond
        Dante. Ruskin's patronage of Rossetti and the subsequent
        cooling in that relationship are also summarized.

296. Dennis, Imogen. "Destruction by Vandals." *Country Life*
        148 (1970): 28.

        Describes the recent destruction of Ford Madox Brown's
        portrait bust of Rossetti, which stood in the garden in
        front of 16 Cheyne Walk. See item 299.

297. Fredeman, William E. "Prelude to the Last Decade: Dante
        Gabriel Rossetti in the Summer of 1872." *Bulletin of
        the John Rylands Library* 53 (1970-71): 75-121, 272-328.

        Discusses the distortion and selectivity of previous
        biographical accounts of Rossetti. Newly available docu-
        ments provide an unvarnished portrait of Rossetti during
        the critical summer when he attempted suicide. Rossetti's
        breakdown was apparently brought on by Buchanan's recently
        published attack on the poet. Included also is a calendar
        of the relevant letters from the Angeli and Penkill papers
        [Note: this article was also issued in separate covers by
        the library, under the same title.]

298. Murray, C.D. "Buchanan's Attack on Rossetti." *Notes &
        Queries* 215 (1970): 37.

        Asks why Rossetti was so sure in advance of publication
        that Buchanan would view *Poems* (1870) so harshly.

299. [Anonymous]. "Rossetti Is Back." *Country Life* 149
     (1971): 589.

     Notes the restoration of the Rossetti bust at the
     Cheyne Walk memorial by a recasting from the original
     mold. See item 296.

300. Bertram Rota Ltd. *Books from the Libraries of Christina,
     Dante Gabriel, and William Michael Rossetti*. Introduc-
     tion by William E. Fredeman. London: Rota, 1973. 48 pp.

     Describes 193 volumes from William Michael's personal
     library, now put up for sale. Since William Michael in-
     herited many books from his brother and sister, this cata-
     log sheds light on Rossetti's book acquisitions too. The
     brief introduction discusses the history of William
     Michael's library.

301. Claiborne, Jay W. "John Ruskin and Charles Augustus
     Howell: Some New Letters." *Texas Studies in Language
     and Literature* 15 (1973): 471-498.

     Guesses that Rossetti may have arranged for Howell to
     become Ruskin's secretary as a way of repairing the broken
     friendship. Howell often betrayed Ruskin's confidences
     to Rossetti.

302. Gomez, Joseph A. "Dante's Inferno: Seeing Ken Russell
     through Dante Gabriel Rossetti." *Literature/Film
     Quarterly* 1 (1973): 274-279.

     Sees Russell's film biography of Rossetti as typical of
     Russell's film style and as perceptive in its grasp of
     Rossetti's character (e.g. the clash between high ideals
     and physical urges). The film's structure involves
     development through parallel characters, scenes, and
     objects. While it takes liberties with the facts, it
     also offers defensible and even exciting interpretations.

303. Pittman, Philip M. "Blake, Rossetti, and Reynolds: A
     Detail." *Notes & Queries* 219 (1974): 215-216.

     Shows that Rossetti read Blake's annotations to Reynolds'
     Discourses only in the early 1860s--not in the late 1840s
     as previously believed.

304. Weintraub, Stanley. "Tudor House." *Whistler: A Biog-
     raphy*. New York: Weybright and Talley, 1974, pp. 92-103.

Chronicles Whistler's close association with Rossetti during the 1860s. Whistler admired the brooding, imperious, but charming Rossetti, whose "moral anarchism" influenced the young American. The two painters also shared passions (blue china), patrons (Leyland), and problems (money).

305. Fredeman, William E. "'From Insult to Protect': The Pre-Raphaelites and the Biographical Fallacy." *Sources for Reinterpretation: The Use of Nineteenth Century Literary Documents: Essays in Honor of C.L. Cline.* Austin: University of Texas Press, 1975, pp. 57-80.

Describes the ways in which the life of Rossetti has been sensationalized to the detriment of useful scholarship. The author narrates the growth of his own interest in the Pre-Raphaelites, including his friendship with Helen Rossetti Angeli and his discovery of the Penkill Papers (see item 297); he also advances his ideas about the proper use of such life documents.

306. Fredeman, William E., ed. *The P.R.B. Journal: William Michael Rossetti's Diary of the Pre-Raphaelite Brotherhood, 1849-1853.* Oxford: Clarendon Press, 1975. 282 pp

An unexpurgated edition of the diary kept by William Michael during the early years of the P.R.B. (see item 123). Although Gabriel later mutilated the diary, destroying (the editor estimates) as much as forty percent of the leaves, this remnant still tells us a great deal about the daily lives of the young Rossetti brothers and their friends. Appendices on *The Germ* and other P.R.B. affairs plus an extensive critical apparatus and notes are also included.

307. Hale, John. *The Love School.* New York: St. Martin's Press, 1975. 207 pp.

A novel treating the loves of young Rossetti, Millais, and Hunt, beginning with the time before they met "Lizzie, Effie, and Annie," respectively. The emphasis is on the social life of Victorian England. Rossetti is a Faustian figure. His life is followed up to the time of his involvement with Jane Morris.

308. LeBourgeois, John. "Morris, Rossetti, and Warrington Taylor." *Notes & Queries* 220 (1975): 113-115.

Uses letters related to a marital crisis of Taylor's

(who was a member of "The Firm") to speculate that it was
Morris' neglect of his wife in favor of work that drew
Rossetti and Jane Morris closer together in 1868.

309. Munro, John M. "D.G. Rossetti, William Bell Scott, Theo.
     Marzials and a Letter That Came Too Late." *Notes &
     Queries* 220 (1975): 441-443.

     Notes how Marzials abandoned poetry in part because of
     adverse criticism by Rossetti, a criticism later softened
     and balanced by a letter from Rossetti to Scott praising
     Marzials.

310. Bury, Shirley. "Rossetti and His Jewelry." *Burlington
     Magazine* 118 (1976): 94-102.

     Discusses, in considerable detail and with illustrations,
     the bequest to the Victoria and Albert Museum of the
     jewelry of the late May Morris. Much of the jewelry
     had been worn by Jane Morris while she posed for Rossetti's
     paintings. Particularly noteworthy are a Burmese gold
     bracelet from *The Beloved*, a Tyrolean belt from *Astarte
     Syriaca*, an emerald ring from *La Bello Mano*, and a heart
     brooch from *Mariana*.

311. Cable, Carol. "Charles Fairfax Murray, Assistant to Dante
     Gabriel Rossetti." *Library Chronicle of the University
     of Texas* 10 (1976): 81-89.

     Uses unpublished letters by Rossetti to show how the
     seventeen-year-old Murray was employed as a studio as-
     sistant and supplier of photographs. Murray became in-
     valuable as a copyist and general factotum.

312. Williamson, Audrey. "Rossetti and Pre-Raphaelitism."
     Artists and Writers in Revolt: The Pre-Raphaelites.
     Philadelphia: Art Alliance Press, 1976, pp. 37-61.

     Intends to show the Pre-Raphaelites as rebels against
     the urban society created by the Industrial Revolution.
     The chapter on Rossetti summarizes his adult life and
     describes the magnetism of his personality, his relation-
     ship with his models, and his inner conflicts.

313. Dobbs, Brian and Judy. *Dante Gabriel Rossetti: An Alien
     Victorian*. Atlantic Highlands, N.J.: Humanities Press,
     1977. 256 pp.

     A short, derivative biography, based on already pub-

lished material. The portrait of the artist is generally
sympathetic. The emphasis is on his struggle in trying
to work in a society hostile to the nature of his genius.

314.   LeBourgeois, John. "The Love and Marriage of William
          Morris: A New Interpretation." *South Carolina Review*
          9, no. 2 (April 1977): 43-55.

          Argues that Morris' failure to outgrow his infatuation
          with his sister Emma, rather than Rossetti's affair with
          Jane, caused the breakdown of Morris' marriage. The theme
          of unrequited love appears very early in Morris' poetry,
          not just in the late 1860s. Letters are used to substan-
          tiate the thesis regarding Emma.

315.   Bornand, Odette, ed. *The Diary of William Michael Rossetti
          1870-1873.* Oxford: Clarendon Press, 1977. 302 pp.

          A hitherto-unpublished successor volume to items 122,
          123, and 124. The original volume was to have contained,
          besides the diary, letters from and to the Rossetti
          brothers, but only the diary portion is printed now.
          The entries allude to such matters as the publication of
          Poems (1870), the "Fleshly School" controversy, Rossetti's
          breakdown in 1872, and Rossetti's activities as a painter.
          See also item 306.

316.   Taylor, Frank, and Glenis A. Matheson. "Handlist of Addi-
          tions to the Collection of English Manuscripts in the
          John Rylands University Library of Manchester, 1952-
          1970." *Bulletin of the John Rylands University Library*
          60 (1977): 213-267.

          Describes recent additions to the collection, in parti-
          cular some items of interest to students of Rossetti's
          life (photographs, letters to him, etc.).

317.   Savage, Elizabeth. *Willowwood: A Novel.* Boston: Little
          Brown, 1978. 214 pp.

          Treats Rossetti's life from 1850 until his attempted
          suicide. The principal foci are Rossetti's relationship
          with Fanny Cornforth and his ambivalent attitudes toward
          Lizzie Siddal.

318.   Trevelyan, Raleigh. *A Pre-Raphaelite Circle.* London:
          Chatto and Windus, 1978. 256 pp.

          A biography of Pauline Lady Trevelyan. Offers many

glances at her Pre-Raphaelite friends, including Rossetti,
who painted *Mary in the House of John* for her.

319. Weintraub, Stanley. *Four Rossettis: A Victorian Biography*.
New York: Weybright, 1978. 303 pp.

Summarizes the lives and loves of the four Rossetti
children (Maria, Dante Gabriel, Christina, and William
Michael), offering more narration than interpretation.
Repeats the view of Rossetti as a gloomy, anxiety-
ridden addict, and uses his poetry as material for biographical speculation.

320. Boos, Florence S. "Old Controversies, New Texts: Two
Recent Books on Pre-Raphaelitism." *Modern Philology*
77 (1979): 172-187.

A comprehensive review-essay focusing on items 144 and
306. Contends that Rossetti's letters to Jane Morris
show that he disliked, even despised, Morris, and that he
found the outer world "monotonous, faithless, and menacing."
Parallels both in diction and theme between the letters
and Rossetti's poems are also noted. The P.R.B. journal
shows William Michael's selflessness and his devotion to
his brother. It also shows how much William Michael and
Coventry Patmore influenced the direction of the P.R.B.

321. Going, William T. "'Goblin Market' and the Pre-Raphaelite
Brotherhood." *Pre-Raphaelite Review* 3 (1979): 1-11.

Claims that Christina Rossetti modeled the characters
in her poem at least partly after the members of the
P.R.B. and their associates. Thus Dante Gabriel becomes
one of the little goblin men, "Brother with queer brother,
/Signaling each to other, /Brother with sly brother."
The use of the name "Lizzie" is also not accidental.

See also items 62, 64, 78, 111, 118-147, 341, 357, 360, 369,
385, 405, 426, 428, 431, 449, 464, 534, 538, 539, 551, 592, 652,
672, 684, 710, 829, 836, 859, 884, 885, 891, 893, 906, 919,
953, 961, 986, 989, 991, 997, 1006, 1018, 1028, 1038, 1043,
1051, 1052, 1054, 1059, 1075, 1082, 1094.

Studies of Rossetti
as a Writer

This section includes critical assessments of Rossetti as a poet and prose writer. Criticisms of specific works may be mentioned, but if the study is devoted solely to an individual work it will be found in Section B. Criticisms of Rossetti published during his lifetime, principally in the form of reviews, can be found in item 11 (sections 27-29).

322. [Anonymous]. "The Poetry of Rossetti." *British Quarterly* 76 (1882): 109-127.

Judges Rossetti adversely as the high priest of a cult which is pernicious for modern poetry. His ballads are dexterous but counterfeit, his lyrics are mediocre in thought and expression, his sonnets are deficient both in music and in genuine inspiration. The "House of Life" poems prove that Rossetti does not understand love and lacks the ability to give a sustained criticism of life.

323. Hamilton, Walter. "Dante Gabriel Rossetti" and "Buchanan's Attack on Rossetti." *The Aesthetic Movement in England*. London: Reeves and Turner, 1882, pp. 54-64.

Predicts that the "Aesthetic poets," i.e. largely the Pre-Raphaelites, will become for the second half of the century what Wordsworth and the Lakers were for the first half. Rossetti is the pre-eminent poet, and the attack on him by Buchanan was the work of an egotistical scribbler.

324. Shairp, J.C. "Aesthetic Poetry: Dante Gabriel Rossetti." *Contemporary Review* 42 (1882): 17-32.

Objects to Rossetti's poetry as work that appeals "to the perfumed taste of overeducated coteries." He lacks manly thought, noble sentiment, and fresh diction. Reprinted also in *Eclectic Magazine* and *Living Age*.

325. Sharp, William. "Dante Gabriel Rossetti and Pictorialism in Verse." *Portfolio* 13 (1882): 176-180.

Defines *suggestiveness* as the prime quality of poetic pictorialism. The poet need not be especially detailed in his descriptions, and his imagery can be highly condensed. Rossetti epitomizes such a poet, as "The Blessed Damozel" demonstrates.

326. Smith, G. Barnett. "Dante Gabriel Rossetti." *Time* 7
      (1882): 163-173.

      Praises Rossetti as a major poet, equal to the early
      Tennyson. His poetry is marked by an artist's sense for
      beauty and by pictorial power. He can be faulted for
      recondite diction and a neglect of simple English themes.

327. Benton, Joel. "Dante Gabriel Rossetti, the Apostle of
      Beauty." *Manhattan* 2 (1883): 249-253.

      Esteems Rossetti's poetry because it is symbolic, misty,
      subtly spiritual yet profoundly human. Sometimes his in-
      trospections lead him to a "morbid and unhealthy laxity,"
      but he is saved by the purity of his devotion to beauty.

328. Waddington, Samuel. "The Sonnets of Rossetti." *Academy*
      25 (1884): 385.

      Notes that the twelve sonnets by which Rossetti is re-
      presented in *English Sonnets by Living Writers* were with
      one exception chosen by the poet himself. Thus they can
      serve as an indication of his judgment of his own best
      work in that form.

329. Sarrazin, Gabriel. "Dante Gabriel Rossetti." *Poètes
      modernes de l'Angleterre*. Paris: Ollendorff, 1885,
      pp. 233-271.

      Makes great claims for Rossetti as a renovator of Eng-
      lish poetry and an apostle of aestheticism. Rossetti,
      like Dante, is an exile always writing a *vita nuova*. His
      visions are poised between the pictorial and the poetic,
      the real and the imaginary. Unfortunately he has more
      images than he does ideas. Short critical comments on
      selected poems can illustrate these general remarks.

330. Buchanan, Robert W. "A Note on Dante Rossetti." *A Look
      Round Literature*. London: World, 1887, pp. 152-161.

      Retracts his earlier abuse: Buchanan now finds Rossetti
      modest, gentle, pure, and delicate. The "Fleshly School"
      judgment was based on a lack of sympathy, since cor-
      rected. Rossetti is a wizard, a necromancer, a sibyl,
      one who uses earthly love--"the noblest pleasure"--to
      reach the heavens. His intentions are always beyond
      any reproach.

331. Horne, Herbert P. "Thoughts Towards a Criticism of the
     Works of Dante Gabriel Rossetti." *Century Guild Hobby
     Horse* n.s. 2 (1887): 91-102.

     Defines "the passion of Love" as the master spirit of
     Rossetti's life, one that accounts for the seeming
     materialism of his poetry and which gives unity to "The
     House of Life." At his best Rossetti is fresh, even
     exotic. But he can also be overly elaborate, too narrow,
     and thus he can never serve as a model.

332. Prideaux, W.F. "Dante Gabriel Rossetti." *Notes & Que-
     ries*, 7th series, 4 (1887): 481-482.

     Calls attention to variants between the texts of the
     first and subsequent editions of Rossetti's poems.
     Examples from "Love's Nocturne," "The Burden of Nineveh,"
     and "The Card Dealer" show how fastidious Rossetti was
     in revising his poetry, usually with good results.

333. Wood, Charles J. "Dante Gabriel Rossetti." *Andover
     Review* 8 (1887): 573-592.

     Presents Rossetti as a seer, a prophet, one who used
     mystical and symbolic language to convey his deep truths
     about the oneness of love and life. His poetry is time-
     less yet shows the earnestness, sincerity, and purity
     characteristic of his age.

334. Bates, Herbert. "A Study of Rossetti's Verse." *Harvard
     Monthly* 7 (1889): 130-137.

     Characterizes Rossetti as a mystic, one who aspires
     toward the unattainable and sees into "the secret sug-
     gestiveness." However his striving is coupled with
     passion, and this is a defect. Furthermore his poetry
     is often victimized by weaknesses in technique, in
     diction, and in poetic strength.

335. Pater, Walter. "Dante Gabriel Rossetti." *Appreciations*.
     London: Macmillan, 1889, pp. 205-218.

     Sees Rossetti's chief qualities as sincerity, trans-
     parency in language, definiteness of imagery, vividness
     in the use of personifications, and feverishness in
     mood. His most distinctive contribution to poetry is
     the addition of fresh poetic material. Reprinted from
     Ward's *English Poets* series (1883).

336.   Patmore, Coventry. "Rossetti as a Poet." *Principle in
       Art*. London: Bell, 1889, pp. 103-111.

       Sees Rossetti as a better poet when he eschews his
       characteristic subtlety of thought and diction. The
       reason for Rossetti's unusual diction is perhaps his
       lack of familiarity with English literature and his de-
       votion to inferior Italian poets, including Dante [!].
       The ballads are Rossetti's best work, and many of the
       sonnets show remarkable insight.

337.   Dawson, William James. "Dante Gabriel Rossetti." *Makers
       of Modern English*. London: Hodder and Stoughton, 1890,
       pp. 341-352.

       Views Rossetti as a poet whose high artistic quality
       was betrayed by "unmanliness" and morbidity. No healthy
       mind could luxuriate so much in over-ripe female charms.
       Rossetti's chief virtues were his melody and his command
       of the romantic and the supernatural.

338.   Sharp, Amy. "Dante Gabriel Rossetti, William Morris,
       and Algernon Charles Swinburne." *Victorian Poets*.
       London: Methuen, 1891, pp. 157-185.

       Sees Rossetti's poetry as escapist, but healthily so:
       like Coleridge he suspends our disbelief, takes us into
       the unknown. Rossetti is the greatest Victorian sonnet
       writer. His work is marked by intensity, mysticism,
       music, diction, and technical mastery.

339.   Walker, John. "Dante Gabriel Rossetti." *Manchester
       Quarterly* 10 (1891): 71-92.

       Points out the perfections in Rossetti's poetry; the
       blemishes will be left for other eyes. These perfections
       include originality, intensity, mysticism, and solemnity.
       Special attention is given to "The Blessed Damozel,"
       "The Cloud Confines," "Jenny," and the ballads. The
       poetry forms "an enduring monument of triumphant achieve-
       ment."

340.   Mabie, Hamilton W. "The Poetry of Dante Gabriel Rossetti.
       Essays in Literary Interpretation. New York: Dodd,
       Mead, 1892, pp. 71-98.

       Charts Rossetti's progress from his "prenatal" [!] edu-
       cation to the conclusion of his "uneventful" [!] life. As

a poet he is subtle, delicate, a lover of beauty and a
devotee of the power of love as it transforms lives. Reprinted from the *Andover Review* (1889).

341. Hodgkins, Louise M. "Dante Gabriel Rossetti." *A Guide
to the Study of Nineteenth Century Authors*. Boston:
Heath, 1893, pp. 66-70.

A study guide prepared by the author for her students
at Wellesley College. Lists biographical facts, friends,
selected poems, and secondary sources.

342. Worsfold, W. Basil. "The Poetry of D.G. Rossetti."
Nineteenth Century 34 (1893): 284-290.

Contends that Rossetti was deficient in ideas, in
architectonics, and in fluidity. But within his narrow
sphere of the soul and its images Rossetti is supreme.
He is the poet of love, of the entire gamut of human
passions, of the union between the spiritual and the
physical.

343. [Anonymous]. "The Poetry of Dante Gabriel Rossetti."
London Quarterly Review 82 (1894): 104-112.

Finds in Rossetti's poetry charm, grace, vigor, originality; his fancy is rich and his technique is emi-
nently pictorial. But at times he is repetitive, in-
direct, deficient in ideas, and incapable of giving a
healthy inspiration to his readers.

344. Jacottet, Henri. "Poètes modernes de l'Angleterre:
Dante Gabriel Rossetti." *Bibliothèque Universelle
et Revue Suisse*, ser. 3, 62-63 (1894): 503-524,
94-114, resp.

Recounts Rossetti's career as a poet, then translates
and explicates sonnets from "The House of Life," selected ballads, and "Jenny." Rossetti is a poet of both
subtlety and humane breadth.

345. Kernahan, Coulson. "A Note on Rossetti." *Sorrow and
Song*. Philadelphia: Lippincott, 1894, pp. 406-412.

Notes the controversy over whether Rossetti expresses
genuine feeling or the self-consciousness of a poseur.
We can accept him if we use the medieval standards of
taste by which he himself wrote, rather than subjecting

him to our own moralistic rejection of his Southern
warmth, his non-didacticism, and his sensuousness.
Revised from an essay in the *Fortnightly Review* (1891).

346. Saintsbury, George. "The Second Poetical Period."
      *A History of Nineteenth Century Literature (1780-
      1895).* London: Macmillan, 1896, pp. 253-316.

      Surveys the major Victorian poets and finds in Ros-
      setti the most direct descendent of the earlier Romantics.
      He is pictorial, mystical, medieval, ornate in his lan-
      guage and cunning in his use of verbal music.

347. Guthrie, William Norman. "Dante Gabriel Rosetti."
      *Modern Poet Prophets: Essays Critical and Inter-
      pretive.* Cincinnati: Clarke, 1897, pp. 115-123.

      Sees "Rosetti" [sic] as an agnostic who nevertheless
      wanted to stimulate faith artificially by means of his
      symbolism. The poet only succeeds in losing his way
      and deluding his readers.

348. Hume, James Cleland. "Rossetti, the Poet, and the Pre-
      Raphaelite Brothers." *Midland Monthly* 7 (1897):
      42-52.

      Judges Rossetti as lacking in health, scope, tone,
      virility, and robustness. Yet he also possesses a
      devotion to beauty and genuine religious feeling; "The
      House of Life" is perhaps the greatest sonnet sequence
      since Shakespeare.

349. Morse, Charles A.L. "Rossetti's Poetry." *Catholic
      World* 65 (1897): 633-640.

      Urges readers to acquaint themselves with a too-much-
      neglected Rossetti, because much of his poetry is ex-
      cellent and fully in tune with the Catholic spirit. He
      is not sensual, not didactic.

350. Nencioni, Enrico. "Opere di Dante Gabriele Rossetti."
      Saggi critici di letteratura inglese. Florence:
      LeMonnier, 1897, pp. 317-322.

      Sees Rossetti's poetry as a continuation of the Roman-
      tic movement. "The Blessed Damozel" shows the poet's
      striving for a personal resurrection, a second birth. He

lacks, however, the large human sympathy which characterizes the very greatest writers.

351. Noble, James A. "A Pre-Raphaelite Magazine." *The Sonnet
      in England and Other Essays*. Portland, Maine: Mosher,
      1898, pp. xv-xxx.

      Recounts the history of *The Germ* and summarizes its
      contents. Rossetti's contributions are judged to be the
      best in terms of quality: he is a poet of beauty, imagi-
      nation, and precision. From *Fraser's Magazine* (1892).

352. Beers, Henry A. "The Pre-Raphaelites." *A History of
      Romanticism in the Nineteenth Century*. New York:
      Holt, 1901, pp. 282-351.

      Finds in Rossetti's poetry the most important influence
      on late nineteenth-century Romanticism. His symbolism,
      medievalism, and aestheticism make his position akin to
      that of Coleridge earlier in the century, i.e. his was a
      seminal mind which guided younger and more proficient
      artists. Rossetti in turn had been influenced by Coler-
      idge and pre-eminently by Keats.

353. Kenyon, James B. "Dante Gabriel Rossetti and His Sister
      Christina." *Loiterings in Old Fields: Literary Sketches*.
      New York: Eaton, 1901, pp. 149-171.

      Sees Rossetti as a "brilliant and unique" poet, a com-
      pound of Keats, Shelley, Poe, and Baudelaire whose most
      distinguishing feature is mysticism. Reprinted from the
      Methodist Review (1893).

354. Payne, William M. "Dante Gabriel Rossetti (1828-1882)."
      Library of the World's Best Literature. Edited by
      C.D. Warner. Vol. 31. New York: Hill, [1902],
      pp. 12411-12415.

      Judges Rossetti to be one of the six major poets of
      the Victorian era. He is a poet dominated by "retro-
      spection, anticipation, and gnomic philosophical
      utterance." His works are rich in imagination and in
      compression. Nineteen selected poems illustrate these
      observations.

355. Spens, J. "The Ethical Significance of Rossetti's
      Poetry." *International Journal of Ethics* 12 (1902):
      216-225.

Believes that Rossetti is a very serious poet, one who
is not "fleshly" at all but rather one who in various
ways explores the issue of "at what point the purely
sensuous passes into the intellectual."

356. Galletti, Alfredo. "Dante Gabriel Rossetti e la poesia
     preraffaellita." *Studi di letteratura straniere.*
     Verona: Fratelli Drucker, 1903, pp. 1-68.

     Offers a general introduction to Rossetti's poetry for
     an audience presumed to be unfamiliar with it; generous
     extracts are included. Reprinted from *Emporium* (1897).

357. Benson, Arthur C. *Rossetti* [*English Men of Letters
     Series*]. London: Macmillan, 1904. 238 pp.

     Offers a romantic view of Rossetti as the poet who al-
     ways dwelt in an atmosphere of beauty "to which the sordid
     acts of real life were but dreary interruptions." Gives
     biographical data with concentration on the literary
     works, and summarizes what the author believes to be
     Rossetti's strengths and weaknesses as a poet. The early
     poems are refreshingly naive, the later ones show Ros-
     setti as a "weaver of strange tapestries." The treatment
     is generally sympathetic, although special emphasis is
     placed on Rossetti's chloral addiction and on his unfor-
     tunate relationship with Lizzie Siddal. Reprinted 1973.

358. Fuller, Edward. "Arnold, Newman, and Rossetti." *Critic*
     45 (1904): 273-276.

     Compares and contrasts the three writers who, different
     as they were in temperament, enjoyed a similar measure
     of popularity in their day and have suffered a similar
     eclipse. Of Rossetti it can be said that Buchanan's
     charges were not unjust: he was not a great poet, and
     "this Hyperion had a strain of the satyr."

359. Henry, Albert S. "Rossetti." *Book News Monthly* 22
     (1904): 1032-1033.

     Reviews item 357 favorably and finds in Rossetti one
     who asks, not British questions about morality, but
     rather Italian questions about beauty.

360. Moulton, Charles W., ed. "Gabriel Charles Dante Rossetti.
     *The Library of Literary Criticism of English and Ameri-
     can Authors.* Vol. 7. Buffalo: Moulton, 1904, pp. 434-4

Prints extracts from several dozen Victorian criticisms of Rossetti. Separate headings: "Personal" (the largest category), "Art," "Blessed Damozel," "Sister Helen," "Jenny," "King's Tragedy," "House of Life," "Sonnets," and "General."

361. Sieper, Ernst. *Das Evangelium der Schönheit in der englischen Literatur und Kunst des XIX. Jahrhunderts.* Dortmund: Ruhfus, 1904, pp. 250-264.

Not examined.

362. Hellings, Emma L. "Rossetti's Treatment of Love." *Poet Lore* 16, no. 1 (Spring 1905): 76-79.

Describes Rossetti's ideas about love as centering on three themes: illumination through the senses; the immortality of the love moment; the desire for eternal union of the lovers.

363. Weygandt, Cornelius. "Two Pre-Raphaelite Poets: William Morris and Dante Gabriel Rossetti." *Book News Monthly* 24 (1906): 687-690.

Rossetti's poetry shows reverence and rapture. His best works are the medieval ballads, which demonstrate that the poet had considerable dramatic powers.

364. Payne, William M. "Dante Gabriel Rossetti." *The Greater English Poets of the Nineteenth Century.* London: Bell, 1907, pp. 284-315.

Weighs the Pre-Raphaelites as equal to the five great Romantic poets. Rossetti is pure, manly, religious, spiritual, a man of deep convictions and a master of poetic technique.

365. Smith, Arnold W. "Neo-Romanticism: Dante Gabriel Rossetti." *The Main Tendencies of Victorian Poetry.* London: Simpkin, 1907, pp. 183-195.

Sees Rossetti as a neo-Romantic by virtue of his use of mystery and his devotion to the past. The detailed coloring in his ballads gives them their peculiar strength. Love is his single theme, but it is treated in a great variety of ways and remains "the one true thing in a world of illusion."

366. Brooke, Stopford A. "Dante Gabriel Rossetti." *Four Vic-*
      torian Poets: Clough, Arnold, Rossetti, and Morris.
      London: Putnam, 1908, pp. 145-204.

      Relates Rossetti to the problem of struggling against
      one's times. Arnold and others accepted this struggle,
      but Rossetti, like Keats before him, escaped, fleeing
      into another world. Yet in his poems Rossetti often
      touches on eternal questions through a masterful use of
      symbol and image, and in this he is thoroughly modern.
      Furthermore he shows a surprising love of order, a "noble
      chastity," and a mystical supernaturalism, although his
      "perfumed air" insures that he will not be ranked as a
      great poet.

367. Fontainas, André. "Dante Gabriel Rossetti, le poète."
      Mercure de France 73 (1908): 193-211.

      Surveys Rossetti's poetic career and includes French
      translations for six of his poems. Sees Rossetti as
      Italian in his origins, his tendencies, and his aspira-
      tions. His poetry is mysterious, incantatory, and more
      lyrical than that of any other English poet except
      Keats. His love for feminine beauty was but an avenue
      to spiritual beauty, and it helped to change the direc-
      tion of modern poetry.

368. Horn, Kurt. *Studien zum Dichterischen Entwicklungsgange*
      DG Rossettis. Berlin: Felber, 1909. 141 pp.

      Summarizes scholarship on Rossetti as a poet and in-
      cludes a list of works. Emphasizes the pictorial nature
      of Rossetti's poetry and combats the views of Max Nordau
      (see item 995) regarding its alleged unhealthiness.
      Also included are German translations of Rossetti's work
      and a study by R.G. Watkin of the relationship between
      Robert Browning and the Pre-Raphaelites (item 600).

369. Kellner, Leon. "Dante Gabriel Rossetti und die Prä-
      raffaeliten." *Die Englische Literatur im Zeitalter*
      der Königin Viktoria. Leipzig: Tauchnitz, 1909,
      pp. 463-482.

      Offers short descriptions of Rossetti's life, his per-
      sonality, and his poetic characteristics. As a poet his
      soul was torn between rationalism and "Catholic" super-
      stition. He became master of a new style in poetry, thus
      influencing others (like Patmore and Marston) just as he
      in turn had been shaped by Elizabeth Barrett Browning.

370. Magnus, Laurie. "Pre-Raphaelitism." *English Literature in the Nineteenth Century.* London: Melrose, 1909, pp. 301-314.

Views the Pre-Raphaelites as Bohemians united by their opposition to unworthy standards. Rossetti's poetic career was affected by his Italianate blood, his idealism, and the shipwreck of his marriage. All led to an increasingly ornate style and to the sacrifice of "universalism to particularism, and concentric to esoteric art."

371. Armstrong, C.B. "Some Poets of the Victorian Era. XI. Dante Gabriel Rossetti." *Academy* 79 (1910): 317-318, 341-342.

Judges Rossetti as a man with a generous heart, and thus devoted to the worship of women. His poems show sensitivity, pain, and longing; his diction and technique are masterful. The principal faults are an over-zealous search for recondite words and prolixity. Based on a Trinity College prize essay, reprinted in the college's Philosophical Society *Publications* (1910).

372. Chapman, E[dward] M[ortimer]. "The Doubters and the Mystics." *English Literature in Account with Religion.* Boston: Houghton Mifflin, 1910, pp. 423-459.

Includes Rossetti among the mystics, although he has a dreamy, anemic, decadent tone. His poetry is permeated by a musical but fragile languor.

373. Foster, Nancy K. "A Word for Rossetti." *Poet Lore* 21 (1910): 322-329.

Pays tribute to Rossetti as one who can create a spell of brooding calm in which color and music interpenetrate to reveal the depths of the spirit. His is a delicate, spiritualizing sorcery, full of pathos, and he is a perfect antidote for modern decadence.

374. Saintsbury, George. "The Pre-Raphaelite School." *A History of English Prosody from the Twelfth Century to the Present Day.* Vol. 3. London: Macmillan, 1910, pp. 307-375.

Praises Rossetti for his prosodic dexterity, especially in the use of names, in the felicity of rhythm, and in the adaptation of the Petrarchan form.

375. Walker, Hugh. "The Pre-Raphaelites." *The Literature of
      the Victorian Era*. Cambridge University Press, 1910,
      pp. 490-512.

      Chronicles Rossetti's development as a poet. The works
      in the 1870 *Poems* are rich in pictorial detail but are
      too ornate to satisfy long. When Rossetti is good he
      is clear, definite, virile; when he is bad he is fanciful,
      artificial. He is the best embodiment of the nineteenth-
      century spirit of art.

376. Saintsbury, George E. "The Poetry of Dante Gabriel
      Rossetti." *Bookman* [London] 40 (1911): 120-127.

      Sees Rossetti's poetry as bedevilled by three enemies:
      belatedness, detraction, and Rossetti's own legend. The
      author recounts his own purchase of *Poems* in the year of
      its publication and his recognition that Rossetti and
      his sister were the best sonnet writers in the language
      after Shakespeare. Illustrated by thirty-six plates
      and photographs.

377. Ulmer, Hermann. *Dante Gabriel Rossettis Versetechnik*.
      Bayreuth: Ellwanger, 1911. 112 pp.

      Not examined.

378. Des Garets, Marie-L. "Dante Gabriel Rossetti, 1828-
      1882." *La Revue Hebdomadaire* 4 (1912): 212-221.

      Contains a short introduction to Rossetti's poetry
      plus translations into French of six of his works.

379. Reed, Edward Bliss. "The Lyric of the Nineteenth Cen-
      tury, Part II." *English Lyrical Poetry*. New Haven:
      Yale University Press, 1912, pp. 447-509.

      Judges Rossetti to be "among our greatest lyricists,"
      a master of technique who treated beauty, love, and
      desolation and who possessed "insight into spiritual
      realities."

380. Sharp, William. "Rossetti in Prose and Verse." *Papers
      Critical and Reminiscent*. New York: Duffield, 1912,
      pp. 38-65.

      Sees Rossetti as a writer who always portrays himself
      and thereby fascinates us. Rossetti, haunted by a vision

of Beauty, is an exponent of the renascence of wonder, although this devotion sometimes leads him to obscurity and to extravagance in diction. His sorrow is deeply serious, even noble. Reprinted from *National Review* and *Eclectic Magazine* (1887).

381. Olivero, Federico. "Il Ritornello nella poesia di Dante Gabriele Rossetti." *Saggi di letteratura inglese.* Bari: Laterza, 1913, pp. 283-294.

Examines Rossetti's use of the refrain, finding that it serves both descriptive and musical functions. "Sister Helen" is used as the chief example. See item 410. Reprinted from *Archiv für das Studien der neueren Sprachen und Literaturen* (1910).

382. Schelling, Felix E. "The Victorian Lyricists." *The English Lyric.* Boston: Houghton Mifflin, 1913, pp. 194-263.

Includes Rossetti among the lyricists: he is the most purely lyrical of all. Untrammelled by rule or precedent, his poetry is rich, spontaneous, visionary. While his feeling is sometimes in excess of his thought, the works as a whole maintain a high and impassioned poetic level.

383. Spurgeon, Caroline F.E. "Love and Beauty Mystics." *Mysticism in English Literature.* Cambridge University Press, 1913, pp. 35-56.

Sees Rossetti's mysticism as a thirst for knowledge of the mystery lurking beyond feminine beauty. But he lacks a metaphysical dimension, perhaps because he became entangled in the "swamp" of sensuous beauty. Reprinted from the *Quarterly Review* (1907).

384. Walker, Hugh, and Mrs. Hugh Walker. "The Turn of the Century." *Outlines of Victorian Literature.* Cambridge University Press, 1913, pp. 73-85.

Judges Rossetti as sometimes too cloying, too enervating, too sensual. Yet he must be numbered among the major Victorian poets, and occasionally he verges on the heroic.

385. Boas, Mrs. F[rederick] S[amuel]. *Rossetti and His Poetry.* London: Harrap, [1914]. 149 pp.

Uses a chronology of Rossetti's poetic career as a

device for reprinting and then commenting on his poems.
The comments on the poems are mostly appreciations of
them and summaries of their themes. Of the poet himself
it is sufficient to say that he was "a genius." Reprinted 1972.

386. Schoepe, Max. *Der Vergleich bei Dante Gabriel Rossetti.*
     Eine stilistische Untersuchung. [*Normannia*, vol. 13.]
     Berlin: Felber, 1914. 152 pp.

     Examines Rossetti's imagery as an approach to style.
     The first part considers and gives examples of the nature
     imagery: earth, stars, times of the day and year, the
     four elements, weather, trees, flowers, animals and birds.
     The second part describes and illustrates imagery drawn
     from human life: bodies, clothes, work, recreation,
     religion, science, mythology. The final section analyzes
     Rossetti's sources, his influence, and the high artistic
     value of his imagery. Supersedes a volume with a similar
     title from the preceding year.

387. Bell, A.F. "Rossetti, Morris, and Swinburne." *Leaders*
     in English Literature. London: Bell, 1915, pp. 214-223.

     Briefly surveys Rossetti's poetic career, with emphasis
     on the ballads and his medievalism.

388. Galletti, Alfredo. "Dante Gabriel Rossetti e il roman-
     ticismo preraffaellita." *Saggi e studi.* Bologna:
     Zanichelli, 1915, pp. 1-94.

     Traces Rossetti's Romanticism to origins in German
     thought, in English literature and folklore, and in
     contemporary poets like Tennyson and Browning. Offers
     detailed summaries, translations, and analyses of the
     major ballads, and praises "The House of Life" as a
     beautiful, delicate, and visionary work. Rossetti was
     trying to recapture the energy and lyricism of the early
     Italians. Reprinted in *Studi di letteratura inglese*
     (1928).

389. Brawley, Benjamin. "Pre-Raphaelitism and Its Literary
     Remains." *South Atlantic Quarterly* 15 (1916): 68-81.

     Charges Rossetti and the Pre-Raphaelite poets with
     being esoteric, blasphemous, and decadent Romantics.
     They "were over-rated in 1870 and are still over-rated."
     In their works Romanticism is not reborn: it dies.

390. Clark, John Scott. "Gabriel Charles Dante Rossetti."
     A Study of English and American Writers. Vol. 3.
     New York: Row Peterson, 1916, pp. 564-574.

     Defines and explains the principal characteristics of
     Rossetti as a poet: devotion to beauty; mysticism;
     medievalism; sensuousness; dramatic power; melancholy;
     archaism.

391. Symons, Arthur. "Dante Gabriel Rossetti." *Figures of
     Several Centuries*. London: Constable, 1916, pp. 201-206.

     Impressionistic judgment of Rossetti as a tragic poet:
     narrow, intensive, one who loved not wisely but too well.

392. Thompson, A. Hamilton. "The Rossettis, William Morris,
     Swinburne, and Others." *The Cambridge History of Eng-
     lish Literature*. Edited by A. Ward and A. Waller.
     Vol. 13. Cambridge University Press, 1916, pp. 110-146.

     Sees Rossetti as influenced by romance and mysticism,
     which ran counter to his Pre-Raphaelite devotion to
     precise detail. His pictorial and dramatic qualities
     are best seen in the ballads "Sister Helen" and "Rose
     Mary." "The House of Life" shows the inner life by per-
     sonifying abstract qualities and by praising the union of
     body and soul.

393. Urech-Daysh, C. *Dante Gabriel Rossetti*. Basel: Hirzen,
     1916. 137 pp.

     Not examined.

394. Malmstedt, A. "Rossetti och 'The Aesthetic Movement.'"
     *Studier i modern Sprakvetenskap utgivna av Nyfilo-
     logiska Sällskapet i Stockholm* 6 (1917): 193-229.

     In Swedish.

395. Olivero, Federico. "Sul simbolismo di D.G. Rossetti."
     Nuovi saggi di letteratura inglese. Turin: Libreria
     Editrice Internazionale, [1917], pp. 173-210.

     Discusses the nature of the symbolism in Rossetti's
     poetry, focusing more on the (high) aesthetic value of
     the symbols rather than on the contexts within which
     the symbols are created. Rossetti is masterful and
     original in his use of symbols.

396. Chudoba, Frantisek. "Básnický odkaz D.G. Rossettiho."
      Básníci, Vestci A Bojounící. Pilsen: Karel, 1920,
      pp. 163-192.

      In Czech.

397. Elton, Oliver. "The Rossettis." *A Survey of English
      Literature, 1830-1880*. Vol. 2. London: Arnold, 1920,
      pp. 1-30.

      Judges Rossetti to be "the surest artist of his time,"
      one with "the steadiest instinct for perfection." His
      earliest verse is the clearest; later work is more often
      turbid or idiosyncratic. His work is of major impor-
      tance to the history of both the English ballad and the
      English sonnet, and his translations and prose writings
      also deserve praise.

398. Trombly, Albert E. *Rossetti the Poet, an Appreciation*.
      [University of Texas Bulletin #2060.] Austin: Uni-
      versity of Texas Press, [1920]. 86 pp.

      Gives a personal and enthusiastic appreciation of Ros-
      setti's major poems. Rossetti is difficult, but his
      technique, his magic, and his command of atmosphere
      justify our attention. His language has melody, sonor-
      ity, color, and virility. His sonnets are "the greatest
      we have had." As a philosopher, he shows religious in-
      sight but not moralism. Reprinted from articles in the
      South Atlantic Quarterly (1919-1920).

399. Woodberry, George E. "A Literary Portrait of Rossetti."
      Studies of a Litterateur. London: Selwyn and Blount,
      1921, pp. 61-65.

      Paints Rossetti as a mystic, one who is absorbed in
      medieval romance and symbolism but who lacks technique
      and form.

400. Hearn, Lafcadio. "Studies in Rossetti" and "Note upon
      Rossetti's Prose." *Pre-Raphaelite and Other Poets:
      Lectures*. New York: Dodd, Mead, 1922, pp. 1-121.

      Believes Rossetti should occupy "the very first rank
      in nineteenth century poetry." The poems are divided
      into three groups (symbolic poems, ballads, and sonnets),
      and detailed explications are offered for several poems
      in each category. Rossetti is both a philosopher and a

mystic. As a prose writer Rossetti shows immense talent
also, as explications of "Hand and Soul" and "St. Agnes
of Intercession" can demonstrate.

401. Shuster, George N. "Ruskin, Pater, and the Pre-
      Raphaelites." *The Catholic Spirit in Modern English
      Literature.* New York: Macmillan, 1922, pp. 166-186.

      Contends that Rossetti did not fully understand the
      early Christian symbolism he was trying to appropriate,
      although he made effective use of it. His poetry is
      too quiet, too pictorial, perhaps because he lacks
      intellectual conviction.

402. Elton, Oliver. "Poetic Romancers after 1850." *A Sheaf
      of Papers.* Boston: Small, 1923, pp. 45-68.

      Describes those who revived the ballad as different
      from medievalists because they lacked distance from the
      subject. Rossetti, however, is the best of the Vic-
      torian revivalists. He is an inventor of forms, and
      his poetic style offers both magic and economy. Al-
      though he has no special philosophy, his works remind
      us of the eternal themes. [Note: this was originally
      written and delivered as the 1914 Warton Lecture on
      English Poetry.]

403. Hearn, Lafcadio. "Definitive Rossetti" and "Some Human
      Frailty." *Essays in European and Oriental Literature.*
      Edited by A. Mordell. New York: Dodd, Mead, 1923,
      pp. 221-235.

      Reviews item 26, finding in the poetry both super-
      natural feeling and a stimulus for biographical inves-
      tigation. The poet broods over the figure of Woman,
      symbolized for him by Lizzie Siddal. [Note: these
      posthumous essays are fragments of drafts.]

404. Symons, Arthur. "Rossetti on the Cornish Coast."
      Bookman [New York] 57 (1923): 604-609.

      Offers an impressionistic New Year's Eve ramble along
      the coast, during which Rossetti's poetry is meditated
      upon and likened--in its subtlety, its mystery, its
      despair, and its obsessiveness--to mystics like Blake,
      St. Theresa, and St. John of the Cross.

405. McQuilland, Louis J. "Dante Gabriel Rossetti and the
      Pre-Raphaelites." *Bookman's Journal* 11 (1924): 60-62.

      Summarizes Rossetti's life and in conclusion has to
      praise him as the poet of nuptial love and spiritual
      beauty.

406. Buchan, John. "Morris and Rossetti." *Homilies and
      Recreations*. London: Nelson, 1926, pp. 272-280.

      Finds Rossetti's most striking qualities to be his
      evenness in quality and his novelty in subject matter.
      He has a studied simplicity which serves as the perfect
      vehicle for his love of beauty.

407. Calverton, V.F. "The Immoral Revolution." *Sex Ex-
      pression in Literature*. New York: Boni and Liveright,
      1926, pp. 247-267.

      Summarizes the public outcry at Rossetti's "fleshly"
      poems, noting how Rossetti--despite his own intentions--
      helped turn poetry toward the physical and away from the
      spiritual.

408. Jones, H. Foster. "Dante Gabriel Rossetti, Medievalist
      and Poet." *Quarterly Journal of the University of
      North Dakota* 16 (1926): 309-323.

      Argues for a favorable reappraisal of Rossetti because
      he (unlike modern writers) was willing to learn from
      the past, because he used the pictorial method, and
      because he inspired other poets.

409. Hearn, Lafcadio. "Two New Schools: Spasmodic and Pre-
      Raphaelite." *A History of English Literature*. Vol. 2.
      Tokyo: Hokuseido Press, 1927, pp. 661-687.

      Relates both schools to the urge to be passionate and
      individualistic. Rossetti as a poet shows the delicacy
      and charm of an Italian and the indifference to modern
      science of a true medievalist. Both qualities make him
      equal or even superior to Tennyson.

410. Ruhrmann, Friedrich G. "Dante Gabriel Rossetti."
      *Studien zur Geschichte und Characteristik des Refrains
      in der englischen Literatur*. Heidelberg: Anglistische
      Forschungen, 1927, pp. 129-150.

      Examines Rossetti's role in the history of English

poetry with special reference to his use of the refrain. Focuses on "Sister Helen." See also item 381.

411. Gosse, Sir Edmund. "Rossetti." *Living Age* 334 (1928): 1077-1080.

Asks why Rossetti is now neglected. The chief reason seems to be the undue attention which is being given to the circumstances of his life. Future generations will appreciate the lucidity, intensity, and purity of his best poetry. An older generation can still recall when Rossetti stood for adventure, romance, and mystery. Reprinted from the Sunday *Times*.

412. Hamilton, George Rostrevor. "Dante Gabriel Rossetti, a Review of His Poetry." *Criterion* 7 (1928): 379-391.

Argues that Rossetti, while he had originality and virtuosity, lacked the transforming power necessary for fusing his disparate material into a genuinely creative poetic vision. "Jenny," "Rose Mary," and "The House of Life" are his greatest achievements; many of the others suffer when subjected to close reading. Rossetti is not a sensualist, but his spiritual perception is too vague, too generalized.

413. Lemmermayer, Fritz. "Dante Gabriel Rossetti, der Romantiker zur hundertsten Wiederkehr seines Geburtsjahres." *Das Goetheanum* 7 (1928): 404-406.

Not examined.

414. Mégroz, Rodolphe L. "Dante Gabriel Rossetti: The Man and His Poetry." *Bookman* [London] 74 (1928): 4-10.

Surveys Rossetti's career as a poet, stressing his untiring efforts at revision and his dedication to both sensuality and mysticism. See item 765, a companion piece on Rossetti as an artist.

415. Monroe, Harriet. "Comment: Rossetti." *Poetry* 32 (1928): 270-277.

Pays tribute to Rossetti on the occasion of his centenary. Rossetti is vivid, stylized, quaint, outside the English open-air current. He is a tragic figure, one who aspires and fails.

416. Shanks, Edward. "Dante Gabriel Rossetti." *London Mer-*
     cury 18 (1928): 67-78.

     Sees Rossetti in his personal life as greedy, exuberant,
     selfish, demanding, and magnetic. As a poet he is ar-
     chaic, unlyrical, unphilosophical. "Fundamental brain-
     work" is simply Rossetti's attempt to give a philosophi-
     cal context to his desire for a woman companion. His
     temperament is original, intense, hypnotic; his place
     in the history of poetry, though small, is secure.

417. Wolff, Lucien. "Le Centenaire de Dante Gabriel Rossetti--
     Rossetti et le Moyen-Age." *Revue Anglo-Américaine*
     (1928): 452-458.

     Contends that Rossetti's poetry shows pure medieval
     mysticism tempered by his own personal melancholy and
     the temperament of the modern artist. Although Rossetti
     lacks a belief in medieval theology and cosmogony, he
     also lacks scientific skepticism; thus his poetry pen-
     etrates the spirit of the earlier age and liberates his
     own imagination in the process.

418. Burgum, Edwin B. "Rossetti and the Ivory Tower."
     Sewanee Review 37 (1929): 431-446.

     Sees Pre-Raphaelitism as an artistic outgrowth of the
     Oxford Movement, the final decay of genre painting.
     Rossetti changed the emphasis to a secular and erotic
     view of woman. As a poet he eventually fell victim to
     his own self-lacerating introspection, to his unfulfilled
     Epicureanism, and to a failure to distinguish life from
     art. Unable to face reality, he deluded himself by a
     search for the perfect phrase.

419. Grierson, Herbert J.C. "Arnold and the Pre-Raphaelite
     Group." *Lyrical Poetry from Blake to Hardy*. London:
     Hogarth Press, 1929, pp. 90-121.

     Defines Rossetti as one who seeks to communicate a
     mood by suggestion and atmosphere, much like Poe. He
     communicates the medieval world skillfully, but weakens
     some of the ballads by over-elaboration.

420. Axmann, M. *Die Präraffaelitische Dichtung im Urteile*
     Ihrer Zeit. Hildesheim: Borgmeyer, 1930.

     Not examined.

421. Littel, Philip. "The Poetry of Rossetti." *Modern Writers at Work*. Edited by Josephine Piercy. New York: Macmillan, 1930, pp. 165-169.

Praises Rossetti as a poet who wears well, as one who knows how to choose his words and structure a poem (despite what *Edinburgh Review* critics and others have said). To read him "is like being shut up with Memory and Desire in a small room." Reprinted from *The New Republic* (1921).

422. Cecil, Lord David. "Gabriel Charles Dante Rossetti." *The Great Victorians*. Edited by H. and H. Massingham. London: Nicholson and Watson, 1932, pp. 437-448.

Lauds Rossetti as the greatest aesthete, one who tried to create a new intellectual and moral background for the artist. Even in failure Rossetti's conscious artistry is important, and he remains "the poet of the silver age." The poetry can be divided into works that philosophize about love and beauty and those that portray them in action.

423. Evans, B. Ifor. "Dante Gabriel Rossetti." *English Poetry in the Later Nineteenth Century*. London: Methuen, 1933, pp. 17-44.

Sees Rossetti as a Victorian Coleridge, one whose symbolic presence exceeds his literary merit. The history of his poetical development is the triumph of "Dantesque visions" over the desire to represent the real world. His chief value lies in the way he liberates Victorian poetry from the duty of commenting on the times.

424. Mégroz, R[odolphe] L. "Pre-Raphaelite Poetry." *Modern English Poetry, 1882-1932*. London: Nicholson and Watson, 1933, pp. 13-36.

Denies that Pre-Raphaelite poetry could be called "sickly," and tries to isolate its peculiar characteristics. Rossetti and his associates begin a renaissance of English poetry by combining the dream-like effects and freshness of color derived from the Romantics with devotion to the occult and an almost classical insistence on precision.

425. Cunliffe, John W. "Mid-Victorian Poets." *Leaders in the Victorian Revolution*. New York: Appleton-Century, 1934, pp. 228-252.

Summarizes Rossetti's career as a poet, finding him "a master of felicitous phrase and melodious meter," one who surrenders himself to the vain but not ignoble pursuit of beauty.

426. Wolff, L[ucien]. *Dante Gabriel Rossetti*. Paris: Didier, 1934. 319 pp.

Offers a general survey of Rossetti's poetic career, with a special emphasis on his absorption with the Beatrice figure (the three central chapters--out of five-- are entitled "A la recherche de Béatrice," "Béatrice," and "Après Béatrice"). The poems are therefore seen in the light of and as comments on Rossetti's relationship with Lizzie Siddal. The alternation of moods in the sonnets, for example, grows out of the alternation of despair and hope in Rossetti's own personal life as he reacts to his wife's tragic death. A final chapter on Rossetti as man and artist judges him to be a mystic whose poetry shows conciseness and a mastery of diction and meter.

427. Osgood, Charles G. "The Pre-Raphaelites." *The Voice of England*. New York: Harper, 1935, pp. 534-550.

Sees Rossetti's poetry as romantic, colorful, musical. All of his work is infused with an "intense but roily emotion"; unfortunately it lacks great ideas.

428. Kunitz, Stanley J., and Howard Haycraft, eds. "Rossetti, Dante Gabriel." *British Authors of the Nineteenth Century*. New York: Wilson, 1936, pp. 532-535.

Gives a brief synopsis of Rossetti's life and concludes he is "anti-rational, superstitious, and impulsive." The poetry is excellent but limited in scope.

429. Weygandt, Cornelius. "Dante Gabriel Rossetti." *The Time of Tennyson: English Victorian Poetry as It Affected America*. New York: Appleton-Century, 1936, pp. 192-216.

Condemns Rossetti for his sublimated and therefore false sensuality, for his rhetoric, for his faulty technique, and for his structural failures, all of which stem from a dark, unstable, "alien" mind. However, he has written a few beautiful poems, especially some of the ballads and "The Blessed Damozel."

430. Troxell, Janet C. "The 'Trial Books' of Dante Gabriel
      Rossetti." *The Colophon* n.s. 3, no. 2 (Spring 1938):
      243-258.

      Identifies no less than six sets of proof which were
      struck between August of 1869 and March of 1870, all
      prior to *Poems* and only two of which, the so-called
      "Trial Books," had ever been described before. These
      proofs show among other things that Rossetti needed to
      exhume the manuscripts from his wife's coffin only to
      establish the text of four poems--all the rest were
      obtained from other sources. Reprinted in the *Prince-
      ton University Library Chronicle* 33 (1972): 177-192.

431. Harrold, Charles F. "Recent Trends in Victorian Studies:
      1932-1939." *Studies in Philology* 37 (1940): 667-697.

      Notes, among other trends, the popularity of sensa-
      tionalized biographies of Rossetti and--more important--
      the new emphasis on sound textual scholarship for the
      poetry.

432. Lucas, F[rank] L[awrence]. "Dante Gabriel Rossetti."
      Ten Victorian Poets. Cambridge University Press, 1940,
      pp. 99-114.

      Gives a dramatic representation of the origin of the
      P.R.B. and its devotion to simple and sincere poetry.
      But in Rossetti the crisp morning air soon gives way
      to "brooding, sultry, thunderous heat." He represents
      the return of Dionysius, of paganism, of a naked devo-
      tion to beauty alone. Reprinted 1976.

433. Grierson, Herbert, and J.C. Smith. "The Pre-Raphaelite
      Group." *A Critical History of English Poetry*. New
      York: Oxford University Press, 1944, pp. 484-495.

      Shows Rossetti evolving from the careful detail and
      plain diction of the early ballads and narratives to
      the deeper color and "aureate" diction of the later
      sonnets. In general he becomes "sophisticated to excess."

434. DeArmond, Anna J. "What is Pre-Raphaelitism in Poetry?"
      Delaware Notes, 19th series (1946): 67-88.

      Echoes Hueffer's claim (in item 717) that in the strict
      sense of the term Pre-Raphaelitism is the naturalism of
      Hunt. The medievalism of Morris is therefore a separate

movement. Rossetti bridges both groups, yet is the
least typical of any Pre-Raphaelite writer. In poetry
the earlier phase is represented by symbolism, descriptive detail, and simplicity of form. The later phase
is represented by mysticism, by psychological realism,
and especially by the love of beauty for its own sake.

435. Masefield, John. *Thanks Before Going: Notes on Some of*
        the Original Poems of Dante Gabriel Rossetti. London:
        Heinemann, 1946. 67 pp.

        Offers a tribute to Rossetti (from the Poet Laureate).
        Includes descriptions of Rossetti's principal poems plus
        critical notes--ranging from one sentence to several
        paragraphs--on each, particularly "The House of Life."
        The notes are prompted by a re-reading of Rossetti, "by
        much the most kindling influence among the young men of
        my time."

436. Cecchi, Emilio. "Dante Gabriel Rossetti." *Scrittori*
        inglesi e americani. Milan: Mondadori, 1947, pp.
        46-51.

        Lauds Rossetti as an extraordinary poet from an extra-
        ordinary family. He joins Tennyson, Browning, and his
        sister Christina as the major English poets of the second
        half of the century.

437. [Anonymous]. "Pre-Raphaelite Poetry." *Times Literary*
        Supplement, 31 July 1948, pp. 421-423.

        Finds the Pre-Raphaelites to be poets obsessed with
        death, even in their youthful poems. Their distinctive
        note is hard to put into words: it has to do with emo-
        tional desires enhanced by social restrictions to an
        ineffable level, it has analogs in Tennyson and the
        Spasmodics, it is "the bitter-sweet distillation of
        emotional exigency." Rossetti adds to this the mystical
        hope that spiritual and physical can intermingle.

438. Cooke, John D., and Lionel Stevenson. "Dante Gabriel
        Rossetti." *English Literature of the Victorian Period*.
        New York: Appleton-Century-Crofts, 1949, pp. 175-181.

        Summarizes Rossetti's career and concludes that in
        both arts he was more important as a stimulus to others
        than as an artist in his own right. The verse is in-
        dividualistic and intense; but it is also too ornate,
        too contrived.

439. Batho, Edith, and Bonamy Dobrée. "Poetry." *The Victorians and After, 1830-1914.* Revised Edition, Vol. 4. London: Cresset Press, 1950, pp. 42-75.

Views Rossetti's poetry as deliberately non-prophetic. He emphasizes instead the primacy of personal feeling, simplicity of expression, and the use of arcane symbolism. As a poet he is overshadowed by his sister.

440. Heath-Stubbs, John. "Pre-Raphaelitism and the Aesthetic Withdrawal." *The Darkling Plain.* London: Eyre and Spottiswoode, 1950, pp. 148-178.

Sees the P.R.B. as the first phase of a movement away from the external world and toward a purely decorative beauty. "The Blessed Damozel" can be analyzed as a poem which uses Christian imagery to create a "pagan dreamworld." Rossetti's poetry is not as good as that of his sister Christina.

441. Hübner, Walter. "Dante Gabriel Rossetti." *Die Stimmen der Meister: eine Einführung in Meisterwerke des englischen Dichtens und Denkens.* Berlin: Gruyter, 1950, pp. 476-479.

Gives brief but sympathetic summaries of three poems which the author sees as typical of Rossetti's work: "The Blessed Damozel," "Sister Helen," and the Willowwood sequence from "The House of Life."

442. Vines, Sherard. "The Pre-Raphaelites and After." *One Hundred Years of English Literature.* London: Duckworth, 1950, pp. 47-56.

Sees Rossetti as developing a slow, studied, and profoundly poetic idiom, although occasionally he is betrayed by an over-reliance on spondees.

443. Westland, Peter. "Pre-Raphaelites and Others." *The Victorian Age.* Vol. 5. Teach Yourself History of English Literature. London: English Universities Press, 1950, pp. 54-87.

Summarizes Rossetti's poetic career. Of Milton's three requisites for poetry--simplicity, sensuousness, and passion--Rossetti is the possessor of at least two. The mawkishness which many associate with Rossetti's eroticism comes from a failure to understand his sacra-

mental view of nature and the body. Yet it is true that
his poetry can be enervating.

444.   Churchill, R[eginald] C. "The Oxford Movement and the
        Pre-Raphaelites." *English Literature of the Nineteenth
        Century*. London: University Tutorial Press, 1951,
        pp. 146-171.

        Does not relate the two movements except through the
        "bridge" figures of Patmore, Dixon, and Christina Ros-
        setti. Dante Gabriel is the mystic poet; in contrast
        with Christina he is "religiose rather than religious."

445.   Groom, Bernard. "Rossetti, Morris, and Swinburne."
        The Diction of Poetry from Spenser to Bridges. Univer-
        sity of Toronto Press, 1955, pp. 252-265.

        Sees Rossetti as a key poet in the history of English
        poetic diction, one who symbolizes the great changes in
        literature which took place around 1870. Rossetti's
        use of several characteristic devices--e.g. approximate
        rhymes, medieval diction, compound nouns, groups of
        "Love" words and "Hell" words--is summarized.

446.   House, Humphry. "Pre-Raphaelite Poetry." *All in Due
        Time*. London: Rupert Hart-Davis, 1955, pp. 151-158.

        Assigns to Rossetti the power of concretizing spiritual
        and mythological issues. This power is derived from
        Dantean symbolism; consequently those who call him the
        father of aestheticism misunderstand his purposes. Re-
        printed from *The Listener* (1948).

447.   Parrott, Thomas Marc, and Robert B. Martin. "Rossetti."
        A Companion to Victorian Literature. New York:
        Scribner's, 1955, pp. 235-240.

        Outlines Rossetti's career as a poet. Although the
        "most sensuous of Victorian poets," he is also a true
        ethical poet influenced by the Christian tradition.

448.   Bush, Douglas. "Minor Poets, Mid-Victorian and Later."
        Mythology and the Romantic Tradition in English Poetry.
        Cambridge, Mass.: Harvard University Press, 1957,
        pp. 396-428.

        Dismisses Rossetti as almost unreadable, a "high priest
        of Victorian paganism" who still leaves us "thirsty for

reality." As a handler of classical myths Rossetti is especially clumsy, making them pretty rather than vital.

449. Doughty, Oswald. *Dante Gabriel Rossetti*. Writers and Their Work Series, No. 85. London: Longmans, Green, 1957. 34 pp.

   Offers a brief summary of the poet's life and an appraisal of his poetry. The conclusion is that Rossetti is "an amateur of genius," especially as a sonneteer.

450. Fairchild, Hoxie Neale. "Dante Gabriel Rossetti." *Religious Trends in English Poetry*. Vol. 4. New York: Columbia University Press, 1957, pp. 390-404.

   Finds Rossetti a pure aesthete whose attitude toward organized religion is one of superstitious rationalism. Hence the paradoxes, e.g. secularism at one time and genuine Catholic feeling at another. Perhaps his final position is that of "a wavering but not altogether unhopeful theist."

451. LoSchiavo, Renato. *La Poesia di Dante Gabriele Rossetti*. Rome: Edizioni di Storia e Letteratura, 1957. 105 pp.

   Devotes separate chapters to the early poetry, *Dante and His Circle*, the 1870 Poems, and the 1881 *Ballads and Sonnets*, with evaluative descriptions of the major poems and translations in each section. As a poet Rossetti is highly individualistic, at once the literary forerunner of *stil nuovo* and the last flowering of nineteenth-century Romanticism.

452. Zanco, Aurelio. "D.G. Rossetti." *Storia della letteratura inglese*. Vol. 2. Turin: Loescher, 1958, pp. 624-646.

   Surveys Rossetti's achievement as a poet. The best poetry can be found in the early ballads and in "The House of Life," especially the latter, which is characterized by a "hot sensuality." The dramatic monologs, on the other hand, are inferior work.

453. Daiches, David. "The Victorian Poets." *A Critical History of English Literature*. Vol. 2. New York: Ronald Press, 1960, pp. 311-329.

   Sees Rossetti as illustrating the confluence of Wordsworthian meditation and Tennysonian pictorialism,

one who knew and could well portray Jenny's London,
among other scenes.

454.   Weatherby, Harold L. "Problems of Form and Content in
        the Poetry of Dante Gabriel Rossetti." *Victorian
        Poetry* 2 (1964): 11-19.

        Criticizes the poetry largely on the grounds that,
        while Rossetti can render genuine feeling and command
        poetic form, he lacks the content which could validate
        that form.

455.   Wright, David H., ed. "Dante Gabriel Rossetti." *Seven
        Victorian Poets*. London: Heinemann, 1964, pp. 93-100.

        Prints nine poems by Rossetti and in the introduction
        judges him as a sentimentalist and prude rather than as
        a *poète maudit*. In general his better-known poems are
        the worst ones; good poetry occurs when he is simple,
        restrained, objective.

456.   Charlesworth, Barbara. "Dante Gabriel Rossetti." *Dark
        Passages: The Decadent Consciousness in Victorian Lit-
        erature*. Madison: University of Wisconsin Press, 1965,
        pp. 3-18.

        Defines Rossetti's sensibility as decadent because of
        his concentration on capturing ecstatic moments. He is
        a "divided man" because these momentary ecstasies never
        bring him to the transcendental realm for which he
        yearns. Uses "Hand and Soul" as the prolegomenon, "The
        House of Life" as the exemplum.

457.   Chew, Samuel, and Richard Altick. "Rossetti and His
        Circle." *A Literary History of England*. Edited by
        A. Baugh. 2nd Edition. Vol. 4. New York: Appleton-
        Century-Crofts, 1967, pp. 1421-1429.

        Chronicles Rossetti's literary career, one which was
        marked by luxuriance coupled with austerity. His dream
        world deliberately fuses the conscious and the sub-
        conscious.

458.   Lucie-Smith, Edward. "Dante Gabriel Rossetti." *The
        Listener* 77 (1967): 788-790.

        Views Rossetti as idealistic, erotic, and hysterical.
        His sensuality marks him off from other Pre-Raphaelite

poets. He is a direct descendent of Keats and the poems often show power and truth; but he is also betrayed by his obsessions and by his vulgarity.

459. Robson, W.W. "Three Victorian Poets." *Collective Essays*. New York: Barnes and Noble, 1967, pp. 200-221.

Assesses the poetry of Rossetti, his sister, and Morris, using as a criterion Arnold's dictum that poetry must be a criticism of life. Rossetti, who receives the most attention, clearly fails: he is too literary, too finished, too sententious, too egocentric. Yet in some poems, most notably "The Blessed Damozel," he can be harsh and direct. Revised from an essay entitled "Pre-Raphaelite Poetry" in vol. 6 of the *Pelican Guide* (1958).

460. Chapman, Raymond. "Escape through Art." *The Victorian Debate: English Literature and Society 1832-1901*. New York: Basic Books, 1968, pp. 228-243.

Sees Rossetti as a prototype of those who fled to art as an escape from the ugliness of Victorian industrialism. As a poet he is "too much a verbal trickster," too much a victim of his own "lotus-eating dreaminess." But he does show versatility and a broad vision.

461. Stange, G. Robert. "The Victorian City and the Frightened Poets." *Victorian Studies* 11 (1968): 627-640.

Contends that most Victorian poets, including Rossetti, were inept at dealing with urban life despite their recognition of its importance. "Jenny" is a repudiation of city life despite the poet's personal attachment to that life.

462. Culler, A. Dwight. "*The Windy Stair:* An Aspect of Rossetti's Poetic Symbolism." *Ventures* 9, no. 2 (Fall 1969): 65-75.

Traces the motif of the winding stairway from its beginning in Rossetti's four sonnets about climbing church towers during his 1849 European tour, through his prose tales, to its apotheosis in "Love's Nocturn," where it becomes a form of private symbolism.

463. Harris, Wendell V. "A Reading of Rossetti's Lyrics." *Victorian Poetry* 7 (1969): 299-308.

Divides the lyrics into two modes, objective and sub-

jective, finding Rossetti's real genius to lie with the
second type. The poet's achievement is less as a
spiritual idealist and more as a dramatist of transient
psychological states.

464. Johnston, Robert D. *Dante Gabriel Rossetti*. New York:
      Twayne, 1969. 167 pp.

      Surveys Rossetti's poetic achievement, from the early
      translations to the late, embittered sonnets (i.e. the
      progression is chronological). Special emphasis is
      given to the theme of love, beginning with the Beatrice
      figure, followed by Lilith and finally by the Siren.
      Rossetti's greatest weakness as a poet is said to be
      his egocentricity. Part of Twayne's "English Authors
      Series."

465. McGann, Jerome J. "Rossetti's Significant Details."
      Victorian Poetry 7 (1969): 41-54.

      Denies that Rossetti is vague and that his Christian
      symbolism has no aesthetic function. Instead, Rossetti
      uses these symbols to remind the reader of the value of
      appearances *per se*. He purges them of their traditional
      meaning so they can suggest the power of erotic love.

466. Cooper, Robert M. *Lost on Both Sides, Dante Gabriel
      Rossetti: Critic and Poet*. Athens: Ohio University
      Press, 1970. 268 pp.

      Acknowledges the fact that Rossetti published very
      little formal criticism, but contends that one can glean
      from his correspondence and elsewhere "a body of criti-
      cism impressive in bulk, quality, and ... basic consis-
      tency." Rossetti as a critic values simplicity, subtlety,
      compression, and clarity, among other virtues. Unfor-
      tunately as a poet he often achieves only a labored
      obscurity. Portrays Rossetti as a kind of artistic
      Jekyll and Hyde, a compound of the genial, energetic,
      ultra-English "good" Rossetti and the gloomy, vengeful,
      Italianate "bad" Rossetti. The rather portentous con-
      clusion is that "where [Rossetti] succeeds, he is a
      success; where he fails, he is a failure."

467. Holberg, Stanley M. "Rossetti and the Trance." *Vic-
      torian Poetry* 8 (1970): 299-314.

      Finds that Rossetti's dreamlike atmosphere pervades
      not just the fantasy poems but also the poems which

represent external reality. Rossetti's motive might be to suggest that the speaker is gripped by emotions too intense for ordinary consciousness.

468. Sambrook, James. "The Rossettis and Other Contemporary Poets." *The Victorians*. Edited by A. Pollard. Sphere History of Literature in the English Language, vol. 6. London: Barrie and Jenkins, 1970, pp. 334-363.

Pronounces Rossetti to be a compound of guilt and idealism, one whose poetry "represents a not altogether successful attempt to spiritualize love." His best poems are those which dramatize a sinister and demonic landscape of memory, like "Willowwood," rather than those of the angelic sphere, like "The Blessed Damozel."

469. Spector, Stephen J. "Love, Unity, and Desire in the Poetry of Dante Gabriel Rossetti." *Journal of English Literary History* 38 (1971): 432-458.

Contends that Rossetti's poetry, unlike the works of the earlier Romantics, portrays a self conscious only of itself and therefore a living tautology, unable to return to the external world. Love isolates rather than liberates, and the desire for unity stems from loneliness in a fragmented world. Concludes with an analysis of selected sonnets from "The House of Life" which dramatize these themes.

470. Vogel, Joseph F. *Dante Gabriel Rossetti's Versecraft.* Gainesville: University of Florida Press, 1971. 111 pp.

Studies Rossetti as a poetic craftsman and concludes that he was both "subtle" and "remarkably fine." Consideration is given to the poet's use of meter, of stanzaic form, and of rhyme and other sound devices. A concluding chapter devotes special attention to "The Blessed Damozel," which the author believes to be "a superb example of prosodic art." The fundamental aim is to banish the view of Rossetti as a dreamy dilettante.

471. Buckley, Jerome H. "Pre-Raphaelite Past and Present: The Poetry of the Rossettis." *Victorian Poetry*. Edited by Malcolm Bradbury and David Palmer. London: Arnold, 1972, pp. 123-137.

Compares the medieval and modern elements in Rossetti's work. Modern themes are significant only insofar as they point to timeless values. Medievalism predominates because it allows the poet to dwell in a "Byzantium of the imagination."

472. Fredeman, William E. "Impediments and Motives: Biography as Unfair Sport." *Modern Philology* 70 (1972): 149-154.

Reviews item 1075, arguing that "it illustrates so dramatically the excesses of so much of contemporary critical writing" about Rossetti's poetry because it repeats Buchanan's error of assuming that the poet and the speaker of his poems must always be one and the same.

473. Howard, Ronnalie R. *The Dark Glass: Vision and Technique in the Poetry of Dante Gabriel Rossetti.* Athens: Ohio University Press, 1972. 218 pp.

Attempts to rescue Rossetti's poetry from those who decry his ritualism or medievalism and from those whose interest is more in biography than in criticism. The arrangement is chronological, although the poems are also treated according to major types (e.g. medieval poems, ballads, narratives). The author's aesthetic principles are avowedly Crocean, defined rather widely. The most important poems are given close readings, and the treatment is generally sympathetic to the poet.

474. Keane, Robert N. "D.G. Rossetti's *Poems*, 1870: A Study in Craftsmanship." *Princeton University Library Chronicle* 33 (1972): 193-209.

Examines in chronological order the proofs of *Poems* (see item 430) to show that Rossetti was a meticulous craftsman: adding, revising, rearranging, correcting, designing. The dominant motives for his changes seem to have been consistency and clarity. Swinburne, Scott, and his brother William Michael were Rossetti's chief advisors and their suggestions were usually accepted.

475. Stevenson, Lionel. "Rossetti as Poet." *The Pre-Raphaelite Poets.* Chapel Hill: University of North Carolina Press, 1972, pp. 18-77.

Offers a retrospective of Rossetti's career as the "first English ... *poète maudit*." Concludes with a discussion of the major types, i.e. ballads, lyrics, and sonnets, in the last of which Rossetti is "pre-eminent among the Victorian poets" because of his mastery of mood and technique.

476. Tierney, Frank M. "The Causes of the Revival of the Rondeau in Nineteenth Century England." *Revue de l'Uni-
versité d'Ottawa* 43 (1973): 96-113.

Attributes the revival of the rondeau in part to Rossetti's interest in medieval art history and in French
literature. Subsequent poets like Swinburne drew from
Rossetti's interest the conviction that the fixed forms
used by medieval poets had real possibility.

477. Jarfe, Günther. "Rossettis dichtungsgeschichtliche
Standort: Tendenzen seiner dichterischen Entwicklung."
Germanisch-romanische Monatsschrift 24 (1974): 88-104.

Sees three phases in Rossetti's work as a poet: the
years 1847-1853, when Rossetti worked productively in
the Romantic tradition; the years 1854-1868, when he
was a tortured devotee of the god of Love; and the years
1869-1882, when he developed a pessimistic philosophy
and a more mannered style.

478. Pittman, Philip M. "The Strumpet and the Snake: Rossetti's Treatment of Sex as Original Sin." *Victorian
Poetry* 12 (1974): 45-54.

Counters the popular view of Rossetti as a sex-obsessed
neurotic. His treatment of sex is natural, healthy,
and deeply moral. The figure of Lilith, as seen in
"Body's Beauty" and "Eden Bower," can substantiate this
claim.

479. Christ, Carol T. *The Finer Optic: The Aesthetic of
Particularity in Victorian Poetry*. New Haven: Yale
University Press, 1975. 171 pp.

Relates the passion for "particularity" (i.e. the preference for the individual rather than the species) in
Tennyson, Rossetti, Browning, and Hopkins. There are
numerous references to Rossetti's works throughout.
Demonstrates Rossetti's sensitivity to detail and his
use of those details to express strong emotion. But
Rossetti's devotion to the particular is only a means
to a greater end, viz. the infinite.

480. Boos, Florence S. *The Poetry of Dante Gabriel Rossetti:
A Critical Reading and Source Study*. The Hague:
Mouton, 1976. 311 pp.

Offers, as the title promises, a summary of Rossetti's

sources and an analysis of his poetic techniques. The
underlying assumption for most of the explications is
that the poet is a guilt-ridden sexist. The fundamental
method is comparison and contrast, both between one
Rossetti poem and another and between Rossetti and other
poets.

481. Going, William T. "The Tennysons and the Rossettis:
      Sonneteering Families." *Scanty Plot of Ground:
      Studies in the Victorian Sonnet*. The Hague: Mouton,
      1976, pp. 40-60.

      Emphasizes the way in which sonnet-writing was a family
      exercise during the 1870s, with only Maria Rossetti among
      the siblings not participating. There are notable sim-
      ilarities in structure and ideas between "The House of
      Life" and "Monna Innominata."

482. Hardesty, William H. "Rossetti's Lusty Women." *Cimarron
      Review*, no. 35 (April 1976): 20-24.

      Says that Rossetti alone of the major Victorian poets
      treats female sexual frustration with sympathy and in-
      telligence. The need of women for physical sex is
      apparent as early as "The Blessed Damozel" in the 1840s
      and as late as the final sonnets of "The House of Life."

483. Prince, Jeffrey R. "D.G. Rossetti and the Pre-Raphaelite
      Conception of the Special Moment." *Modern Language
      Quarterly* 37 (1976): 349-369.

      Explains the fusion of sensuality and religious sacra-
      mentality in Rossetti's sonnets. They are an extrapo-
      lation of Romantic monism, especially Keats' doctrine
      of intensity.

484. Bentley, D.M.R. "Political Themes in the Work of Dante
      Gabriel Rossetti." *Victorian Poetry* 17 (1979): 159-179.

      Argues that Rossetti is not indifferent to political
      issues, as has been supposed. The early sonnets, "The
      Burden of Nineveh," and "The King's Tragedy" show both
      Rossetti's liberalism and his political pessimism,
      attitudes which are nonetheless defined by a Christian
      framework.

485. Dowson, Carl. *Victorian Noon: English Literature in
      1850*. Baltimore: Johns Hopkins University Press,
      1979. 268 pp.

The study as a whole defines Victorian literary culture in mid-century. There are references to Rossetti
throughout, with particular emphasis being given to
The Germ and his contributions to it. Periodical publication was gaining in importance, a fact the author
believes is not now sufficiently appreciated by scholars.

See also items 28, 30, 36-39, 151, 157, 203, 226, 241, 251,
252, 292, 315, 980-1099.

SECTION B: CRITICISM OF INDIVIDUAL LITERARY WORKS

i. "The Blessed Damozel"

486.   Ciccotti, Ettore. *La Fanciulla beata di Dante Gabriele*
       Rossetti e un giudizio di Max Nordau. Milan:
       Kantorowicz, 1893. 29 pp.

       Contains an Italian translation of Rossetti's "The
       Blessed Damozel" plus Max Nordau's condemnation of it
       (see item 995) and the translator's reply.

487.   Tyrrell, R.L. "A Literary Causerie: The Growth of a
       Poem." *Academy*, no. 1771 (1906): 356-358.

       Offers the first description of Rossetti's successive
       revisions of "The Blessed Damozel." For a fuller treat-
       ment see item 488 and especially items 492 and 500.

488.   Prideaux, William Francis. "Palgrave's 'Golden Treasury.'"
       Notes & Queries, 10th series, 8 (1907): 393.

       Answers a query from the November 2nd issue regarding
       the publication history of "The Blessed Damozel"; this
       item is in turn augmented by a note in the December 7th
       issue. See also items 492 and 500.

489.   McKillop, Alan D. "*Festus* and *The Blessed Damozel*."
       Modern Language Notes 34 (1919): 93-97.

       Finds in Bailey's poem, which Rossetti knew well, a
       source for the cosmic imagery in Rossetti's poem and
       also for the central situation of an earthly lover
       lamenting a beloved in heaven.

490. Williams, Stanley T. "Two Poems by Rossetti." *Studies
     in Victorian Literature*. New York: Dutton, 1923,
     pp. 183-198.

     Finds the poet of "The Blessed Damozel" to be charac-
     terized by charm, simplicity, and dreamy melancholy.
     The poet of "Jenny" is anguished by the desecration of
     his ideal of womanhood. Neither voice will appeal much
     to a modern audience. Revised from the *Texas Review*
     (1921).

491. Waller, Ross Douglas. "The Blessed Damozel." *Modern
     Language Notes* 26 (1931): 129-141.

     Traces the antecedents of Rossetti's poem to his read-
     ings in Poe, Dante, Petrarch, Blake, and Shelley. Dante
     is especially important, as numerous parallel passages
     testify.

492. Knickerbocker, K[enneth] L[eslie]. "Rossetti's 'The
     Blessed Damozel.'" *Studies in Philology* 29 (1932):
     485-504.

     Contends that the published final version of the poem
     emerged only after numerous alterations over a period of
     years--it did not appear magically from a boy of nineteen
     Furthermore, its successive revisions show the influence
     both of events in Rossetti's later life, such as his
     wife's death and his occult studies, and of his wide
     reading in Dante and the English Romantics.

493. Sanford, John Albert. "The Morgan Manuscript of Ros-
     setti's 'The Blessed Damozel.'" *Studies in Philology*
     35 (1938): 471-486.

     Claims that the manuscript was written later than its
     signed date (1847) and incorporates later revisions. It
     is therefore worthless for scholarly purposes. [But see
     items 500 and 501.]

494. Jackson, Elizabeth. "Notes on the Stanza of Rossetti's
     'The Blessed Damozel.'" *Publications of the Modern
     Language Association* 58, no. 4. (December 1943):
     1050-1056.

     Sees the stanzaic form of the poem as derived from the
     ballad stanza by way of Coleridge, with the addition of
     a tendency to vary the iambic pattern with spondees
     rather than anapests.

495. Shen, Yao. "Accident or Universality?" *Western Humani-*
      ties Review 10 (1955): 77-79.

      Notes the similarities in theme (lover's longing) and
      situation (beloved in a monotonous heaven) between Ros-
      setti's poem and "A Song of Unending Sorrow" by the
      ancient Chinese poet Pai Chii Yi.

496. Lauter, Paul. "The Narrator of 'The Blessed Damozel.'"
      Modern Language Notes 73 (1958): 344-348.

      Contends that the poem's true nucleus is not the damo-
      zel but the narrator, the earthly lover. Rossetti, like
      Poe, concentrated on the delusions of the bereaved man.
      The tone is melancholy because the possibility of bliss
      is doubted.

497. Vogel, Joseph S. "'White Rose' or 'White Robe' in 'The
      Blessed Damozel'?" *English Language Notes* 1 (1963):
      121-123.

      Demonstrates that both sense and grammar support "rose"
      rather than "robe" in line three of the second stanza.

498. Langford, Thomas A. "Rossetti's 'The Blessed Damozel,'
      71." *Explicator* 30 (1971): item 5.

      Sees the poem alluding to Matthew 18:19--the situation
      is ironic, the damozel's hope for reunion with her be-
      loved may be frustrated.

499. Brown, Thomas H. "The Quest of Dante Gabriel Rossetti
      in 'The Blessed Damozel.'" *Victorian Poetry* 10 (1972):
      273-277.

      Notes three distinct voices in the poem--omniscient
      narrator, earthbound lover, and damozel--all of which
      coalesce into a single consciousness, one which engages
      in a quest to discover the reality of the supernatural.
      The poet captures a moment of vision, as in other Ro-
      mantic poets like Tennyson and Keats; but Rossetti,
      unlike the others, remains ambiguous about the value of
      such a vision.

500. Fredeman, William E. "Rossetti's 'The Blessed Damozel':
      A Problem in Literary History and Textual Criticism."
      English Studies Today, 9th series (1973): 239-269.

      Proposes that the two American printings of "The Blessed

Damozel" contain emendations by the poet. Shows how
Rossetti continued to modify the poem after its initial
composition. See item 501 for a parallel treatment.

501.   Peterson, Carl A. "The Pierpont Morgan Manuscript of
       Rossetti's 'The Blessed Damozel': Dating, Authenticity,
       Significance." *Papers of the Bibliographic Society
       of America* 67 (1973): 401-429.

       Identifies the Morgan Library manuscript of the poem
       as the one sent by Rossetti to Browning in 1855. Sees
       this manuscript as an intermediate draft between two
       printed versions, one in which the poet continued to
       re-think his use of the parenthetical speeches by the
       earthbound lover. See also item 500.

502.   Burch, Francis F. "Rossetti's 'The Blessed Damozel,' 71."
       Explicator 37 (1979): 5.

       Replies to Lanford (item 498), arguing that Rossetti,
       independent of Dante and Poe, creates his own earthly
       paradise where human love need not be related to divine
       love. The line need not be read ironically.

See also items 29, 285, 325, 339, 350, 360, 388, 429, 440, 441,
459, 468, 470, 473, 480, 492, 518, 609, 642, 995, 1065, 1078,
1099.

ii.   Other Ballads

503.   Watts[-Dunton], Theodore. "Rossetti's Unpublished Poems."
       Athenaeum, no. 3578 (1896): 683.

       Announces the intention to publish later several Ros-
       setti poems, including "Jan Van Hunks," which would have
       been part of a collaborative venture with the author.
       Reprinted later in the author's *Old Familiar Faces* (1916).

504.   Walker, Elizabeth B. "The Ballads of Dante Gabriel
       Rossetti." *Citizen* 4 (1898): 76-77.

       Sees Scott and Keats as the starting points for Ros-
       setti's ballads, those "cloud boats" for escaping the
       nineteenth century. When Rossetti's ballads are compared
       to earlier ones, we find the latter touch us more deeply.

505. Jiriczek, Otto L. "Zum Erstdruck von D.G. Rossettis 'Sister Helen.'" *Germanisch-Romanische Monatsschrift* 3 (1911): 247.

Corrects William Michael Rossetti on the first appearance of the poem in the *Düsseldorf Artists' Album* and explains the contents of that volume. See item 31.

506. Horn, Kurt. "*The Staff and Scrip* von D.G. Rossetti." *Zeitschrift für französischen und englischen Unterricht* 26 (1927): 575-591.

Gives a German translation of the poem and extracts of letters from William Michael Rossetti to the author. Discusses the two main currents of Rossetti's poetry (medieval romances and ballads) and the context of "The Staff and the Scrip," together with its connection to the poet's own tormented love for Lizzie Siddal.

507. Förster, Max. "Die älteste Fassung von D.G. Rossettis Ballade 'Sister Helen.'" *Die Leipziger Neunundneunzig: Festschrift des Leipziger Bibliophilen-Abends*. Leipzig: [privately printed], 1929, pp. 116-139.

Discusses the appearance of "Sister Helen" in the *Düsseldorf Artists' Album* (1854). But see item 31.

508. Marchbank, W. "A Rossetti Ballad." *Times Literary Supplement*, 27 February 1930, p. 166.

Notes--contrary to a *TLS* review--that "Jan Van Hunks" had appeared in print before, in a 1912 pamphlet, and that a manuscript of it was now in the author's possession. See also the follow-up letter by G.C. Moore-Smith in the issue for 6 March, p. 190.

509. Smith, Simon Nowell. "Rossetti Manuscripts." *Times Literary Supplement*, 10 September 1931, p. 683.

Corrects a number of factual errors in Baum (item 47) regarding the manuscripts and publication history of "Jan Van Hunks."

510. Symons, Arthur. "Notes on Two Manuscripts." *English Review* 54 (1932): 514-520.

Describes the original manuscripts of a Swinburne poem and of "Eden Bower" (formerly in Symons' possession).

511.   Howe, Merrill L. "Some Unpublished Stanzas by Dante
       Gabriel Rossetti." *Modern Language Notes* 48 (1933):
       176-179.

       Publishes five stanzas from an early draft of "The
       King's Tragedy," stanzas which Rossetti later excised,
       apparently because they seemed too sentimental.

512.   ["T.O.M."] "Echoes of Poe in Rossetti's 'Beryl Song.'"
       Notes & Queries 168 (1935): 77.

       Sees, in lines 27 and 32 of Rossetti's poem, echoes of
       Poe's "Annabel Lee" and "To One in Paradise."

513.   Ray, S.N. "Rossetti's 'Border Song.'" *Modern Language
       Notes* 58 (1943): 246.

       Picks up on Howe (item 511), tracing the discovery of
       the poem through various notes by W.F. Prideaux and E.
       Walford in *Notes & Queries* (1894-1895).

514.   Culler, Dwight and Helen. "Sources of 'The King's
       Tragedy.'" *Studies in Philology* 41 (1944): 427-441.

       Claims that the main source for the poem is a prose
       chronicle entitled "The Dethe of the Kynge of Scotis,"
       an edition of which had been published by the Maitland
       Club in 1837. Rossetti owned a copy of this edition.

515.   Baum, Paull F. "Rossetti's 'The White Ship.'" [Duke
       University] *Library Notes*, no. 20 (1948): 2-6.

       Compares the two manuscripts of the poem owned by the
       Duke University Library, one representing an early stage
       and another a late stage in the poem's composition.
       Together they show how the poem grew from a cartoon
       through successive accretions to its final form. Also
       gives a collation of the later manuscripts and the stan-
       dard printed text.

516.   Hyder, Clyde K. "Rossetti's *Rose Mary*: A Study in the
       Occult." *Victorian Poetry* 1 (1963): 197-207.

       Shows how the poem gives evidence of Rossetti's great
       familiarity with occult lore regarding beryl stones and
       scrying. It also uses motifs, situations, and moods
       analogous to those found in the poet's other works, and
       there is some indication of borrowings from Dante, Keats,

Coleridge, and Tennyson, so the poem is not as singular as it first appears to be. Nevertheless the poem is a remarkable work of art.

517. Fisher, Benjamin F. IV. "Rossetti's 'William and Marie': Hints of the Future." *English Language Notes* 9 (1971): 121-129.

Prints the text of the ballad and comments on how it demonstrates Rossetti's use of such devices as archaic diction, approximate rhyme, and Gothic violence.

518. Trail, George Y. "A Modern Reading of 'Sister Helen.'" *Proceedings of the Conference of College Teachers of Texas.* Edited by J.F. Kobler. Denton: Conference of College Teachers of Texas, 1973, pp. 28-32.

Sees "The Blessed Damozel" as an examination of the viability of static, classical notions of order as these are opposed to eternal recurrence, and proposes an equally radical reading for "Sister Helen." In the latter poem Christian concerns are treated with crushing irony and Victorian notions of virginity are satirized. The poem is highly sophisticated in its psychology and its treatment of witchcraft. Thus we come to a greater respect for Rossetti's skill and subtlety.

519. Bentley, D.M.R. "Rossetti's Bride-Chamber Talk." *Wascana Review* 11, no. 2 (Fall 1976): 83-97.

Shows how in "The Bride's Prelude" Rossetti consciously uses rich, pictorial details as emblems of the bride's troubled sexual history. Furthermore the central metaphor of sunlight entering the darkened bridal chamber serves to distinguish the two sisters, to heighten our awareness of Alöyse's guilt, and to give the poem a thematic unity centered around the idea of shame.

520. Rubenstein, Jill. "The Framework of Belief in Rossetti's Tales of Damnation." *Pre-Raphaelite Review* 1, no. 1 (November 1977): 2-15.

Demonstrates Rossetti's manipulation of form, structure, point of view, and metaphorical patterns in order to create a framework within which the reader can believe the supernatural events of "Sister Helen" and "Rose Mary." The reader maintains aesthetic distance, as does the poet; violence and innocence combine to create a world

which we do not accept but which we believe the characters in it accept.

See also items 31, 32, 44, 176, 339, 344, 360, 363, 381, 388,
392, 410, 412, 429, 441, 452, 461, 473, 478, 480, 484, 995,
and 1065.

iii.   Dramatic Monologs: "Jenny" and "A Last Confession"

521.   Kingsland, William G.   "Rossetti's 'Jenny': With Ex-
       tracts from an Hitherto Unpublished Version of the
       Poem." *Poet-Lore* 7 (1895): 1-6.

       Gives an account of a manuscript of "Jenny" in T.J.
       Wise's Ashley Library, a fragment which differs markedly
       from the first published version and which apparently
       predates that version.

522.   DeVane, William Clyde.   "The Harlot and the Thoughtful
       Young Man: A Study of the Relation Between Rossetti's
       Jenny and Browning's *Fifine at the Fair*." *Studies
       in Philology* 29 (1932): 463-484.

       Summarizes the Rossetti-Browning friendship and ex-
       plains Rossetti's psychotic reaction to Browning's 1872
       presentation copy of *Fifine* as being a result of the
       inordinate value Rossetti placed on "Jenny." Also,
       Rossetti was convinced that Browning was linked with
       Buchanan and that *Fifine* hinted at a personal connection
       between Rossetti and the young speaker of his poem.
       Browning *was* sympathetic to Buchanan and he often wrote
       poems responding to situations found in other poets, so
       Rossetti's conclusions were not at all far-fetched.

523.   Howarth, R.G.   "On Rossetti's 'Jenny.'" *Notes & Queries*,
       15th series, 173 (1937): 20-21.

       Argues that the source of the poem was not the youth-
       ful poet's own experience but rather *The Memoirs of
       Harriette Wilson* (1825).

524.   Howard, Ronnalie Roper.   "Rossetti's *A Last Confession*:
       A Dramatic Monologue." *Victorian Poetry* 5 (1967): 21-29

       Contends that the poem is a success because the drama-
       tic monolog form allows Rossetti to indulge in super-

natural trappings without committing himself to them.
A paragraph-by-paragraph analysis shows how Rossetti
combines irony, symbolism, and multiple perspectives to
achieve an aesthetic whole.

525. Gordon, Jan B. "A Portrait of 'Jenny': Rossetti's
       Aesthetics of Communion." *Hartford Studies in Liter-*
       ature 1 (1969): 89-106.

       Sees "Hand and Soul" as a means of interpreting "Jenny,"
       which is really more a poem about poetry than it is about
       prostitution. The poem dramatizes two of Rossetti's most
       important aesthetic ideas: specifically, the relationship
       of the creator and his self-begotten image, and the evo-
       lution from naturalism through abstract moralism to an
       ironic allegory of the aesthetic act.

526. Seigel, Jules P. "*Jenny*: The Divided Sensibility of a
       Young and Thoughtful Man of the World." *Studies in*
       English Literature 9 (1969): 677-693.

       Finds in the ambivalence of the speaker--in his vacil-
       lation between passion and compassion--the poem's great-
       est strength, a strength which justifies Rossetti's own
       high regard for it in the face of moral strictures from
       Ruskin and Buchanan.

527. Nelson, James G. "The Rejected Harlot: A Reading of
       Rossetti's 'A Last Confession' and 'Jenny.'" *Victor-*
       ian Poetry 10 (1972): 123-129.

       Offers an unsympathetic interpretation of the speakers
       in both poems, finding in them a conflict between their
       love of fleshly beauty and their bent for moralizing.
       In "Jenny" Rossetti's strategy is to second the moralizing
       while at the same time revealing in subtle ways his own
       aesthetic inclinations.

528. Keane, Robert N. "Rossetti's 'Jenny': Moral Ambiguity
       and the 'Inner Standing Point.'" *Papers on Language*
       and Literature 9 (1973): 271-280.

       Shows how the speaker of the poem exhibits "a tension
       between moral propriety and humane sensitivity," thus
       allowing the reader to form his own conclusions. The
       poet is just as critical of the speaker as he is of the
       prostitute.

529.   Peterson, Carl A.   "Rossetti's *A Last Confession* as
       Dramatic Monologue."   *Victorian Poetry* 11 (1973):
       127-142.

       Reappraises the poem as a successful dramatic monolog,
       one which gives us a clearly-defined speaker in a moment
       of crisis.   Traces motifs such as the dagger and the
       girl's laughter, showing how manuscript revisions demon-
       strate Rossetti's concern with these image patterns.

530.   Christie, James W.   "A Pre-Raphaelite Dispute: 'Rosabell,'
       'Jenny,' and Other Fallen Women."   *Pre-Raphaelite
       Review* 1, no. 2 (May 1978): 40-48.

       Denies the influence of William Bell Scott's poem
       either on Rossetti's "Jenny" or on his painting *Found*.
       In fact, Rossetti takes pains to ignore or even mock
       Scott's central concerns and to offer a fresh, un-
       sentimental, non-dogmatic treatment.

531.   Hersey, G.L.   "Rossetti's 'Jenny': A Realist Altar-
       piece."   *Yale Review* 69 (1979): 17-32.

       Sees the poem as a dramatic monolog but also as an
       ecphrasis, i.e. a rhetorical/poetic description of a
       real or imagined work of visual art.   Rossetti creates
       an imaginary painting, complete with an iconic main
       panel, a narrative predella, a floral frame, and an
       inscription (the lines on lust).   The poem is also a
       Social Darwinist lecture on prostitution.

532.   Shrimpton, Nicholas.   "Rossetti's Pornography."   *Essays
       in Criticism* 29 (1979): 323-340.

       Discusses Rossetti's "Jenny" as a poem dealing with
       prostitutes, i.e. pornography in the earliest sense of
       that term.   "Jenny" is not social realism or dramatic
       monolog; instead it is the last flowering of a great
       Romantic genre, the Coleridgean conversation poem.   This
       form allows Rossetti to experiment with ideas, to ex-
       plore the workings of the mind, with no commitment to
       an intellectual process or to a moral significance.   The
       poem is neither autobiographical nor sentimental but
       rather an artistic *tour-de-force*.

See also items 339, 344, 360, 412, 452, 453, 456, 473, 480,
984, 1004, and 1010.

iv. "The House of Life."

533. Boyle, J.R. "Rossetti's Sonnets." *Notes & Queries*, 7th series, 7 (1889): 258.

Identifies, in response to an earlier inquiry (p. 228), the seer of "True Woman III" as Emmanuel Swedenborg, whose *De Coelo et Inferno* (1758) is the source for the passage.

534. Laughlin, Clara E. "Dante Gabriel Rossetti and 'The House of Life.'" *Stories of Authors' Loves*. Vol. 1. Philadelphia: Lippincott, 1902, pp. 317-322.

Views the sequence as a tribute to Rossetti's beloved woman, Lizzie Siddal. Their relationship is summarized, including the burial and subsequent exhumation of the poems. Rossetti saw Lizzie as his Beatrice, and Dante was his model for creating a poetic tribute. Reprinted from the *Delineator* (1901) and *Book-Lover* (1902).

535. Pantini, Romualdo. "La 'Casa di Vita' di Dante Gabriele Rossetti." *L' Italia Moderna* 2 (1904): 527-538.

Not examined.

536. Suddard, Sarah Mary. "The House of Life." *Keats, Shelley, and Shakespeare: Studies and Essays in English Literature*. Cambridge University Press, 1912, pp. 261-278.

Sees the sonnet sequence as a late flowering of the Renaissance, a period into which Rossetti enters instinctively and breathes his own life. He tries to conciliate the visible and immaterial worlds and to celebrate the complete ideal of love. Rossetti's conception of love is healthy, philosophically solid, and strikingly original. As a poet, however, he is not supple and he writes only fragments.

537. Wagschal, Friedrich. "E.B. Brownings *Sonnets from the Portuguese* und D.G. Rossettis *House of Life*." *Zeitschrift für französischen und englischen Unterricht* 13 (1914): 207-217.

Contrasts the two sonnet sequences, noting that Rossetti was much enamored of Mrs. Browning's poetry. He preferred a two-strophe form, presenting two facets of a single thought, while she preferred the single-strophe

form as suitable for a lyrical outpouring. She wrote
from "inspiration," he from "conception"; she was personal, he visionary. Mrs. Browning's tact can be set
against Rossetti's want of reserve.

538. Tisdel, Frederick M. "Rossetti's 'House of Life.'"
      Modern Philology 15 (1917): 257-276.

      Uses the poem as a means of explicating Rossetti's
      mysterious life. After the sonnets are dated and ar-
      ranged in chronological order, the picture emerges of
      a tragic and noble figure, a man torn between an old
      and new love and suffering a genuine remorse until he
      is able to purify and idealize his emotional life.

539. Wallerstein, Ruth C. "Personal Experience in Rossetti's
      'House of Life.'" *Publications of the Modern Language
      Association* 42 (1927): 492-504.

      Claims that the sonnets are mostly autobiographical
      and deal with Rossetti's love for his wife. Internal
      evidence, such as the parallels between Rossetti's
      letters and the lover's anguish in "Hope Overtaken,"
      and external evidence, such as the dating of the Willow-
      wood group, support this view. [But see item 281.]

540. Jonson, G.C. Ashton. "'The House of Life.'" *Poetry
      Review* 22 (1931): 343-359.

      Compares Rossetti's sonnet sequence with Shakespeare's
      sonnets. Both perfected their form, both believed in
      "fundamental brainwork," both wrote autobiographically.
      Rossetti is more pictorial, Shakespeare more personal.

541. Bowra, C.M. "The House of Life." *The Romantic Imagi-
      nation*. Cambridge, Mass.: Harvard University Press,
      1949, pp. 197-220.

      Sees Rossetti as a "conscious imitator of the Romantic
      outlook," one who expressed in his sonnets the deepest
      concerns of his life. The poet's use of a highly Latinate
      vocabulary can be defended because it gives "Miltonic"
      majesty and suits the principal theme of the sequence,
      i.e. the pursuit of beauty. The sonnet sequence repre-
      sents "what was most powerful in Rossetti's creative
      being" and is an impressive achievement. Reprinted in
      Victorian Literature: Modern Essays in Criticism, ed.
      Austin Wright (1961).

542. Lindberg, John. "Rossetti's Cumaean Oracle." *Victorian Newsletter*, no. 22 (1962): 20-21.

    Explicates the sonnet "The One Hope." Its imagery associates it with the legend of the Cumaean Sibyll, hence with anxiety about the unknown co-existing with hope for a better future. The themes pervading the entire sequence are thus eternal and cyclical.

543. Robillard, Douglas J. "Rossetti's 'Willowwood' Sonnets and the Structure of *The House of Life*." *Victorian Newsletter*, no. 22 (1962): 5-9.

    Contends that the four Willowwood sonnets are central to the carefully planned structure of the entire work: they offer a "lustral rite," they represent an epiphany for the poet, and they darken the tone in anticipation of the second half of the sequence.

544. Vogel, Joseph F. "Rossetti's *The House of Life*, LXXVIII." *Explicator* 21, no. 8 (April 1963): item 64.

    Suggests that the last line of "Death's Songsters" has the poet exhorting his soul to resist the seductive song of death.

545. Buttel, Helen. "Rossetti's 'Bridal Birth.'" *Explicator* 23, no. 3 (November 1964): item 22.

    Sees the poem as creating a birth metaphor by which Rossetti could unite his spiritual and sensual desires, devotion to the second leading to a higher type of the first.

546. Vogel, Joseph F. "Rossetti's 'Memorial Thresholds.'" *Explicator* 23, no. 4 (December 1964): item 29.

    Reads the sestet of the sonnet as concluding that the poet must be granted a reunion with the beloved and renewal of his earlier passionate experience.

547. Fredeman, William E. "Rossetti's 'In Memoriam': An Elegiac Reading of *The House of Life*." *Bulletin of the John Rylands Library* 47 (1965): 298-341.

    Examines the poem's structure in light of its compositional history, finding it a unified whole which mirrors the structure of the Petrarchan sonnet and is therefore

a house in the architectural rather than the zodiacal
sense. Biographical claims about the sequence are in
general not very helpful in understanding it as a work
of art. Instead we should view the sequence as an artistic and personal statement about death--hence elegiac,
a retrospective monument to the synthesized moments of
a representative human being. Included also is a chart
listing for each sonnet its date of publication, date of
composition, and position in the three published versions of the sequence.

548. Kendall, J.L. "The Concept of the Infinite Moment in
       The House of Life." *Victorian Newsletter*, no. 28
       (1965): 4-8.

       Contends that Rossetti's obsession with frozen moments
       of time gives a thematic unity to "The House of Life."
       Time means frustration, dilution, the undermining of
       order, and Rossetti chooses, not the frantic activity
       recommended by Browning, but rather the savoring atti-
       tude which salvages love and beauty from time's destruc-
       tion. This theme is traced in nineteen sonnets from
       the sequence, with allusions to others.

549. Talon, Henri Antoine. *D.G. Rossetti: "The House of Life;"*
       Quelques aspects de l'art, des themes et du symbolisme.
       Paris: Lettres Modernes, 1966. 86 pp.

       Gives detailed explications of seven sonnets, all
       chosen because they illustrate Rossetti's virtuosity
       as a sonneteer. A second part of the monograph is de-
       voted to aspects of Rossetti's symbolism: his use of
       personal experience; the images drawn from nature (woods
       and flowers); the eternal circle; the creation of arch-
       etypes.

550. Eldredge, Harrison. "On an Error in a Sonnet of Ros-
       setti's." *Victorian Poetry* 5 (1967): 302-303.

       Points out that lines 4-6 of "The Dark Glass" presume
       a simile ("dark names"="loud sea") which is not in fact
       stated in the poem.

551. Lees, Francis Noel. "The Keys Are at the Palace: A Note
       on Criticism and Biography." *Literary Criticism and*
       Historical Understanding: Selected Papers from the
       English Institute. Edited by Phillip Damon. New York:
       Columbia University Press, 1967, pp. 135-149.

Sees "The Hill Summit" as an example poem for determining how much "biographical air" can be legitimately
pumped into a poem. Argues for a separation of poetry
and biography in literary criticism, even though they
are clearly interdependent. Reprinted from *College
English* (1966).

552. Going, William T. "The Brothers Rossetti and *Youth* and
Love." *Papers on Language and Literature* 4 (1968):
334-335.

Uses one of William Michael Rossetti's "Democratic
Sonnets" to support Doughty's contention (item 281)
that Love and not Youth was originally tripled with
Change and Fate in "The House of Life."

553. Hume, Robert D. "Inorganic Structure in *The House of
Life*." *Papers in Language and Literature* 5 (1969):
282-295.

Follows Robillard and Fredeman (items 543 and 547) in
seeing a clear structure to the sequence, but the structure is inorganic (i.e. the parts do not follow one
another organically) and it is not necessarily autobiographical. Part I consists of three movements centering on the delights of love, premonitions of loss,
and grief, respectively. Part II has four movements
centering on art, philosophy, the poet's feelings, and
death, respectively.

554. Miyoshi, Masao. "Broken Music: 1870." *The Divided Self:
A Perspective on the Literature of the Victorians*.
New York: New York University Press, 1969, pp. 227-285.

Discusses Rossetti's love for the past and his dramatization of it in "The House of Life," where his beloved
becomes the object of a "Dantean passion." The motif
of the double is tied to this Dantean desire for fusion
of earth and heaven, self and other.

555. Baker, Houston A., Jr. "The Poet's Progress: Rossetti's
The House of Life." *Victorian Poetry* 8 (1970): 1-14.

Argues that the sequence shows the speaker progressing
from narrow ideals, based primarily on an idealization
of physical love, to a broader ideal in which love becomes spiritualized. Rossetti repudiates aestheticism;
he stresses impersonal poetry and a life of striving.

556. Ryals, Clyde de L. "The Narrative Unity of *The House of Life*." *Journal of English and Germanic Philology* 69 (1970): 241-257.

Argues that the sonnet sequence develops through the presentation of lyrical moments. Part I focuses on love, Part II on art, and both on mutability. The ending suggests that the pilgrim must struggle to avoid the conclusion that life is meaningless.

557. Barth, J. Robert, S.J. "Mysticism in Rossetti's 'House of Life.'" *Barat Review* 6 (1971): 41-48.

Claims that the mystical qualities noted by Savarit (see item 1068) can be attributed just as plausibly to the Dantean tradition rather than the Gnostic one. Four elements are especially noteworthy: an incarnational emphasis on material beauty; the conviction that matter is symbolic; the equivalence of human love and divine love; the fulfillment of all love in a future time.

558. Adlard, John. "Rossetti's 'Willow-Wood': A Source?" *Notes & Queries* 217 (1972): 253-254.

Cites *Cuzner's Hand-Book to Froome-Selwood*, published in 1867, as a source for the local place-name "Willow-Wood." Christina had stayed in Froome-Selwood in 1853 and 1854.

559. Greene, Michael E. "The Severed Self: The Dramatic Impulse in *The House of Life*." *Ball State University Forum* 14, no. 4 (Autumn 1973): 49-58.

Contends that the sequence is a culmination of Rossetti's interest in dramatic techniques. The sonnet form allowed the objective representation of the poet's inner states. He could also use multiple personalities, invent scenes, and allow abstractions to assume human form. The disintegration of individual sonnets mirrors the disintegration of the soul.

560. Jarfe, Günther. *Kunstform and Verzweiflung: Studien zur Typologie der Sonettgestalt in Dante Gabriel Rossettis 'The House of Life.'* Bern: Lang, 1973. 144 pp.

Begins with a history of the critical reception of "The House of Life" as a prolegomenon to a full-scale examination of the sequence. Divides the sonnets into four

types, with six, twenty, twenty-four, and forty-eight
sonnets in each, respectively; this framework allows
for detailed explications of selected sonnets. There
is a further categorization according to whether the
sonnet has an amplifying structure or a dramatic structure. Topics discussed include: allegorical and dramatic elements in the work; the concept of "the moment";
the progression from love to the loss of love and the
concomitant destruction of the poet's personality; and
Rossetti's high position in the history of the English
sonnet.

561. Parrington-Jackson, P.A. "Rossetti, 'The House of Life.'"
     Notes & Queries 218 (1973): 221.

     Requests help in the preparation of a projected anno-
     tated edition of the sonnet sequence.

562. Magnier, M. "La *Maison de vie* de Dante Gabriel Rossetti
     et l'Italie." *Revue de Littérature Comparée* 50 (1976):
     303-311.

     Traces the Italian, especially Dantean, parallels in
     selected sonnets from the sequence.

563. Spector, Stephen J. "Rossetti's Self Destroying 'Moment's
     Monument': 'Silent Noon.'" *Victorian Poetry* 14 (1976):
     54-58.

     Claims that even in Rossetti's most serene sonnet a
     reader can detect a Romantic restlessness and dis-
     satisfaction. No moment is exempt.

564. Bentley, D.M.R. "'The Song-Throe' by D.G. Rossetti."
     Notes & Queries 24 (1977): 421-422.

     Argues that the sonnet is based on the myth of Apollo
     and Marsyas.

565. Jarvie, Paul, and Robert Rosenberg. "'Willowwood,'
     Unity, and *The House of Life*." *Pre-Raphaelite Review*
     1, no. 1 (November 1977): 106-120.

     Sees the action of the Willowwood sonnets as arche-
     typal for the rest of the sequence. The scene is con-
     stantly re-created, further isolating the speaker and
     deepening his misery. The overtones of evil, of un-
     fulfillment, of passivity, of disunity--all these are

typical too. The sequence has no coherent progression and no optimistic conclusion, despite what other critics have tried to show.

566. Bentley, D.M.R. "Rossetti's Pre-Raphaelite Manifesto: The 'Old and New Art' Sonnets." *English Language Notes* 15 (1978): 197-203.

Finds in three sonnets of 1848-1849 an embodiment of the Pre-Raphaelite theory of art. Rossetti at this time believed in art as the handmaiden of religion and the artist as the husbandman of God.

See also items 28, 281, 322, 331, 344, 348, 360, 388, 392, 412, 435, 441, 452, 468, 469, 473, 480-482, 610, 629, 989, 1013, 1031, 1078, and 1085.

v. Other Poems

567. St. Johnston, Alfred. "Rossetti's 'Sudden Light.'" *Academy* 25, no. 624 (1884): 279.

Shows and analyzes the textual variants in three published versions of the poem, i.e. the versions of 1863, of 1870, and of 1881.

568. Hardinge, William M. "A Note on the Louvre Sonnets of Rossetti." *Temple Bar* 91 (1891): 433-443.

Observes that in three of the four sonnets Rossetti misinterprets the subject, in all cases giving it a modern, mystical, and highly personal treatment. His use of rhyme and color, wherein he suits the poem to the painting, is also noteworthy.

569. ["Comestor Oxoniensis"]. "Rossetti's 'Ruggiero and Angelica.'" *Notes & Queries*, 9th series, 9 (1902): 425.

Calls attention to Rossetti's use of the words "geomancy" and "teraphim" in the sonnet. The former word is of Rossetti's own coinage--perhaps it means necromancy; the latter is a Jewish cult.

570. Metzdorf, Robert F. "The Full Text of Rossetti's Sonnet on *Sordello*." *Harvard Library Bulletin* 7 (1953): 239-243.

Prints for the first time the sestet, and thus the complete text, of Rossetti's "Sonnet on a first reading of 'Sordello.'" The text was found in an edition of *Sordello* owned by Thomas Woolner and dated 1849. The lines sum up Rossetti's love for the early, Shelleyean Browning.

571. Kodama, Sanechika. "D.G. Rossetti's 'One Dream Alone.'" *Dōshisha Daigaku Jimbungaku*, no. 35 (1958): 1-15.

In Japanese.

572. Bracker, Jon. "Notes on the Texts of Two Poems by Dante Gabriel Rossetti." *Library Chronicle of the University of Texas* 7, no. 3 (Summer 1963): 14-16.

Corrects line 8 of "Antwerp and Bruges" ("along," not "alone") in Doughty's edition of Rossetti's poems (see item 34) and seconds Doughty's notion of a variant reading for a line in "The Orchard Pit."

573. Nelson, James G. "Aesthetic Experience and Rossetti's 'My Sister's Sleep.'" *Victorian Poetry* 7 (1969): 154-158.

Views the poem as a successful attempt to create an "aesthetic domestic idyll," perceived and arranged by the sensitive young narrator. Despair is transmuted into beauty, personal experience becomes aesthetic experience.

574. Thomas, Robert. "Graphics: *Chimes* by Rossetti and Skiöld." *Art and Artists* 4 (1970): 55.

Describes the Circle Press publication entitled *Chimes*, which reprints seven Rossetti poems exhibiting "an unusual sense of sound relationships," plus accompanying visual images by Birgit Skiöld which unite with the poems to give a "satisfactory whole."

575. Hobbs, John N. "Love and Time in Rossetti's 'The Stream's Secret.'" *Victorian Poetry* 9 (1971): 395-404.

Analyzes the poem as a series of psychological actions in which the speaker reveals his emotional ambivalence: he is torn between an optimistic desire for reunion and a tortured awareness of his beloved's absence.

576. Hollander, John. "The Poem in the Eye." *Shenandoah*
      23, no. 3 (Spring 1972): 3-32.

      Discusses the *ut pictura poesis* tradition and its
      modern manifestations. Offers special praise for
      Rossetti's "Antwerp to Ghent," which transforms still
      picture into motion, sensation into rushing image, much
      as a movie might do.

577. Patterson, Kent. "A Terrible Beauty: Medusa in Three
      Victorian Poets." *Texas Studies in Language and
      Literature* 17 (1972): 111-120.

      Shows how Rossetti, in contrast to Morris and Swin-
      burne, emphasizes the power of the artist to create
      beauty from even a terrible reality. His "Aspecta
      Medusa" is but another example of his fascination with
      the "dark woman" motif.

578. Sussman, Herbert. "Rossetti's Changing Style: The
      Revisions of 'My Sister's Sleep.'" *Victorian News-
      letter*, no. 41 (1972): 6-8.

      Compares the use of Christian symbolism in the *Germ*
      version of the poem and the less conventional use of it
      in the version printed two decades later in *Poems*. See
      also item 581.

579. Hammond, L. Kenneth. "Dante Gabriel Rossetti's 'The
      Orchard Pit.'" *Victorians Institute Journal* 2 (1973):
      23-26.

      Sees the prose sketch of the poem as indicating that
      Rossetti was ambivalent about the sexual content of the
      poem. The pit itself represents the female genitalia,
      and the attitude toward it is both violent and com-
      pulsive. Both fascination and repulsion are apparent
      too in the poetic fragment, which Rossetti perhaps
      could not finish for deeply personal reasons.

580. Stuart, Donald C. III. "Bitter Fantasy: Narcissus in
      Dante Gabriel Rossetti's Lyrics." *Victorians Institute
      Journal* 2 (1973): 27-40.

      Describes Rossetti's treatment of the Narcissus myth
      in a number of his poems but with special concentration
      on "The Stream's Secret." Rossetti combined in himself
      Narcissus and the idealizing troubador. Narcissus in

this case is a positive figure, a seeker after self-
consciousness. A detailed analysis of the poem shows
it to be an example of that dialog of the mind with
itself that Arnold feared; this dialog might in turn
be based on Rossetti's knowledge of meditation techniques.

581. Bentley, D.M.R. "The *Belle Assemblée* Version of 'My
     Sister's Sleep.'" *Victorian Poetry* 12 (1974): 321-334.

     Announces a hitherto-unrecorded printing of the poem
     and shows how Rossetti manipulated its Christian sym-
     bolism during this and later revisions. See item 578.

582. Keane, Robert N. "Rossetti: The Artist and 'The Por-
     trait.'" *English Language Notes* 12 (1974): 96-102.

     Relates the poem to Rossetti's artistic interests and
     shows how work on it progressed from 1847 through the
     publication of *Poems* in 1870. The earlier emphasis on
     "sunlit love" is transmuted into a poem centering on
     mystery and loss.

583. Bright, Michael H. "The Influence of Browning's 'My
     Last Duchess' on Rossetti's 'The Portrait.'" *American
     Notes & Queries* 13 (1975): 99-100.

     Points out the similarities in situation, commencement,
     painterly verisimilitude, wonderment, and diction between
     the two poems, Rossetti's being written when he was nine-
     teen and much enthused with Browning's work.

584. Greene, Michael E. "Rossetti's 'Absurd Trash': 'Sir
     Hugh the Heron' Reconsidered." *Tennessee Studies in
     Literature* 20 (1975): 85-91.

     Sees in this poem, written by Rossetti at age twelve,
     adumbrations of the poet's later subjects, such as mysti-
     cism, romantic heroines, and the intermingling of sacred
     and profane elements. Rossetti's development was to be
     marked by a refinement of early responses rather than by
     genuine change.

585. Peters, John U. "Rossetti's 'My Sister's Sleep,' 13-16."
     Explicator 35, no. 2 (Winter 1976): 29-30.

     Calls attention to the Eucharist symbolism in these
     lines, a symbolism Rossetti had secularized from an
     earlier draft of the poem. Further developed in item 589.

586. Crabbe, John K. "Dante Gabriel Rossetti's 'Five English
        Poets': Another Side of the Anti-Lyric." *Pre-Raphaelite
        Review* 1, no. 1 (November 1977): 39-46.

        Analyzes Rossetti's five-sonnet sequence as an example
        of Cadbury's "anti-lyric," i.e. a group of poems which
        posit a single exterior narrator and a common theme.
        The unifying theme here is the tragic fate of the poet.

587. Bentley, D.M.R. "Rossetti's 'Sunset Wings.'" *Explicator*
        37, no. 1 (1978): 39.

        Argues that "sunset wings" are allegorical representa-
        tions of the time just before death and that, while Hope
        is now replaced by Sorrow, the possibility of an after-
        life is not negated.

588. Nassar, Christopher S. "Rossetti's 'Astarte Syriaca':
        A Neglected Sonnet." *Pre-Raphaelite Review* 2, no. 1
        (November 1978): 63-65.

        Praises the late sonnet as a blending of form and con-
        tent which shows Rossetti's final, despairing view of
        the nature of sexual passion. The Syrian goddess, behind
        her beautiful mask, is cruel, man-destroying.

589. Peters, John U. "'My Sister's Sleep': Rossetti's Mid-
        night Mass." *Victorian Poetry* 17 (1979): 265-268.

        Contends that the religious symbolism of the poem is
        unified around the Christian Eucharist; the secular ac-
        tivities in the poem correspond to the ritual of the
        mass. For an earlier version of this thesis, see item
        585.

See also items 47, 332, 339, 360, 400, 462, 473, 480, 484,
598, 633, 640, 1071, 1083, 1087, 1093, and 1099.

vi. "Hand and Soul"

590. Wilkins, W. "Dante Rossetti's 'Hand and Soul.'" *Academy*
        21 (1882): 323.

        Asks when the story appeared in the *Fortnightly Review*,
        as Hall Caine (item 148) claims. Answered (p. 341) by
        G. Barnett Smith: the year was 1870, although variant
        versions appeared earlier in *The Germ* and in a pamphlet.

591. Gurney, Alfred. "Dante Gabriel Rossetti: A Painter's
Day-Dream, and the Vision That Ensued." *Monthly
Packet*, 3rd series, 9 (1885): 185-193.

Discusses "Hand and Soul" as the prolegomenon to any
study of the artist's work. The allegory is interpreted
religiously: Rossetti has a lofty aim, and those who
accuse him of despair or license err.

592. Morse, B.J. "A Note on the Autobiographical Elements
in Rossetti's 'Hand and Soul.'" *Anglia* 54 (1930):
331-337.

Recapitulates the argument of Rossetti's story and
contends that Chiaro is young Rossetti, Pisano is Ford
Madox Brown, and the "figura mistica" painting is based
on a Rossetti drawing of 1848.

593. Ryals, Clyde de L. "The 'Inner Experience': The Aesthetic
of Rossetti and Isak Dinesen." *Revue des Langues Vi-
vantes* 26 (1960): 368-374.

Compares "Hand and Soul" with Dinesen's "Young Man
with the Carnation." Rossetti sees art as a self-
fulfilling manifestation of God, whereas Dinesen sees
it as a God-assigned destiny for the artist.

594. Forsyth, R.A. "The Temper of Pre-Raphaelitism and the
Concern with Natural Detail." *English Studies in
Africa* 4 (1961): 182-190.

Uses Rossetti's "Hand and Soul" as an example of Pre-
Raphaelite goals, i.e. the union of naturalistic detail
(method, or "Hand") and social concern (intention, or
"Soul").

595. Gordon, Jan B. "The Imaginary Portrait: Fin-de-Siècle
Icon." *University of Windsor Review* 5, no. 1 (Fall
1969): 81-104.

Names Rossetti as the initiator of the imaginary portrait genre later brought to fruition in Pater, Wilde,
Symons, and others. "Hand and Soul" shows typical qualities: the painting which reflects the creator's torment;
the tale which centers on the growth of the artist; the
raising of art to the level of religious faith. Rossetti also anticipates Wilde's claim that life eventually
comes to imitate art.

596.   Bentley, D.M.R. "Rossetti's 'Hand and Soul.'" *English
       Studies in Canada* 3 (1977): 445-457.

       Views the story as an intensely metaphorical prose
       poem about art. Rossetti's admiration for Charles Wells
       shows through in his interest in the moral implications
       of art and in Catholic ritual (an interest diminished
       in later versions of the story). A summary of the con-
       tents shows that Chiaro's moral failures were arrogance,
       self-centeredness, and the pursuit of fame. The artist
       should paint the moral essence of man.

See also items 24, 27, 38, 149, 400, 456, 462, 525, 617, 699,
1058, and 1084.

SECTION C: RELATIONSHIPS WITH OTHER WRITERS

Included in this section are: general studies of influences on
Rossetti's poetry (source studies for particular poems will be
found in Section B); studies of Rossetti's relationships with
contemporary writers; and studies of Rossetti's influence on
writers who came after him.

597.   Milner, George. "On Some Marginalia Made by Dante
       Gabriel Rossetti in a Copy of Keats' Poems." *Man-
       chester Quarterly* 2 (1883): 1-10.

       Prints and then comments on the marginalia found in
       Rossetti's copy of the 1868 Moxon Keats. *Endymion*
       elicits mostly negative comments; *Hyperion* is "the crown
       of Keats' genius"; numerous short judgments are also
       recorded.

598.   Armes, William D. "DeQuincey and Rossetti." *Critic* 17
       (1890): 328.

       Calls attention to a parallel between a passage on
       music in "The Confessions of an English Opium Eater"
       and Rossetti's sonnet "The Monochord." Did Rossetti
       read and admire the Romantic prose writer?

599.   Kuhns, Oscar. "Matthew Arnold and Rossetti." *Dante
       and the English Poets from Chaucer to Tennyson*. New
       York: Holt, 1904, pp. 198-217.

Summarizes the growth of Rossetti's interest in Dante, his translations of Dante, his use of Dantean materials in his own poetry, and his influence on the revival of English interest in Dante.

600. Watkin, Ralph G. *Robert Browning and the English Pre-Raphaelites*. Breslau: Fleischmann, 1905. 63 pp.

Describes the personal relationships and reciprocal influences of Browning and the Pre-Raphaelites, principally Rossetti. Rossetti's letter to Browning in 1850 and their subsequent friendship followed years of youthful hero-worship by Rossetti. Browning in turn showed, in poems like "Old Pictures in Florence," the effect of Pre-Raphaelite principles. Traces the many parallels between Browning's poetry and Rossetti's.

601. Compton-Rickett, Arthur. "Keats and Rossetti." *Personal Forces in Modern Literature*. London: Dent, 1906, pp. 112-139.

Sees both poets as marked by congruity of matter and manner, by the power of transfiguring commonplaces through the use of color, and by the mingling of the sensuous and the supernatural. Their personalities show as many similarities as their work, and both were devotees of beauty. Reprinted 1968.

602. Ranftl, Johann. "Romantik und Prärafaelismus." *Historisch-politische Blätter für das katholische Deutschland* 138 (1906): 449-468.

Traces the Pre-Raphaelites and Rossetti back to their Romantic origins, especially in the works of such poets as Campbell, Blake, Hunt, and Keats.

603. Routh, James. "Parallels in Coleridge, Keats, and Rossetti." *Modern Language Notes* 25 (1910): 33-37.

Denies that there are any significant parallels in rhythm, sentiment, or subject between Keats and Rossetti (but see items 605, 612, 628, and 630). Finds "The White Ship" and "Rose Mary" to be indebted in style, form, and subject to "The Ancient Mariner" and "Christabel," respectively.

604. Willoughby, Leonard A. *Dante Gabriel Rossetti and German Literature*. London: Fowde, 1912. 32 pp.

Describes Rossetti's knowledge of German literature,
which was extensive, and his use of it in translations
and in original works, ranging from the youthful
"Sorrentino" (1843) to "Body's Beauty." Reprinted 1968;
also in *Oxford Lectures on Literature* (1924).

605. Villard, Léonie. *The Influence of Keats on Tennyson and
Rossetti.* Saint-Étienne: Mulcey, 1914. 94 pp.

Explains how Rossetti's purchase of an edition of
Keats's poems in 1848 led both to a new direction for
the P.R.B., which began to illustrate subjects from
Keats, and to an increasing emphasis on beauty in
Rossetti's own poetry. Rossetti's sensuousness, color,
visual detail, and diction all show Keats's influence.
But Rossetti lacks Keats's breadth and humanity.

606. Browning, Robert. *Critical Comments on Algernon Charles
Swinburne and D.G. Rossetti.* London: privately printed
by T.J. Wise, 1919. 17 pp.

The second of three Browning letters printed in this
little volume contains Browning's objection to the
"effeminacy" of Rossetti and the Pre-Raphaelites.

607. Van Roesbroeck, Gustave L. "Rossetti and Maeterlinck."
Modern Language Notes 34 (1919): 439-441.

Points to Rossetti's "An Old Song Ended" as a possible
source for Maeterlinck's well-known "Et s'il revenait
un jour" inasmuch as they have similar subjects, treatments, and atmospheres.

608. Broers, Bernarda C. "Dante and Rossetti" and "Dante
Gabriel Rossetti." *Mysticism in the Neo-Romantics.*
Amsterdam: Paris, 1923, pp. 56-86.

Traces the influence of Dante's concept of "mystic
union" on Rossetti, who then blends this concept with
the doctrines of aestheticism. Rossetti as a poet is
spiritual, not sensual, and aestheticism for him only
means restoring Beauty to its proper place of honor.

609. Drinkwater, John. "Tennyson's Influence." *Victorian
Poetry.* New York: Doran, 1924, pp. 102-141.

Finds Rossetti to be a poet working in the Tennysonian
tradition. A comparison of "The Lady of Shalott" and

"The Blessed Damozel" shows these similarities, but
Rossetti is more artificial, more ethereal.

610. Galimberti, Alice. "Gli esuli.--Il culto di Dante in
        casa Rossetti." *Dante nel pensiero inglese*. Florence:
        LeMonnier, 1924, pp. 179-198.

        Describes the interest in Dante exhibited by the entire
        Rossetti family. Dante Gabriel's translations, especi-
        ally of the *Vita Nuova*, are imbued with the Dantean
        spirit, as is his own "House of Life."

611. Holthausen, Ferdinand. "D.G. Rossetti und die Bibel."
        Germanisch-Romanische Monatsschrift 13 (1925): 310-
        312 and 14 (1926): 73-76.

        Shows how numerous passages in Rossetti's poems draw
        their inspiration and even their wording from passages
        in the Bible. The preponderance of biblical citations
        comes from the Old Testament authors.

612. Shine, Wesley Hill. "The Influence of Keats upon Ros-
        setti." *Englische Studien* 61 (1927): 183-219.

        Argues contrary to Routh (item 603) that Rossetti
        knew Keats's poems intimately and that he shared Keats's
        mysticism and supernaturalism. Separate sections are
        devoted to four types of parallels: themes, situations,
        descriptions, and tropes. Within each section numerous
        examples of parallel passages buttress the case. See
        also items 628 and 630.

613. Turner, Albert Morton. "Rossetti's Reading and His
        Critical Opinions." *Publications of the Modern Lan-
        guage Association* 42, no. 1 (March 1927): 465-491.

        Summarizes Rossetti's reading, which was primarily in
        Dante, the Italian lyric poets, contemporary French
        novelists, and Goethe among foreign authors, and the
        ballad writers, Shakespeare, Milton, Donne, Burns, Blake,
        Scott, Coleridge, Byron, and Keats among English poets.
        Critical enthusiasms among his contemporaries included
        Tennyson, both Brownings, Morris, Swinburne, Patmore,
        and Dickens.

614. Arrieta, Rafael Alberto. "Dante Gabriel Rossetti."
        Dickens y Sarmiento: otros estudios. Buenos Aires:
        Al Ateneo, 1928, pp. 63-82.

Explores the literary relations between England and
Italy as manifested in the case of Rossetti. Begins
with a short history of Anglo-Italian literary relations
from Chaucer through the Brownings. Rossetti's treatment of Italian subjects and of Dante made Italy more
real for Victorian Englishmen and at the same time gave
expression to a character which was by nature Italian.

615.   Bachschmidt, Friedrich W. *Das italienische Element in
       Dante Gabriel Rossetti*. Breslau: Walter, 1930.   83 pp.

       Not examined.

616.   Farmer, Albert J. "Le Mouvement préraphaélite: Rossetti
       et Morris." *Le Mouvement aesthétique et "decadent" en
       Angleterre (1873-1900)*. Paris: Champion, 1931, pp.
       15-21.

       Shows how the sensuality and mystery which color Ros-
       setti's poetry influenced younger poets and contributed
       to the creation of a literary climate in which decadence
       could flourish.

617.   Rosenblatt, Louise. "La Defense du beau." *L'Idée de
       l'art dans la littérature anglaise pendant la période
       victorienne*. Paris: Champion, 1931, pp. 89-120.

       Demonstrates how Rossetti (among others) influenced
       aestheticism by his short story "Hand and Soul," by his
       contribution to the cult of Keats, by his avoidance of
       didacticism, and by his contribution to the revival of
       the decorative arts.

618.   Klenk, Hans. *Nachwirkungen Dante Gabriel Rossettis*.
       Berlin: Bachmann, 1932.   62 pp.

       Studies Rossetti's influence on contemporary and later
       poets, specifically on his sister, Patmore, Marston,
       Watts-Dunton, O'Shaugnessy, Dowson, and Davidson. Ros-
       setti became a model for these writers, both as man and
       as artist. They adapted his ideas, his mystic dream-
       world, his tragic sense of fate, his pictorialism, and
       his diction. Specific examples from each of the other
       poets are provided.

619.   Morse, B.J. "Dante Gabriel Rossetti and William Blake."
       Englische Studien 66 (1932): 364-372.

Argues that Rossetti unintentionally tried to purify Blake's rhyme and rhythm, thus having a pernicious effect on later editions of Blake's work. Rossetti was sympathetic to Blake because of their parallel careers and parallel opinions. Rossetti's use of repetitions, of specters, and of overt sexuality may owe something to the earlier master.

620. Klinnert, Adelheid. *Dante Gabriel Rossetti and Stefan George*. Würzburg: Mayr, 1933. 105 pp.

Examines the similarity in poetic philosophy between Rossetti and George, especially their rejection of materialism and their devotion to art and its services. A comparison of the two poets in terms of their ideas about religion, love, and nature also reveals many similarities; but on political ideas--or rather Rossetti's lack of them--there is a sharp break. See also item 625.

621. Las Vergnas, R. "Le Britannisme de Rossetti." *Revue Anglo-Américaine* 11 (1933): 129-135.

Objects to the emphasis of Dupré (item 1029) and others on Rossetti's stylistic kinship with Dante. Rossetti was thoroughly British and his Italy was seen mostly through Browning's eyes. His poetic dramatizations of chivalry, supernaturalism, and the ideal of service were indebted to Scott and Tennyson. Only in the sonnets was Dante's influence paramount.

622. Morse, B.J. "Dante Gabriel Rossetti and Dante Alighieri." *Englische Studien* 68 (1933): 227-248.

Claims that, despite what his brother later said, Rossetti was interested in Dante from the very beginning and learned much from his father. But Rossetti's interests in Dante were unorthodox by earlier standards, especially his concentration on the Ideal Woman; these interests should be attributed more to his intellect than to his "blood."

623. Olivero, Federico. *Il Petrarca e Dante Gabriele Rossetti*. Florence: Tipocalcografia Classica, 1933.

Not examined.

624. Howe, M[errill] L. "Rossetti's Comments on *Maud*." *Modern Language Notes* 49 (1934): 290-293.

Quotes from unpublished letters by Rossetti to William
Allingham in which Rossetti criticizes *Maud* for being
artificial and stylistically overloaded, although the
poem does have "glorious" parts. Rossetti also notes
the inordinately violent antipathy Tennyson expressed
towards those who had criticized his work.

625. Farrell, Ralph. "Rossetti." *Stefan Georges Beziehungen*
     zur englischen Dichtung. Berlin: Ebering, 1937,
     pp. 183-191.

     Comments on George's translations of Rossetti's
     sonnets, both the successes and the failures, largely
     by means of a favorable comparison of George's ren-
     derings with those of Otto Hauser. The equivalences
     which George sought for Rossetti's enjambment, tone,
     diction, and rhythm are also discussed. See item 620.

626. Jervis, H. "Carlyle and *The Germ*." *Times Literary*
     Supplement, no. 1907 (1938), p. 544.

     Records a letter by Carlyle dated 31 March 1850 in
     which he praises *The Germ*.

627. Koziol, Herbert. "D.G. Rossettis Reime." *Archiv für*
     das Studien des neueren Sprachen und Literaturen 177
     (1940): 98-99.

     Traces Rossetti's use of such accentuated-unaccentuated
     rhymes as "garlanded/thread" to his reading in early
     English poetry and above all in the folk ballads.

628. Ford, George H. "Rossetti." *Keats and the Victorians*.
     New Haven: Yale University Press, 1944, pp. 91-145.

     Shows how Rossetti's aestheticism and a concomitant
     shift in taste helped to secure Keats an audience in
     the years after 1850. Rossetti's interest in sensuous
     beauty and his indifference to politics and controversy
     account for his affection for the earlier poet. Ros-
     setti's poetry was deeply influenced by Keats, although
     not in specific images or lines (see item 612).

629. Praz, Mario. "La Belle Dame Sans Merci." *The Romantic*
     Agony. Translated by A. Davidson. Oxford University
     Press, 1951, pp. 187-286.

     Contains several references (*passim*) to Rossetti's

influence on Swinburne and to his love of the sad and the cruel, especially in "Willowwood."

630. Unwin, Rayner. "Keats and Pre-Raphaelitism." *English* 8 (1951): 229-335.

Claims that the thought of Rossetti parallels the thought of Keats: both reverted to the Middle Ages for inspiration, both valued detail, both were great colorists, both stressed the paramount importance of love, both used archaicisms, both were devoted to nature. But in each case Keats exhibited the greater range.

631. Decker, Clarence R. "'The Fleshly School'--Baudelaire in England." *The Victorian Conscience*. New York: Twayne, 1952, pp. 63-77.

Shows how Rossetti shared the opprobrium bestowed on Baudelaire for his rebelliousness, his sensuality, his amorality, and his candor about sexual matters. Rossetti's brooding over the attacks by Buchanan and others led to his early demise.

632. West, T. Wilson. "D.G. Rossetti and Ezra Pound." *Review of English Studies* n.s. 4 (1953): 63-67.

Claims that Pound's early poetry was heavily influenced by Rossetti in three ways: the use of personification, the poetic mood, and the love idealism.

633. [Runden, John P.] "Rossetti and a Poe Image." *Notes & Queries* 203 (1958): 257-258.

Speculates that Poe influenced Rossetti. One piece of evidence is the similarity in situation, treatment, and diction between Poe's "To Helen" and Rossetti's "The Portrait."

634. Mellown, Elgin W. "Hopkins, Hall Caine, and D.G. Rossetti." *Notes & Queries* 204 (1959): 109-111.

Explains that in 1881 R.W. Dixon persuaded Hopkins to submit three sonnets to Hall Caine for inclusion in *Sonnets of Three Centuries*. The poems were rejected by Caine on the advice of "an eminent critic," revealed now to have been Rossetti.

635. Jackson, Elizabeth R. "Proust et les Pré-Raphaélites." *Revue des Sciences Humaines* n.s. 117 (1965): 93-102.

Focuses on Proust's 1903 review of a book by William
Michael Rossetti because in it Proust crystallizes
themes later used in *The Remembrance of Things Past*. Of
special importance is the idea of an artist seeing a type
of ideal beauty incarnated in a woman--an idea Proust was
borrowing from his reading of Dante Gabriel Rossetti.

636. Luke, David. "The Eve of St. Mark: Keats's 'ghostly
      Queen of Spades' and the Textual Superstition."
      Studies in Romanticism 9 (1970): 161-175.

      Discusses, among other topics, Rossetti's role first
      in popularizing Keats's poem and then in supplying the
      legend upon which it was based.

637. Adams, Elsie B. "The Pre-Raphaelites and Shaw." *Bernard
      Shaw and the Aesthetes*. Columbus: Ohio State University
      Press, 1971, pp. 14-23.

      Traces the evolution of Shaw's attitude towards and use
      of the Pre-Raphaelites. Shaw called himself a "Pre-
      Raphaelite dramatist," used Rossettian costumes, and
      rebelled against Academicianism. He praised Rossetti's
      moralism and sense of color, but decried his stylization
      and lack of technical skill.

638. Banerjee, Ron D.K. "Dante Through the Looking Glass:
      Rossetti, Pound, and Eliot." *Comparative Literature*
      24 (1972): 136-149.

      Sees Rossetti as an exemplar of the kind of "subjec-
      tive" and "personal" interpretation of Dante character-
      istic of the late nineteenth century--an interpretation
      against which Pound and Eliot rebelled when they develop-
      ed their own critical theories.

639. Grylls, Rosalie G. "Rossetti and Browning." *Princeton
      University Library Chronicle* 33 (1972): 232-250.

      Retells the story of Rossetti's friendship for the
      older poet, his enthusiasm over Browning's poetry, and
      then his eventual disaffection. Prints ten letters
      from Rossetti to Browning covering the period 1863-1872.

640. Fisher, Benjamin F. IV. "Rossetti and Swinburne in
      Tandem: 'The Laird of Waristoun.'" *Victorian Poetry*
      11 (1973): 229-239.

Analyzes a collaborative poem written in 1861, finding
in it a combination of Rossetti's pictorialism and supernaturalism and Swinburne's lyricism and visionary interests.

641.   Spector, Stephen J. "The Unattributed *Blackwood's* Review
       of D.G. Rossetti's *Poems*, 1870." *Notes & Queries* 221
       (1976): 398.

       Identifies the reviewer as Mrs. Margaret Oliphant, the
       well-known novelist.

642.   Findlay, L.M. "D.G. Rossetti and *Jude the Obscure*."
       Pre-Raphaelite Review 2, no. 1 (November 1978): 1-11.

       Suggests that certain motifs in Hardy's last novel
       stem from his reading of Rossetti. Examples of such
       motifs include the physical barrier (wall, bar), the
       Lady Lilith figure (Arabella), marriage as a prison
       (*La Pia*, Susan). "The Blessed Damozel" in particular
       seems key.

See also items 121, 122, 126, 182, 204, 205, 209, 220, 224,
244, 262, 265, 267, 273, 276, 279, 284, 295, 300, 309, 336,
352, 353, 368, 369, 388, 404, 418, 444, 446, 474, 480, 483,
489, 491, 492, 494-496, 498, 502, 504, 512, 514, 516, 522,
523, 533, 537, 542, 548, 554, 557, 558, 562, 564, 580, 583,
593, 595, 596, 646, 648, 651, 652, 655, 729, 874, 886, 896,
899, 918, 941, 946, 954, 987, 1005, 1007, 1013, 1020, 1022,
1023, 1027, 1032, 1038, 1043, 1046, 1048, 1053, 1054, 1058,
1060, 1065, 1068, 1084, 1095, and 1097.

SECTION D: ROSSETTI AS TRANSLATOR

643.   Guthrie, William Norman. "IV. A Great Translator" and
       "V. A Curious Instance." *Sewanee Review* 17 (1909):
       392-404.

       Calls Rossetti "the supreme English translator" and
       illustrates the claim by comparing his renderings of
       selected passages with those of Shelley, Longfellow,
       Andrew Lang, and others. Rossetti paraphrases only
       after he has visualized the subject afresh. This visualiz-
       ing power is best seen in Rossetti's translation entitled
       "The Leaf." But see items 644-646.

644.   Rossetti, William Michael. "Rossetti as Translator: Two
        Letters." *Sewanee Review* 17 (1909): 405-408.

        Explains the circumstances behind Rossetti's trans-
        lation of "The Leaf" (item 643), viz. his reading of
        Leopardi and his ignorance of the fact that Leopardi
        was borrowing from Arnault. Whether Rossetti "visualized'
        very much, as Guthrie contends, is questionable. See
        also items 645 and 646.

645.   Trombly, Albert E. "A Translation of Rossetti's." *Mod-
        ern Language Notes* 38 (1923): 116-118.

        Claims that Rossetti's "The Leaf" is a translation
        from Arnault rather than from Leopardi--but see item 646.

646.   Baum, Paull F. "Rossetti's 'The Leaf.'" *Modern Lan-
        guage Quarterly* 2 (1941): 187-189.

        Contends that Rossetti's translation was based, not
        just on Arnault's original (see item 645), and not just
        on Leopardi's version (see items 643 and 644), but
        rather on *both*.

647.   Simonini, R.C., Jr. "Rossetti's Poems in Italian."
        Italia 25 (1948): 131-137.

        Discusses the seven poems Rossetti wrote in Italian
        and the four English translations he provided. A com-
        parison of the originals with their translations shows
        that Rossetti translated concept-by-concept rather
        than line-by-line.

648.   Lang, Cecil Y. "The French Originals of Rossetti's
        'John of Tours' and 'My Father's Close.'" *Publications
        of the Modern Language Association* 64, no. 5 (December
        1949): 1219-1222.

        Identifies the originals as "Jean Renaud" and "Les
        trois princesses," both of which had appeared in a
        collection by Gérard de Nerval (1808-1855) and are here
        reprinted. See also item 649.

649.   Bellinger, Rossiter. "Rossetti's Two Translations from
        'Old French.'" *Modern Language Notes* 65 (1950):
        217-223.

        Identifies the originals of "John of Tours" and "My

Father's Close" as "Jean Renaud" and "Derrier' chez mon
père," respectively. There is also speculation about
the sources Rossetti used--but see item 648 which, although earlier, seems to be more definitive on this
point.

650. Doughty, Oswald. "Dante Gabriel Rossetti as Translator."
Theoria, no. 5 (1953): 102-112.

Summarizes Rossetti's activities as a translator of
German, French, and Italian poetry. Contends that his
unconscious absorption of Italian poetry explains Rossetti's medievalism and romanticism, both in poetry and
in real life. As a translator Rossetti hated pedantry
and so gave himself considerable latitude; yet he is
intense, vigorous, and--usually--successful.

651. Paolucci, Anne. "Ezra Pound and D.G. Rossetti as Translators of Guido Cavalcanti." *Romanic Review* 57 (1960):
256-267.

Compares Rossetti's translations with Pound's and finds
the latter more accurate and more faithful to both the
style and the spirit of the original. Rossetti is some-
what easier to read, however.

652. Omans, Glen A. "Some Biographical Light on Rossetti's
Translations of Villon." *Victorian Newsletter*, no.
31 (1967): 52-54.

Contends that Rossetti's translations of Villon were
undertaken in the spring of 1870 to help fill out his
projected volume of poetry. Therefore Swinburne's translations are the prior works, despite what has been usually
believed, and Swinburne may in fact have instigated
Rossetti's work.

653. Gitter, Elisabeth T. "Rossetti's Translations of Early
Italian Lyrics." *Victorian Poetry* 12 (1974): 351-362.

Claims that Rossetti's translations often reveal more
about his own techniques and thematic obsessions than
they do about the intentions of the original poet.

654. Baird, J.L., and Garrett McCutchan. "Love, Lures,
Hawks, and the Gentle Art of Translation." *Italia*
53 (1976): 236-247.

   Argues that Rossetti's translation of the medieval
Italian sonnet "Tapina me, ch' amava uno sparviero"
turns a good poem into a bad one. Rossetti's reputation as a translator is unduly high, at least as
regards his Italian works; he did not know the language
well and was insensitive to its delicacies of meaning.

655.   Lange, Bernd-Peter. "Swinburne und Rossetti als Über-
       setzer von Villons 'Ballade pour prier Notre Dame.'"
       Arcadia 12 (1977): 17-30.

   Summarizes the renewed interest in Francois Villon
during the Victorian period, and evaluates Rossetti and
Swinburne as translators of the French medieval poet.
Rossetti is charged with conventionality and a neglect
of nuance; Villon has been subverted in the interest of
furthering Rossetti's own characteristic themes.

See also items 19, 23, 25, 40, 52, 287, 397, 451, 464, 599,
604, 610, 952, 973, 981, and 1009.

Studies of Rossetti
as an Artist

SECTION A: GENERAL CRITICISM--ART

This section includes critical assessments of Rossetti as an artist. Criticisms of individual paintings and drawings may be mentioned, but if the study is devoted solely to a single work it will be found in Section B. Criticisms of Rossetti as an illustrator and as a designer of book-bindings, stained glass windows, picture frames, and furniture will be found in Section D.

656. [Anonymous]. "The Linnell and Rossetti Pictures at Burlington House." *London Society* 43 (1883): 217-221.

   Proclaims Rossetti to be an artist only for a select initiated few because of his arcane symbolism and his monotonous, "unhealthy" sentiments. He does have originality and a fine sense of color.

657. Barrington, Emilie Isabel. "The Painted Poetry of Watts and Rossetti." *Nineteenth Century* 13 (1883): 950-970.

   Compares the two artists as painters of poetic insight. They see the inner truth, not just the outer shells. Watts is pre-eminent in form, Rossetti in color. Watts is a solitary figure, Rossetti the chief of a school. Watts has dignity and a sense for beauty; Rossetti has earnestness, sensitivity, and a hint of the demoniac. Both are antitheses to modern French art.

658. [Beavington-Atkinson, J.] "Rossetti and Alma-Tadema-- Linnell and Lawson." *Blackwood's Magazine* 133 (1883): 392-411.

   Believes that Rossetti's paintings show almost unparalleled conflicts of mind and changes of character. His career recapitulates the history of Italian art, with early naturalism giving way to the Renaissance voluptuousness of Giorgione or Titian. His pictures on Dantean subjects, such as *Dante's Dream*, afford the material by which Rossetti ultimately will be judged.

659. Colvin, Sidney. "Rossetti as a Painter." *Magazine of Art* 6 (1883): 177-183.

   Judges Rossetti to be a great Romantic painter, drawn to the medieval age by its curiosity and strangeness. His art falls into three periods: 1847-1862, dominated by narrative and dramatic works; 1862-1870, dominated by

single female heads which Rossetti often made into
personifications of intellectual qualities; and 1870-
1882, dominated by the mysterious but warped and sickly
figures of his decline.

660.   Duret, Théodore. "Les expositions de Londres: Dante
       Gabriel Rossetti." *Gazette de Beaux-Arts* 28 (1883):
       49-58.

       Finds Rossetti a complex figure whose aestheticism ran
       counter to the utilitarian and puritan tendencies of his
       countrymen. His originality, as manifested in the sybil-
       line women he painted, draws our praise.

661.   G[urney], A[lfred]. *A Dream of Fair Women: A Study of
       Some Pictures by Dante Gabriel Rossetti*. London:
       Kegan Paul, 1883. 46 pp.

       Draws upon the recent Royal Academy exhibition, offer-
       ing impressionistic studies of the paintings which con-
       stitute the "beauty-haunted chambers" of Rossetti's
       imagination. The assessments are favorable.

662.   Hannay, David. "The Paintings of Mr. Rossetti."
       National Review 1 (1883): 126-134.

       Assesses Rossetti's paintings exhibited at the Royal
       Academy and finds them monotonous in style and feeble
       in execution. Even his vaunted skill as a colourist
       comes from avoiding challenges, and his symbolism is
       trite.

663.   Monkhouse, Cosmo. "Rossetti's Pictures at the Royal
       Academy" and "Rossetti at the Burlington Club." *The
       Academy* 23 (1883): 14-15, 50-51.

       Reviews the two exhibitions and finds Rossetti to be
       a painter who, while flawed in technique, excels in the
       use of color and symbol. The vanity of human wishes is
       Rossetti's theme. Perhaps his best work is the un-
       finished *Found*.

664.   Ruskin, John. "Realistic Schools of Painting: D.G.
       Rossetti and W. Holman Hunt." *The Art of England:
       Lectures Given in Oxford*. Orpington: Allen, 1883,
       pp. 1-35.

       The inaugural Slade lecture, delivered 9 March 1883.

Pays tribute to Rossetti as one who changed both the
direction and the temper of modern art. Relates his
color techniques to the medieval art of manuscript illumination.

665. Stephens, Frederic G. "The Earlier Works of Dante
Gabriel Rossetti." *Portfolio* 14 (1883): 87-91, 114-
119.

Analyzes selected works in the Royal Academy exhibition and finds in the earlier works previsions of Rossetti's later genius. The works of 1849-1853 give
evidence of the influence of Rossetti's more technically
inclined friends, especially Brown. Considerable attention is given to specific early pictures, particularly
Michael Scott's Wooing, *The Sun May Shine*, *Ecce Ancilla
Domini!*, *The Girlhood of Mary Virgin*, *The Parable of
Love*, and *The Laboratory*. Rossetti's distinguishing
motives as an artist are a dramatizing energy and a subtle
mysticism.

666. Tirebuck, William E. "Dante Gabriel Rossetti." *Art
Journal* 45 (1883): 27-28.

Proclaims Rossetti one of the immortals, a genius who
combined a new beauty with a new seriousness and who
portrayed abstract emotion better than any other living
artist. His weaknesses are indefinite idealism and a
recoil from nature.

667. Chesneau, Ernest A. "The Pre-Raphaelites." *The English
School of Painting*. Translated by L. Etherington.
London: Cassell, 1884, pp. 179-237.

Pays tribute to Rossetti's influence, even though his
lack of public exhibitions makes it impossible for a
foreigner like the author to assess the work directly.
See also items 141, 143, and 683.

668. Merriman, Helen B. "The English Pre-Raphaelite and
Poetical School of Painters." *Andover Review* 1 (1884):
594-612.

Judges Rossetti to be a painter who was defeated by
his own esoteric symbolism, so that his originality
finds expression only in remote and vapid portraits of
women. His art suffered also from his seclusion in
Chelsea. Yet at his best Rossetti is a master of color

and expression, and his achievements are certainly not
negligible.

669.   Carr, J[oseph] Comyns. "Rossetti's Influence in Art."
       Papers on Art. London: Macmillan, 1885, pp. 196-230.

       Finds in Rossetti a mixture of strength and refinement,
       one who changed the direction of contemporary English
       painting. Perversely we are attracted to his later and
       least successful works; his art degenerated from the
       time of *Lady Lilith* onward. Reprinted from *The English
       Illustrated Magazine* (1883).

670.   [Anonymous]. "PreRaphaelitism." *Spectator*, no. 3015
       (1886): 484-485.

       Sees the Pre-Raphaelites as true Victorians rather
       than as posthumous medievalists. Their concern was to
       attack commercialism, conventions, and sentimentalists.

671.   Chuiko, Vladimir Viktorovich. *Dorafaelsky i ikh pos-
       liĕdovateli v Anglii*. St. Petersburg: 1886.

       In Russian. Reprinted from *Vestnik iziãshchnykh
       iskustv* (1886).

672.   Hunt, William Holman. "The Pre-Raphaelite Brotherhood:
       A Fight for Art." *Contemporary Review* 49 (1886):
       471-488, 737-750, 820-833.

       Recounts the origins of the P.R.B. with emphasis on
       the author's own role. Rossetti appears as a subtle
       but fiery "proselytizer" and as a talented but rather
       undisciplined artist. His personality, manner, and
       appearance are described in some detail. Rossetti was
       not a true Pre-Raphaelite in terms of its original
       principles, as an examination of his pictures will show.

673.   Quilter, Harry. *Sententiae Artis: First Principles of
       Art for Painters and Picture Lovers*. London:
       Isbister, 1886. 398 pp.

       Offers paragraph-length comments on a wide variety of
       topics, some of which relate to Rossetti. Included
       among the latter are *Found*, Rossetti's sense of beauty,
       and Blake as a precursor of Rossetti and the Pre-
       Raphaelites. Claims that Rossetti sometimes produced
       watercolors in a fortnight without the use of models.

674. Frith, William P. "Crazes in Art: Pre-Raphaelitism and Impressionism." *Magazine of Art* 11 (1888): 187-191.

As the title implies, the Pre-Raphaelites are seen as travelling on the wrong path. They may be sincere, but Rossetti and his colleagues mistake means for ends, according to the well-known painter of *Derby Day*.

675. Rod, Edouard. "Les Préraphaélites anglais." *Études sur le dix-neuvième siècle*. Paris: Perrin, 1888, pp. 47-97.

Tries to educate a French audience about the history and importance of the Pre-Raphaelite Movement. Rossetti's early retreat from public exhibition is the most singular fact about his career, especially since that retreat only seemed to augment his influence. Reprinted from *Gazette des Beaux-Arts* (1887), translated in *Connoisseur* (1888).

676. Forsyth, Peter T. "Rossetti." *Religion and Recent Art: Expository Lectures on Rossetti, Burne-Jones, Watts, Holman Hunt, and Wagner*. London: Simpkin, Marshall, 1889, pp. 5-52.

Makes Rossetti into an apostle of the "religion of natural passion," one who reacted to the agnosticism of the age by finding refuge in a devotion to physical love. Rossetti paints not a character but a sensibility, in this case a sensibility tinged with melancholy.

677. Parkes, Kineton. *The Pre-Raphaelite Movement*. London: Reeves and Turner, 1889. 52 pp.

Relates the P.R.B. to the Oxford Movement, the Gothic Revival, and even Socialism. Hunt's role must be emphasized at the expense of Rossetti's. Pre-Raphaelitism is like the measles--a temporary illness from which England is recovering yet one which is ultimately beneficial to the patient. Reprinted from *Ruskin Reading Guild Journal* (1889).

678. Lillie, Mrs. L.C.W. "Two Phases of American Art." *Harper's Magazine* 80 (1890): 206-216.

The second phase is the "American P.R.B.," i.e. those New Yorkers associated with the *New Path*. They appreciated Rossetti's art and kept up on his activities by corresponding with Ruskin.

679. Redgrave, Richard and Samuel. "The Pre-Raphaelites."
      A Century of Painters of the English School. 2nd
      Edition. London: Sampson, Low, 1890, pp. 371-388.

      Aims at being a popular rather than a scholarly ac-
      count. The chapter on the P.R.B. excludes painters
      still living, like Burne-Jones and Holman Hunt. Ros-
      setti's career is summarized briefly, as is his dreamy
      medievalism.

680. Shields, Frederic G. "A Note upon Rossetti's Method of
      Drawing in Crayons." *Century Guild Hobby Horse* n.s. 5
      (1890): 70-73.

      Recounts how the author introduced Rossetti to a new
      type of French charcoal about the year 1864. Rossetti's
      method was to shade with this charcoal, then skim with
      chalk, then reshade with the charcoal, and then high-
      light with pipe clay. All was done on special blue-
      grey paper or green paper and was easily defaced.

681. Child, Theodore. "A Pre-Raphaelite Mansion." *Art and
      Criticism: Monographs and Studies*. New York: Harper,
      1892, pp. 305-343.

      Reprints an 1890 *Harper's Magazine* article describing
      Frederick Leyland's home at 49 Prince's Gate, Kensington.
      Assesses Rossetti's technique as exemplified in the pic-
      tures on display, finding him a master of arrangement
      and composition but one whose genius manifested itself
      in works with "hermetic significations." Leyland was
      Rossetti's long-time art patron--see item 147.

682. Gurlitt, Cornelius. "Die Präraphaeliten, eine britische
      Malerschule." *Westermanns Illustrierte Deutsche
      Monatshefte* 72 (1892): 106-136, 253-282, 327-345,
      480-496.

      Popularizes the P.R.B. for the German public in four
      installments with the headings "Beginning" and "Develop-
      ment." Separate sections in the latter are devoted to
      Watts, Brown, Hunt, Rossetti, Burne-Jones, and later
      followers like Richmond, Strudwick, and Marie Spartali.
      Rossetti is seen as a thoroughly urban man, imbued with
      the Catholic spirit and a genuine simplicity, yet

handicapped by inadequate technique and narrow-minded
critics. We must take him on his own terms.

683. Chesneau, Ernest A. "Peintres anglais contemporains:
        Dante Gabriel Rossetti." *L'Art* 59 (1894): 207-226.

        Reviews Rossetti's life and his achievements in
        paintings. The art can be divided into three periods:
        1848-1860, mysticism; 1860-1870, solitary women; 1870-
        1882, larger assemblages of people. *Dante's Dream*,
        described in some detail, is his best work. Rossetti
        is assured of an important place in the history of
        English painting.

684. Stephens, Frederic G. *Dante Gabriel Rossetti*. London:
        Seeley, 1894. 96 pp.

        Claims for Rossetti the leading place among the poet-
        painters, although "the palette served his purpose better
        than the pen." This lengthy retrospective monograph by
        an original member of the P.R.B. offers glimpses of Ros-
        setti in his early days, painting *Ecce Ancilla Domini!*
        in the Cleveland Street studio, meeting Lizzie Siddal,
        visiting the parental house on Charlotte Street. Thirty-
        five black-and-white illustrations accompany the text,
        and the author comments on each of them. *Proserpine* and
        The Bride are seen as the best works. Reprinted 1979.

685. Sartorio, G.A. "Nota su Dante Gabriele Rossetti, pittore."
        Convito 2 (1895): 121-150 and 4 (1895): 261-286.

        Summarizes Rossetti's career and his major achievements,
        with illustrations. Part of a series on chief modern
        painters.

686. Deleted.

687. Hueffer, Ford Madox. *Rossetti: A Critical Essay on His
        Art*. London: Longmans, 1896. 192 pp.

        The most extensive and intensive assessment of Rossetti
        as a painter at the time of its publication. Sums up
        Rossetti as a "Robin Hood of the Arts," a passionate
        painter who charms the viewer but lacks the mastery of
        technique. Uses a chronological framework but tries to
        avoid biographical interpretations. Certain pictorial

motifs, such as the preoccupied, rapt expression and
the penchant for filling up empty canvas with symbolic
objects, are also traced. Fifty-three black-and-white
illustrations; reprinted 1976.

688.   Low, Will H. "A Century of Painting." *McClure's Maga-*
       zine 7 (1896): 65-72.

       Describes Rossetti as a revolutionary artist, a man
       with a richly endowed nature who led a movement in
       painting that accomplished two important goals: painters
       returned to nature, and sentiment replaced anecdote.

689.   Mourey, Gabriel. "The Pre-Raphaelites." *Across the*
       Channel: Life and Art in London. Translated by G.
       Latimer. London: Allen, 1896, pp. 196-208.

       Offers a brief section on each of the major Pre-
       Raphaelite figures, including Rossetti, whose artistic
       career is summarized.

690.   Temple, Sir Alfred George. "Dante Gabriel Rossetti."
       The Art of Painting in the Queen's Reign. London:
       Chapman and Hall, 1897, pp. 113-123.

       Surveys Rossetti's career, including the history of
       the composition of his major works. His distinguishing
       trait is spirituality. Three plates.

691.   [Ady, Julia M.] "English Art in the Victorian Age."
       Quarterly Review 187 (1898): 209-233.

       Compares Rossetti to his peers and finds him weak in
       technical achievement but powerful in his personality
       and thus immensely influential.

692.   Bazalgette, Léon. "La Banquerante du Préraphaélitisme."
       L'Esprit nouveau dans la vie artistique, sociale, et
       religieuse. Paris: Société d'editions scientifiques,
       1898, pp. 93-118.

       Damns the "incontestable mediocrity" of the Pre-
       Raphaelites, which can be blamed partly on Ruskin's
       bad advice. Ruskin is at heart a realist while the
       painters, especially Rossetti, are at heart idealists.
       The Pre-Raphaelites dehumanize their subjects.

693. Hueffer, Ford Madox. "The Millais and Rossetti Exhibitions." *Fortnightly Review* 69 (1898): 189-196.

Sees Rossetti as far more poetic than his Pre-Raphaelite colleague. Rossetti depends far less on his subject and so his imagination has freer reign. Both men cured British art of its somberness and gave it a new kind of artistic honesty.

694. Kennedy, H.A. "The Pre-Raphaelite Movement." *Artist* 21 (1898): 25-40.

Attributes the influence of the Pre-Raphaelites to their intellectual energy, their many-sided intensity, and their devotion to raising the lot of the artist. Rossetti's gift is his power to imagine, to create. His vividness and subtlety make him a master of atmosphere.

695. Bell, Mrs. Arthur. "Gabriel Charles Dante Rossetti." *Representative Painters of the XIXth Century*. London: Sampson, Low, Marston, 1899, pp. 25-29.

Sees Rossetti's figures as sad, weary, abstracted, mystic, and sensual. He is indifferent to landscapes--only atmosphere counts.

696. Cary, Elisabeth L[uther]. "Rossetti and the Pre-Raphaelites." *Critic* 37 (1900): 320-326.

Printed from advance sheets for the author's book (item 1006). Describes Rossetti's early training as a painter and his distinctiveness compared to the creed of the P.R.B. and its other members. Five black-and-white illustrations.

697. Fred, W. [=Alfred Wechsler]. *Die Prae-Raphaeliten: Eine Episode englischer Kunst*. Strassburg: Heitz, 1900. 152 pp.

Not examined.

698. Ruettenauer, Benno. "Die Romantik und der Präraphaelismus." *Symbolische Kunst*. Strassburg: Heitz, 1900. 180 pp.

Not examined.

699. [Anonymous.] "The Pre-Raphaelite Brotherhood: Dante
      Gabriel Rossetti." *Werner's Magazine* 27 (1901):
      193-202.

      Recapitulates Rossetti's career for a popular audience,
      using six black-and-white illustrations and a complete
      reprinting of "Hand and Soul." The general theme is
      that Rossetti's lack of faith made him responsible for
      his own downfall. [Very unreliable. Some astounding
      factual errors, e.g. that Rossetti did not meet Hunt
      until 1852, that Browning was once Rossetti's boarder,
      and that the "Fleshly School" controversy took place in
      the early 1860s.]

700. Bate, Percy H. *The English Pre-Raphaelite Painters:
      Their Associates and Successors*. Revised Edition.
      London: Bell, 1901. 124 pp.

      Offers eighty-nine reproductions of works by the Pre-
      Raphaelites, and in its commentary includes one chapter
      on Rossetti as "Pre-Raphaelite and Idealist" and two on
      "The Rossetti Tradition" as seen in such painters as
      Burne-Jones and Stanhope. The focus is on the original
      P.R.B., with Rossetti cast as the visionary whose painted
      dreams could not be confined by the principles adhered
      to by such a staunch Pre-Raphaelite as Hunt.

701. Hoppin, James M. "Dante Gabriel Rossetti." *Great Epochs
      in Art History*. Boston: Houghton Mifflin, 1901, pp.
      210-219.

      Claims for Rossetti a place in history as one of the
      great exemplars of the human mind. But despite his
      influence he lacks objectivity and faith.

702. Muthesius, Hermann. "Dante Gabriel Rossetti." *Kunst
      und Kunsthandwerk* 4 (1901): 373-389.

      Sees Rossetti's paintings as the product of a true
      poet, one who creates fantasies and whose portraits of
      women fulfill his sister's description: "Not as she is,
      but as she fulfills his dream." Rossetti is responsible
      for the modern artistic Renaissance in England.

703. Henley, William Ernest. "Rossetti." *Views and Reviews.
      Essays in Appreciation: Art*. London: Nutt, 1902, pp.
      139-144.

Attacks Rossetti for his "bastard issues" and "vicious methods." He failed in two arts. As an artist his temperament was unhealthy, excessive, affected, and his work will soon be forgotten.

704. MacColl, Dugald S. "English Art, Grand, Philistine and 'Decadent.'" *Nineteenth Century Art*. Glasgow: MacLehose, 1902, pp. 109-144.

A description of material in the fine art collection at the 1901 Glasgow International Exhibition. The section on Rossetti (pp. 137-141) values him for his attempts to batter the self-assurance of English art and for his passionate mysticism, best seen in the drawings and engravings.

705. Sharp, William. "Rossetti." *Progress of Art in the Century*. The Nineteenth Century Series, vol. 22. London: Linscott, 1902, pp. 211-230.

Views Rossetti as a painter whose ultimate expression was in his use of color and symbol. His art can be divided into four periods: early Pre-Raphaelitism; watercolors; portraits of women; decline. In his third and greatest period he created a new and tragic beauty.

706. Deleted.

707. Hartley, C.G. [=Catherine G. Gallichan]. "The Pre-Raphaelites: Gabriel Charles Dante Rossetti." *Pictures in the Tate Gallery*. London: Seeley, 1905, pp. 63-76.

Reviews Rossetti's career by proceeding chronologically through the pictures in the Tate Gallery, especially *Ecce Ancilla Domini!* and *Beata Beatrix*. The interplay of symbolism, mysticism, and feminine beauty marks the passing years.

708. Jessen, Jarno [=Anna Michaelson]. *Rossetti*. Künstler-Monographien, no. 77. Bielefeld und Leipzig: Velhagen und Klasing, 1905. 95 pp.

This lengthy monograph, accompanied by seventy black-and-white illustrations, offers a chronological description of Rossetti's career as a painter. That career

can be divided into three parts: the "gothic" period
(1850s), when Rossetti was absorbed in medieval subjects,
mostly Dantean or Arthurian; the "renaissance" period
(1860s), when Rossetti painted beautiful women; and a
final period (1870-1882), when Rossetti warped everything to his own exaggerated ideal of beauty. Rossetti
can be likened to Titian as a revolutionary influence
on his contemporaries.

709. Sickert, Bernhard. "The Pre-Raphaelite and Impressionist
        Heresies." *Burlington Magazine* 7 (1905): 97-102.

        Contrasts the two schools, finding differences in tem-
        perament and in subject. The Pre-Raphaelites, although
        interesting by virtue of their intense humanity, erred
        in trying to combine naturalism and narrative. Even the
        "exquisite" Rossetti did not see that a beautiful sub-
        ject also requires a beautiful interpretation.

710. Vitale, Zaira. "Le Modelle di D.G. Rossetti." *Revista
        d' Italia*, anno VIII, vol. 2 (1905): 448-459.

        Discusses such models as Janey Morris, Christina
        Rossetti, Lizzie Siddal, Ruth Herbert, Annie Miller,
        Marie Stillman, Alexa Wilding, Aggie Monetti, and Elene
        Smith, and the pictures they are associated with.

711. [Anonymous.] "The Pre-Raphaelite Brotherhood." *Quar-
        terly Review* 204   (1906): 352-374.

        A review essay of eight recent books on the P.R.B.
        Asks what Pre-Raphaelitism was and concludes that it
        was "a return to Nature--it was nothing more and nothing
        less." The second generation, which wed medievalism
        and truth-to-nature, was the more profound of the two.
        Rossetti, its leader, was however almost totally devoid
        of painting skill.

712. Dupouey, Charles M.D.P. *Notes sur l' art et la vie de
        D.G. Rossetti*. Paris: Chapelot, 1906.   81 pp.

        Not examined.

713. Housman, Laurence. "The Spirit of Pre-Raphaelitism."
        Magazine of Fine Arts 1 (1906): 406-415.

        Sees Pre-Raphaelitism as "a great movement toward
        naturalistic romance," one which concentrated on the

drama of the human face. Despite Hunt's claims (item 194), Rossetti was the force behind these advances.

714. Jessen, Jarno [=Anna Michaelson]. *Präarafaelismus.*
     Die Kunst, vol. 45. Berlin: Marquardt, [1906]. 65 pp.

   Chronicles the early days of the P.R.B., its break-through, its opposition, and its influence. Separate consideration is given to Rossetti, the "proselyte" of Pre-Raphaelitism. His work is characterized by melancholy, but his achievements make him pre-eminent among his colleagues.

715. March-Phillipps, L. "Pre-Raphaelitism and the Present." *Contemporary Review* 89 (1906): 704-713.

   Sees Pre-Raphaelitism as an assertion of intellectual freedom and therefore allied with other kinds of emancipations. Unfortunately Rossetti soon turned it aside into medievalism. He tried to make painting a mystery and thus he cut it off from human life. Only Morris perceived the real spirit of original Pre-Raphaelitism. Reprinted in *Living Age* (1906).

716. Singer, Hans W. *Dante Gabriel Rossetti.* Langham Series of Art Monographs, vol. 14. London: Siegle, 1906. 73 pp.

   Bemoans the fact that later Pre-Raphaelitism (Burne-Jones) is better known abroad than the earlier phase dominated by Rossetti. He is the sublime genius, the forerunner of aestheticism because he had no moral purpose. His art is characterized by "sensuous emotionalism" and derives its inspiration from the artist's wife, even after her death when his style became more mechanical. The major paintings are listed and their present location specified. Thirteen black-and-white illustrations. Originally published in German (1905).

717. Hueffer, Ford Madox. *The Pre-Raphaelite Brotherhood: A Critical Monograph.* London: Duckworth, 1907. 147 pp.

   Responds to Hunt's memoirs (item 194) by stressing the Overbeckian origins of the P.R.B.'s taste and the role of Rossetti in forming it and holding it together. The works produced by the P.R.B., including Rossetti's,

have more historical than aesthetic value. Rossetti
soon withdrew from the true Pre-Raphaelite impulse, i.e.
a return to nature, by devoting himself to watercolors.

718. Lawrence, Frederic. "The Romanticists Around Dante
      Gabriel Rossetti." *London Quarterly Review* 108 (1907):
      269-282.

      Locates the P.R.B. in the midst of a great decline in
      English painting. Rossetti had the special gift of
      being truthful to the inner nature as well as the outer;
      he protested against the artificiality of his day, es-
      pecially science, on behalf of the reality of the
      imagination.

719. Agresti, A[ntonio]. *I Preraffaelliti; contributo alla
      storia dell' arte.* Turin: Societá Tipografico-Editrice
      Nazionale, 1908. 190 pp.

      Not examined.

720. Cary, Elisabeth L[uther]. "Rossetti's Water Colours."
      Scrip: Notes on Art 3 (1908): 173-178.

      Recounts Rossetti's efforts in the watercolor medium,
      which often involved considerable pains for him and
      showed great freshness of observation. Comments on a
      recent exhibition at the Pennyslvania Academy.

721. Dayot, Armand. "Préraphaélisme." *La Peinture anglaise
      de ses origines à nos jours.* Paris: Laveur, 1908,
      pp. 179-215.

      A brief history, with illustrations, of the P.R.B.
      Rossetti is represented by six plates and a short but
      laudatory commentary.

722. Meier-Graefe, Julius. "The English Reaction." *Modern
      Art, Being a Contribution to a New System of Aesthetics.*
      Vol. 2. Translated by Simmonds and Chrystal. London:
      Heinemann, 1908, pp. 187-265.

      Views the P.R.B. as a "wild aberration" from what the
      author views as the central and revolutionary achieve-
      ment of nineteenth-century art: the abandonment of
      naturalism in favor of subjectivism. Rossetti had a
      sweet nature but was overly conventional, insipid, un-
      intellectual.

723.   Phythian, John Ernest. "The Pre-Raphaelite Brotherhood"
        and "The Course of Pre-Raphaelitism." *Fifty Years of*
        Modern Painting, Corot to Sargent. New York: Dutton,
        1908, pp. 16-51, 129-189.

        Shows how Rossetti diverged from the other Pre-
        Raphaelites by his lack of interest in scientific na-
        turalism and by his comparative disregard of subject.
        He became the leader of what is termed the "romantic"
        side of Pre-Raphaelitism, the side which emphasized the
        role of color, which lived in the past, and which found
        in beautiful women the most appropriate subject for art.

724.   Pissaro, Lucien. *Rossetti.* New York: Stokes, 1908.
        80 pp.

        Finds Rossetti's chief value to be not in his subjects
        ("What is a noble subject anyway?") but in his ability
        to portray his own life in art. Offers a retrospective
        of Rossetti's career, one which showed how an artist can
        be betrayed by medievalism. Eight full-color plates.
        Also included in *Leaders of the English Pre-Raphaelites*
        (1908).

725.   Rambosson, Yvanhoé. "Les Préraphaélites et quelques
        peintres recents." *Histoire de la peinture: La*
        Peinture anglaise. Paris: Nilsson, [1908].

        Not examined.

726.   Rose, George B. "Rossetti." *Pathfinder* 2, no. 9 (March
        1908): 2-5.

        Praises Rossetti as a colorist and as a "splendid
        draughtsman," despite what others may say. Realists
        will not like him, but his oriental beauties are poignant
        treasures for the wise.

727.   Ross, Robert. "Rossetti: An Observation." *Burlington*
        Magazine 13 (1908): 116-123.

        Defends Rossetti as "the greatest personality in the
        English school" besides Turner. He could not draw or
        use oil well. Instead his genius, like Michaelangelo's,
        lay in the force he exerted on others, including Brown,
        Ruskin, Whistler, and a host of other contemporaries.
        Rossetti must be rescued from his imitators and seen for

what he is: the "fortuitous avatar" by which Italy came
to England. *The Blue Bower* and *Lady Lilith* are his
best works.

728. Armstrong, Sir Walter. "Painting--From the Pre-Raphaelite
      Revolt to the Present Day." *Art in Great Britain and
      Ireland*. London: Heinemann, 1909, pp. 229-248.

      Blames Rossetti for the decline in technical ability
      of English artists in the last half century. Rossetti's
      watercolors are his best work.

729. Knight, William A. "The Pre-Raphaelites, Especially
      Dante Gabriel Rossetti, with Reminiscences." *Six
      Lectures on Some Nineteenth Century Artists, English
      and French*. Chicago: Art Institute, 1909, pp. 95-125.

      Traces the neglected literary origins of the P.R.B.,
      especially Carlyle and the early Ruskin. Recounts an
      afternoon spent in Rossetti's company in May of 1871,
      during which the artist defended Millais and spoke of
      the need to combine idealism and realism.

730. Mourey, Gabriel. "Rossetti." *D.-G. Rossetti et les
      Préraphaélites anglais*. Paris: Laurens, [1909],
      pp. 20-47.

      The book concentrates, despite its title, on Pre-
      Raphaelitism as a whole. The chapter on Rossetti sum-
      marizes his personality and his achievements as an
      artist. His career shows constant growth, although
      Beata Beatrix is perhaps the high point.

731. Symons, Arthur. *Dante Gabriel Rossetti*. London:
      International Art, [1909]. 60 pp.

      A monograph with fifty-four illustrations. Sees Ros-
      setti as the contented inhabitant of a dreamworld domi-
      nated by an obsession with love, an obsession which--
      literally--killed him. The Pre-Raphaelites were best
      as illustrators, although only Rossetti bears comparison
      with their great French contemporaries, the Impressionists
      Rossetti is distinguished by imagination, emotion, and
      intellectual passion, but his weakness in technique
      betrays him.

732. Braschi, A. *I Preraffaellitti*. Milan: Vallardi, 1910.

      Not examined.

733. Agresti, Antonio. "Dell' arte prerafaellistica." *La Vita Nova di Dante Alighieri con le illustrazioni di D G Rossetti*. 2nd Edition. Turin: 1911, pp. xxxi-xlvii.

    Traces the history of the P.R.B., including its influence on the decorative arts. Rossetti is especially effective in translating Dante's love ideal, both visually and poetically. Reprints also item 1009.

734. Dick, Stewart. "Rossetti and the Pre-Raphaelites." *Master Painters, Being Pages from the Romance of Art*. London: Foulis, 1911, pp. 249-270.

    Summarizes the history of Pre-Raphaelitism and the artistic contributions of its acknowledged leader, Rossetti.

735. Fryer, Alfred C. "The Religious Art of a Painter Poet." *The Religious Thoughts of Some of Our Poets*. London: Mowbray, 1911. 152 pp.

    Not examined.

736. MacFall, Haldane. "Rossetti (1828-1882)." *A History of Painting*. Vol. 3. London: Jack, 1911, pp. 117-121.

    Blames Rossetti for setting back English art. He "painted literature and wrote colour" and succeeded only in becoming a "primitive-academic."

737. Chester, Austin. "The Art of Dante Gabriel Rossetti." *Windsor Magazine* 35 (1912): 571-586.

    Finds Rossetti to be characterized by bold originality, spirituality, a passionate instinct for beauty, and the "intensity of Southern fervor." His career is summarized, a career in which he rose to heights "scaled only by genius." Seventeen illustrations, with special emphasis on *Astarte Syriaca*, *The Blessed Damozel*, *Dante's Dream* (in color), and *Beata Beatrix*.

738. Singer, Hans W. *Der Prae-Raphaelitismus in England*. Munich: Oldenbourge, 1912. 126 pp.

    Covers the founding of the P.R.B., its rise, and its subsequent influence. Rossetti receives the primary emphasis: he is its chief figure both personally and artistically. His education, his role in the events of

1848-1854, his relationship to Lizzie Siddal, his influence on Burne-Jones and other painters, and his
achievements in painting are all summarized.

739. Agresti, Antonio. "I Preraffaellitti." *Rassegna Con-
temporanea*, ser. II, 6 (1913).

Not examined.

740. Bell, Clive. "Alid ex Alio." *Art*. London: Stokes,
1914, pp. 181-195.

Congratulates the P.R.B. on its desire for revolt, but
unfortunately the revolution produced "a great many bad
pictures and a little thin sentiment." Symbolism was
their strong suit, but far too much time was spent in
looking backwards in time, imitating rather than ima-
gining.

741. Fry, Roger. "Rossetti's Water Colours of 1857." *Burlington Magazine* 29 (1916): 100-109.

Reproduces and discusses five watercolors, including
The Blue Closet, *The Wedding of St. George and Princess
Sabra*, and *The Tune of Seven Towers*. Praises Rossetti
as a forerunner of the twentieth century, as an inspired
artist who came the closest of anyone in his time to a
close-knit unity of design. He is at his best when
painting the accessories of his drama rather than the
central figures of his theme. [For Fry's later view,
see item 781.]

742. Linton, John. "Dante Gabriel Rossetti." *The Cross in
Modern Art: Descriptive Studies of Some Pre-Raphaelite
Paintings*. London: Duckworth, 1916, pp. 41-66.

Studies *The Girlhood of Mary Virgin*, *Ecce Ancilla
Domini!*, and *Beata Beatrix* to show how they expressed
the moral and spiritual forces of the time. In all
three paintings the artist sees the divine in the ordinary, thus grasping the true meaning of the Incar-
nation. We witness the perennial mysteries of birth,
of death, and especially of love.

743. MacColl, D.S. "The New Rossettis at the National
Gallery." *Burlington Magazine* 29 (1916): 80-81.

Describes the eleven Rossetti paintings acquired by

the National Gallery from the George Rae estate. For
too long Rossetti has been neglected--he is "a great
English master."

744. Wood, T. Martin. "The True Rossetti." *Studio* 69 (1916):
      3-15.

      Contends that Rossetti's best work as an artist was
      in watercolor, and illustrates this claim with eleven
      reproductions from the Rae Collection.

745. Carr, Joseph William Comyns. "The Ideals of England."
      The Ideals of Painting. New York: Macmillan, 1917,
      pp. 369-442.

      Among the ideals is the reverence for life, nature,
      and art as seen in the Pre-Raphaelites. Rossetti's
      greatest achievement is "to vindicate the right of
      poetic imagination to enter the arena of pictorial
      design." His earliest years are his best, in part
      because he usually worked on a smaller scale.

746. Phelps, Mrs. J.Q. "The Mysticism of Rossetti." *Fine
      Arts Journal* 37 (1919): 37-40.

      Not examined.

747. Maguinness, Irene. "Revolt from Convention: The Pre-
      Raphaelite Brotherhood and Its Influence." *British
      Painting.* London: Sidgwick and Jackson, 1920, pp. 203-
      223.

      Observes that Rossetti was the first to abandon Pre-
      Raphaelite principles by turning to the expression of
      ideas and ideals. Occasionally his imagination outran
      his powers of execution.

748. Marriott, Charles. "Impressionism and Pre-Raphaelitism."
      Modern Movements in Painting. London: Chapman and
      Hall, 1920, pp. 89-97.

      Compares and contrasts the two movements. Both are
      heresies, the former intellectual, the latter moral.
      The Pre-Raphaelites had an advantage in subjects, the
      Impressionists in treatment. Both groups are realists
      at heart, simply adapting themselves to the climate of
      their very different homelands.

749.   Charpentier, John. *La Peinture anglaise ... Le Pré-*
       raphaélisme. Bibliothèque internationale de critique,
       no. 42. Paris: La Renaissance du Livre, 1921. 180 pp.

       Not examined.

750.   Sapori, Francesco. *Dante Gabriele Rossetti, Pittore.*
       I maestri dell' arte, no. 27. Turin: Celanza, 1921.

       Not examined.

751.   Alton, John. "The Pre-Raphaelites at Millbank." *New*
       Statesman 21 (1923): 141-142.

       Notices two recent Tate Gallery exhibitions on the
       1860s, both of which featured the Pre-Raphaelites, who
       are dismissed as "mistletoe on the bough [of art],"
       beautiful but parasitical. Rossetti is not excepted.

752.   Dick, Stewart. "Dante Gabriel Rossetti." *Our Favorite*
       Painters. London: Foulis, 1923, pp. 143-180.

       Finds Rossetti to be distinguished by "intense emo-
       tional significance" and by the deeply personal nature
       of his art. The works based on Lizzie Siddal are the
       best.

753.   Vinciguerra, Mario. *Il Preraffaellismo inglese.* Bologna:
       Zanichelli, 1925. 156 pp.

       Not examined.

754.   Gerwig, Henrietta. "Dante Gabriel Rossetti." *Fifty*
       Famous Painters. New York: Crowell, 1926, pp. 310-317.

       Summarizes Rossetti's career and labels him as an
       artist whose profuse imagination turned out to be a
       tormenting and ultimately fatal gift.

755.   Manson, J[ames] B[olivar]. "The Pre-Raphaelites." *Hours*
       in the Tate Gallery. London: Duckworth, 1926, pp. 73-89

       Comments favorably on seven Rossetti watercolors: they
       are remarkably inventive illustrations of literature, al-
       though as examples of technique they are deplorable and
       show that Rossetti lacked restraint. The Llandaff
       Cathedral triptych gives us Rossetti at his best. Four
       oils are dismissed as valuable only for the poetical
       imagination seen in them.

756. Waugh, Evelyn. *P.R.B.: An Essay on the Pre-Raphaelite*
         Brotherhood, 1847-1854. [Stratford-upon-Avon]: Alastair
         Graham, 1926.

         Not examined.

757. Bell, Clive. "The Pre-Raphaelites." *Landmarks in Nine-*
         teenth Century Painting. London: Chatto and Windus,
         1927, pp. 107-117.

         Ridicules Rossetti and the P.R.B. for their moralism,
         i.e. for trying to do in painting what Ruskin tried to
         do in prose. They were silly and incompetent, and their
         influence was baneful. Reprinted from *New Republic* and
         Nation and Athenaeum (1925).

758. Hind, C[harles] Lewis. "The Pre-Raphaelite Brotherhood."
         The Great Painters in Art and Life. London: Newnes,
         [1927?]. 198 pp.

         Not examined.

759. Bateman, Arthur B. "Rossetti, the Pre-Raphaelites, and
         a Moral." *London Quarterly Review* 149 (1928): 223-233.

         Contends that Rossetti was stultified by his membership
         in the P.R.B. and that the failure of the Brotherhood to
         recognize his genius led to its absorption in meaning-
         less slogans.

760. Carter, A.C.R. "An Auction Causerie: Rossetti Recalled."
         Studio 96 (1928): 76.

         Recalls attending the William Graham sale at Christies'
         in April of 1886, and attributes to Rossetti the revival
         of interest in early Italian art.

761. Chamberlain, Arthur B. "Dante Gabriel Rossetti." *Hours*
         in the Birmingham Art Gallery. London: Duckworth,
         1928, pp. 81-89.

         Offers appreciations of the major Rossetti works on
         display in the permanent collection.

762. Cortissoz, Royal. "Dante Gabriel Rossetti." *Scribner's*
         Magazine 84 (1928): 617-625.

         Rossetti, like all the Pre-Raphaelites, is fertile as

a designer but weak as a painter. He is lofty, intense, and visionary, although often turgid and technically weak

763. Hunziker, Marguerite. "A Century of Rossetti." *Mentor* 16, no. 4 (May 1928): 37-40.

Portrays Rossetti as generous, unpretentious, and affectionate. His paintings depict spiritual rather than physical qualities because he portrays his dream world. Six black-and-white illustrations.

764. Manson, J[ames] B[olivar]. "Dante Gabriel Rossetti." *Apollo* 7 (1928): 257-258.

Judges Rossetti to be a fine designer and an inspiration to others. But he was also a bad painter, given to sentimentality and vulgarity. Two watercolors, *The Passover in the Holy Family* and *Dr. Johnson at the Mitre*, are among his best, the former because of its clear sincerity, the latter because of its humor.

765. Meldrum, David S. "Rossetti as a Painter." *Bookman* [London] 74 (1928): 10-14.

Surveys Rossetti's career as a painter, which was largely governed by his own kind of home-grown Impressionism, although he failed to discipline his genius sufficiently. Twenty-seven plates and photographs.

766. Rigillo, M. "Dante Gabriele Rossetti e il Preraffaelismo." *Rassegna Nazionale*, anno 50, vol. 3 (1928): 3-7.

Not examined.

767. Waugh, Evelyn. "Dante Gabriel Rossetti: A Centenary Criticism." *Fortnightly Review* 129 (1928): 595-604.

Evaluates Rossetti by examining five pictures painted at different stages of his career. *Ecce Ancilla Domini!* shows tenderness, austerity, and a commitment to the Pre-Raphaelite revolt against the baroque. The Oxford Union fresco signifies Rossetti's involvement with exquisite medievalism. *Beata Beatrix* shows Rossetti's mysticism, *Monna Vanna* his eroticism and hedonism. *Proserpine* dramatizes the frustration and the melancholy sense of exile which colored Rossetti's last years.

768. Beza, Marcu. "The Pre-Raphaelites." *From Confucius to Mencken*. Edited by F. H. Pritchard. New York: Harper, 1929, pp. 805-811.

Offers impressionistic treatments of several Pre-Raphaelite paintings, including Rossetti's *Ecce Ancilla Domini!*, *Sibylla Palmifera*, *Lady Lilith*, and *Paolo and Francesca*. His thirst for beauty leads him to an archetypal woman both sensuous and profoundly melancholy. Reprinted in *World's Best Essays* (1929).

769. Cundall, H[erbert] M. "The Pre-Raphaelite Brotherhood and Its Influence." *A History of British Water Colour Painting*. 2nd Edition. London: Batsford, 1929, pp. 84-89.

Summarizes the watercolor work of Hunt, Millais, and Rossetti. The latter shows mystic intensity and an opulent sense of decoration.

770. Lambotté, Paul. "Les Préraphaélites." *La Peinture anglaise*. Paris-Bruges: Brouwer, [1929], pp. 69-77.

Sees the P.R.B. as misguided enthusiasts whose art was cerebral and artificial. The principal influence of those who campaigned under Rossetti's banner was felt in the decorative arts.

771. Luxardo, Lelio. *Preraffaelliti e Preraffaelismo in Inghilterra, note critiche*. Bologna: Zanichelli, 1929.

Not examined.

772. Manson, J[ames] B[olivar]. "The Pre-Raphaelites." *The Tate Gallery*. London: Jack, 1930, pp. 80-92.

Discusses the Rossetti paintings in the Tate Gallery: four watercolors and three oils. Rossetti shows design and imagination, but he is betrayed by vulgarity and a lack of technical skill. He should have stuck to poetry. A revision of item 755.

773. Johnson, Charles. "Pre-Raphaelites: Rossetti and His Influence." *English Painting from the Seventh Century to the Present Day*. London: Bell, 1932, pp. 267-277.

Finds in the early Rossetti both freshness and creativity. But the later paintings inspire only nausea, partly because of the artist's own degeneration, partly

because the use of oils allowed Rossetti the fatal op-
portunity to revise his work.

774.   Baker, C.H. Collins. "The Pre-Raphaelite Movement and
       Burne-Jones." *British Painting*. London: Medici
       Society, 1933, pp. 201-206.

       Views the P.R.B. as obsolete from the very beginning.
       Rossetti can be faulted as "flaccid with hot-house
       eroticism" and a dangerous influence on others.

775.   Binyon, Laurence. "Rossetti and the Pre-Raphaelites."
       English Water-Colours. London: Black, 1933, pp. 176-
       186.

       Sets Rossetti's admittedly limited achievement against
       the mean and shabby cultural milieu in which he found
       himself. Rossetti's main contribution to watercolor art
       was a new coloring technique which gave special intensity
       to his pictorial conceptions.

776.   DeMontmorency, Miles F. "The Pre-Raphaelite Movement."
       A Short History of Painting in England. London: Dent,
       1933, pp. 188-207.

       Nominates Rossetti as the most remarkable member of the
       P.R.B., a true and highly individualistic genius. His
       work is marked especially by intensity and a sense for
       color.

777.   Rothenstein, John. "The Pre-Raphaelites." *An Intro-
       duction to English Painting*. London: Cassell, 1933,
       pp. 174-197.

       Prefers Rossetti's drawings and watercolors to his
       oils because the former have more expression and atmos-
       phere. Rossetti's pathos makes him northern, not
       Italianate.

778.   Seiler, Magdalene. *DG Rossettis künstleristische Ent-
       wicklung*. Greifswald: Mitan, 1933. 126 pp.

       Not examined.

779.   Underwood, Eric Gordon. "Pre-Raphaelitism--The Men."
       A Short History of English Painting. London: Faber,
       1933, pp. 167-180.

Outlines Rossetti's career, which was marked by lofti-
ness, elaboration, and picturesque medievalism.

780. Wilenski, R[eginald] H. "The Pre-Raphaelite Movement."
English Painting. London: Faber, 1933, pp. 220-229.

Contrasts the genuine excitement of Rossetti's passion
for Lizzie Siddal, as expressed in his sketches and
paintings of her, with the "hysterical" excitement of
his passion for Janey Morris. Rossetti and Hunt are the
only original artists among the P.R.B.; Millais is too
philistine.

781. Fry, Roger. "The Pre-Raphaelites." *Reflections on
English Painting*. London: Faber, 1934, pp. 107-111.

Decries the works of the P.R.B. as redolent of the
hothouse. Their confusion, artificiality, and crudity
owed much to Rossetti's passionate convictions. For
Fry's earlier view, see item 741.

782. Oppe, A[dolf] P[aul]. "The Pre-Raphaelites." *Early
Victorian England, 1830-1865*. Edited by G.M. Young.
Vol. 2. London: Oxford University Press, 1934, pp.
159-176.

Relates the P.R.B. to its artistic milieu and finds
that its revolt "was but the commonplace attitude of
young students who saw their instructors daily ignoring
their precepts in practice." Rossetti's chief contri-
bution was medievalism, which in turn was an outgrowth
of his lack of technique.

783. Smith, Solomon C.K. "The Pre-Raphaelites." *Painters of
England*. London: Medici Society, [1934], pp. 85-96.

Sees Rossetti as too weak in technique ever to fulfill
his potential. His work decays steadily after *Ecce
Ancilla Domini!*

784. Burroughs, Bryson. "1935 Views the Pre-Raphaelites."
American Magazine of Art 28 (1935): 6-13.

Describes the author's early devotion to Rossetti's
solemnity, aloofness, and originality. The artist became
too commercial, however, especially in his later years.

785. Laurie, A[rthur] P[illans]. "The Technique of Rembrandt,
      Turner, the Pre-Raphaelites, and the French Impres-
      sionists." *New Light on Old Masters*. London: Sheldon
      Press, 1935, pp. 92-107.

      Describes the Pre-Raphaelite technique of preparing
      the canvas with white primer, adding white lead (in
      oil) and varnish, and laying on the final colors over
      the still-wet surface. The color thus obtained is bril-
      liant and pure, but tends to scale.

786. Dali, Salvador. "Le Surréalisme spectral de l'éternel
      féminin préraphaélite." *Minotaure*, no. 8 (1936): 46-49.

      Sees the Pre-Raphaelites as proto-surrealists and shows
      how they used small chains and geodesic lines in their
      paintings. Rossetti is represented in the discussion by
      Beata Beatrix.

787. Rosenberg, Isaac. "The Pre-Raphaelite Exhibition." *The
      Collected Works of Isaac Rosenberg*. London: Chatto
      and Windus, 1937, pp. 256-258.

      Fragments from an unpublished article on the Tate Gal-
      lery exhibition of 1911-1912. Compares the P.R.B. and
      Alfred Stevens as two types of Victorian revolutionaries.
      The works by Rossetti are clearly the "cream" of the
      exhibition; he has been too much neglected.

788. Mourey, Gabriel. "Les Préraphaélites et les peintres
      anglais du XIXe siècle." *Visages du Monde*, no. 54
      (1938): 89-92.

      Not examined.

789. Reitlinger, Henry S. "The Pre-Raphaelites." *From
      Hogarth to Keene*. London: Methuen, 1938, pp. 83-91.

      Places Rossetti's artistic value as midway between
      those who damn and those who extol. His watercolors
      show "a singularly gem-like and luminous intensity,"
      but after Lizzie Siddal's death his inspiration waned.

790. Rey, Robert. "Les Préraphaélites." *La Renaissance* 21,
      no. 2 (April 1938): 15-24, 47.

      Shows how the P.R.B. was a natural outgrowth of English
      puritanism and mysticism. Rossetti was cultured, origi-

nal, visionary. He deserted the Brotherhood's vow of
chastity by falling in love with Lizzie Siddal, whose
death hastened his decline.

791. Leroy, Alfred. "L'École des Préraphaélites (1848-1900)."
Histoire de la peinture anglaise (800-1938). Paris:
Michel, [1939], pp. 291-309.

Portrays Rossetti as a nervous, hypersensitive aesthete,
a combination of the nordic and the mediterranean tem-
peraments. His vision is too narrowly circumscribed.

792. Pickford, R[alph] W. "The Pre-Raphaelite Painters."
The Psychology of Cultural Change in Painting.
British Journal of Psychology Monograph Supplement,
no. 26. Cambridge University Press, 1943, pp. 17-23.

Uses Bartlett's theories about the inter-relation of
psychology and culture to study the Pre-Raphaelites and
their cultural milieu. Rossetti's sensuousness and his
fascination with idealized women "suggest that his art
was largely inspired by his attachment to his mother."
His paranoia in turn stemmed from a failure to adapt to
the dominant culture.

793. Spender, Stephen. "The Pre-Raphaelite Literary Painters."
New Writing and Daylight 6 (1945): 123-131.

Argues that the Pre-Raphaelites, while they formed the
greatest movement in Victorian art, were nevertheless
guilty of holding to "the cult of a misconceived medievalism" which prevented them from facing the social facts
of life and which resulted, for Rossetti at least, in
morbidity. Rossetti is the only modern painter who has
ever caught the true medieval spirit.

794. Armfield, Maxwell. "Tempera and the Pre-Raphaelites."
Tempera Painting Today. London: Pentagon Press, 1946,
pp. 43-46.

Denies that the Pre-Raphaelites were innovative in
their use of egg tempera. They were material and sen-
timental rather than spiritual; only Rossetti's *Ecce
Ancilla Domini!* is an exception.

795. Buck, Richard D. "A Note on the Methods and Materials
of the Pre-Raphaelite Painters." *Paintings and Drawings of the Pre-Raphaelites and Their Circle*. [Cam-
bridge, Mass.]: Fogg Museum of Art, 1946, pp. 11-19.

Faults the P.R.B. members for their ignorance about
the technical aspects of their craft, an ignorance which
earlier generations could avoid by lengthy apprentice-
ships and which later generations could avoid by avail-
ing themselves of empirical data. [Note: remainder of
this booklet is an exhibition catalog--see item 96.]

796.   Grigson, Geoffrey. "The Pre-Raphaelite Myth." *The Harp*
       of Aeolus and Other Essays on Art, Literature, and
       Nature. London: Routledge, 1947, pp. 89-95.

       Accuses the P.R.B. and its followers of being frauds,
       in other words artists who created a myth for themselves
       but who were essentially "compromisers and cowards."
       Rossetti alone has some redeeming virtue. Reprinted
       from *Architectural Review* (1947).

797.   Mayne, Jonathan. "The Pre-Raphaelites at Birmingham."
       The Listener 38 (1947): 26-27.

       Observes that the current Birmingham exhibition shows
       Rossetti deviating from his P.R.B. colleagues right from
       the very beginning. His works give the primitive feeling
       of "mysterious, shut-in terror." Furthermore, his draw-
       ings vindicate him from the charge of being an amateur
       draughtsman.

798.   Minondo, Venancio. *Dante Gabriel Rossetti en el Pre-*
       rafaelismo. Buenos Aires: Editorial Ideas, 1947.

       Not examined.

799.   Robsjohn-Gibbings, Terence H. "Art into Music." *Mona*
       Lisa's Mustache: A Dissection of Modern Art. New York:
       Knopf, 1947, pp. 24-39.

       Finds the P.R.B. as practitioners of the occult, led by
       "Svengali" Rossetti. As chief sorcerer Rossetti tried
       to use medievalism as a way to spellbind and then destroy
       the middle class.

800.   Bliss, Douglas Percy. "Pre-Raphaelite Centenary."
       Scottish Art Review 2, no. 1 (January 1948): 2-6.

       Intends to arouse interest in the Pre-Raphaelites, who
       have been sneered at unfairly. Rossetti was their lead-
       er, the leavening agent whose mystical and erotic ladies
       moved them away from realism toward symbolism.

801. Carter, Charles. "The Pre-Raphaelites as Religious
      Painters." *Quarterly Review* 286 (1948): 248-261.

      Observes that Rossetti and his associates produced
      religious paintings "which must be regarded as among
      the most significant to be painted in this country
      since the Reformation." But their literalness and
      didacticism prevented them from achieving greatness.

802. Cook, Olive. "The Pre-Raphaelites." *The Saturday Book*,
      no. 8 (1948): 127-128.

      Contends that the Pre-Raphaelites were subconsciously
      guided by the English preference for literary anecdotes
      in paintings. An extravagantly unreal work such as
      Fazio's Mistress shows the dangers inherent in such an
      interest.

803. Gere, John. "Pre-Raphaelite Drawings." *Alphabet and
      Image*, no. 6 (1948): 18-32.

      Attempts a summing-up of Pre-Raphaelitism as the final
      expression of Romanticism and therefore self-destructive.
      Rossetti, deep, complex, and subtle, is better as a
      draughtsman than as a painter. Six of the eleven il-
      lustrative plates are of his works.

804. Gere, John. "Pre-Raphaelites at the Tate." *Burlington
      Magazine* 90 (1948): 325-326.

      Bemoans the inclusion of *Ecce Ancilla Domini!* and *The
      Girlhood of Mary Virgin* in the Tate Gallery exhibition
      because of their "fumbling insipidity." Nevertheless
      Rossetti was the only real genius of the movement and
      his exhibited drawings show delicacy, sincerity, and
      genuine sensitivity.

805. Wilenski, R[eginald] H. [The Pre-Raphaelite Movement.]
      Outline of English Painting. New York: Philosophical
      Library, 1948, pp. 98-113.

      Sees Pre-Raphaelitism as constituted by Rossetti the
      romantic, Millais the naturalist, and Hunt the puritan.
      Rossetti drew beautifully during his years with Lizzie
      Siddal, but the later paintings are the "hypertrophic"
      work of a man coarsened by drugs and self-indulgence.

806.   Giartosio de Courten, Maria L. "La 'fratellanza pre-
        raffaellita' cent'anni dopo." *Nuova Antologia* 447
        (1949): 380-395.

        Commemorates the centenary of the founding of the
        P.R.B. by retelling the story of its formation and by
        describing current publications devoted to it. Ros-
        setti is judged to be the greatest of the three found-
        ing painters. But he was much misunderstood by his
        contemporaries; these misunderstandings, especially
        as they apply to his religious attitudes, are summarized.

807.   Mills, Ernestine. "Rossetti's Method of Oil Painting."
        Apollo 49 (1949): 49.

        Provides extracts from the notebooks which Frederic
        Shields kept while he was learning oil painting tech-
        niques from Rossetti. The entries reveal Rossetti's
        methods, particularly his theories of color and glazing,
        and his golden rule: "always get [the work] looking
        harmonious in its own stage."

808.   Rothenstein, Elizabeth. "The Pre-Raphaelites and Our-
        selves." *Month* n.s. 1 (1949): 180-198.

        Uses the Tate Gallery exhibition as a point of depart-
        ure for a revaluation of the P.R.B. The Pre-Raphaelites
        had a valid insight about the importance of the signi-
        ficant moment, an insight similar to Hopkins' in poetry;
        but they were not great enough artists to fulfill it.
        As for Rossetti, he was a failed Promethean, a mock
        mystic.

809.   Newton, Eric. "Pre-Raphaelite." *In My View*. London:
        Longmans, 1950, pp. 240-244.

        Defends the P.R.B. against accusations that they were
        too literary. The chief virtue of Rossetti and his
        colleagues was their enthusiasm, "the urgency behind
        the sentiment."

810.   Bertram, Anthony. "The Pre-Raphaelites and Their Com-
        panions." *A Century of British Painting, 1851-1951*.
        New York: Studio, 1951, pp. 15-37.

        Sees the original P.R.B. as "a temporary grouping of
        incompatibles." What we now call Pre-Raphaelitism, i.e.
        exotic emotionalism, stems from Rossetti. When life did

not provide what his art demanded, and when he could not
reconcile his religiosity and his sensuality, he took to
chloral.

811. Hubbard, Hesketh. "The 1850's." *A Hundred Years of
British Painting 1851-1951*. London: Longmans, 1951,
pp. 1-58.

Describes the professional situation for painters
during Rossetti's first decade as an adult. Rossetti's
work was hampered by his impatience and by his devotion
to a "goitrous" type of feminine beauty.

812. Short, Ernest. "The Pre-Raphaelites (1848-1898)." *A
History of British Painting*. London: Eyre and Spottiswoode, 1953, pp. 190-204.

Sees Rossetti as the English Delacroix, one who combines the mystical and the erotic. His impact was more
as an inspirer of others than as a great painter in his
own right.

813. Shipp, Horace. "The Pre-Raphaelites." *The English
Masters*. London: Sampson and Low, 1955, pp. 189-208.

Gives a brief synopsis of Rossetti's career. He was
the "gifted amateur," one who lacked the technical
ability to carry on once his initial rapture had been
exhausted.

814. Garland, Madge. "Rossetti's Models." *The Changing Face
of Beauty--Four Thousand Years of Beautiful Women*.
New York: Barrows, 1957, pp. 134-135.

Illustrates Rossetti's conception of the "Pre-
Raphaelite beauty," using drawings of Lizzie Siddal,
Janey Morris, Ruth Herbert, Alexa Wilding, and Fanny
Cornforth.

815. Orpen, Sir William. "The Pre-Raphaelites." *The Outline
of Art*. London: Newnes, [1957], pp. 257-272.

Recounts the history of the P.R.B. Rossetti, forsaking
the naturalism of Hunt and the anecdotal triviality of
Millais, devoted himself to medievalism. His oils of the
mid-1860s are judged to be his best work.

816. Young, Vernon. "From Pre-Raphaelitism to Bloomsbury."
      The Turn of the Century. New York: Art Digest, 1957,
      pp. 99-114.

      Attacks the P.R.B. for a lack of creativity, the re-
      sult of working in a mercantile and puritan environment.
      Rossetti became the painter of passive and cruel *femmes
      fatales*.

817. Greenwood, Julia. "Young and Angry, Then and Now."
      The Listener 60 (1958): 13-14.

      Focuses on Lizzie Siddal as a way of introducing the
      P.R.B. and its chief concerns. Rossetti is the key
      figure because of his dictatorial nature and the unex-
      pectedness of his work.

818. Boase, T.S.R. "The Pre-Raphaelites." *The Oxford History
      of English Art*. Vol. 10. Oxford: Clarendon Press,
      1959, pp. 275-298.

      Outlines in considerable detail the historical context
      within which the P.R.B. arose and against which they
      triumphed. The "Protestant accuracy" of Hunt can be
      contrasted to the "Catholic imagination" of Rossetti.

819. Canaday, John. "Outside France, 1850-1900." *Mainstreams
      of Modern Art*. New York: Holt, 1959, pp. 280-324.

      Views Pre-Raphaelitism as the most idealistic and most
      self-defeating form of Romanticism in English art. Their
      horror of the present led to an obsession with the sur-
      face forms of the past. Rossetti epitomizes the move-
      ment by his "personal emotionalism." His devotion to
      the archetypal woman is his greatest strength.

820. Lamaitre, Henri [=Aurelian Digeon]. "D.G. Rossetti and
      the Brotherhood." *The 'English Manner' in Painting*.
      New York: Universe Books, 1959, pp. 163-172.

      Finds the P.R.B. to be characteristically English
      because of their conviction that art must have a moral
      or a literary content. Rossetti's best art is his
      earliest.

821. Hudson, Derek. "The Pre-Raphaelites." *The Forgotten
      King and Other Essays*. London: Constable, 1960, pp.
      144-152.

Sees Rossetti as the poet of the movement, given over to emotional intensity rather than naturalism. His tendency is to the mystic and medieval. Reprinted from the *Times Literary Supplement* (1948).

822. Procter, Ida. "Dante Gabriel Rossetti." *Masters of British Nineteenth Century Art*. London: Dobson, 1961, pp. 127-142.

Contains a summary of Rossetti's career and a brief location list. Intended mainly for younger readers.

823. Woodward, John O. "Later Nineteenth Century." *British Painting, a Picture History*. London: Studio Vista, 1962, pp. 125-141.

Sees Rossetti as a believer in "do it yourself medievalism," with Lizzie Siddal as both his Guinevere and his Beatrice. Two plates.

824. [Grylls], Rosalie Mander. "Rossetti's Models." *Apollo* 78 (1963): 18-22.

Describes Rossetti's three most important models: Lizzie Siddal, who embodied spirituality, Fanny Cornforth, who embodied sensuality, and Janey Morris, who embodied both. The three lesser models were Marie Stillman, Ruth Herbert, and Alexa Wilding. The remarkable aspect of Rossetti's treatment of all six models is that they seem to have no expression, no character.

825. Coates, Robert M. "Boom or Bust." *New Yorker*, 13 June 1964, pp. 102, 104-109.

Sees the recent rise in popularity of the P.R.B. as owing to their baroque qualities, matching the age's taste. Rossetti could paint well when he got beyond his "swaying, goitrous females."

826. Reynolds, Graham. "The Pre-Raphaelites." *Victorian Painting*. London: Studio Vista, 1966, pp. 94-116.

Sees the P.R.B. as crystallizers of earlier trends toward shocking the bourgeois and capturing modern life. Rossetti is a genius who squandered his gifts by emotional dissipation. The best works are the early Dante illustrations, completed bfore the dissipation had fully set in. Three plates.

827. Barilli, Renato. *I Preraffaelliti*. Milan: Fabri, 1967.
      100 pp.

      Contains six color plates of Rossetti's work, includ-
      ing *Astarte Syriaca* and *Dantis Amor*. The introduction
      pictures Rossetti as torn by the polarity of the medie-
      val period vs. the banal modern age. He is dominated
      by his obsession with langorous, enigmatic women. His
      chief characteristic is aestheticism, as opposed to the
      social anecdotalism of Millais and the devotionalism of
      Hunt.

828. Bell, Quentin. "Hard-Edge Pre-Raphaelism" and "From
      Rossetti to Art Nouveau." *Victorian Artists*. London:
      Routledge, 1967, pp. 28-39, 65-76.

      The earlier chapter describes the impact of the P.R.B.,
      especially in its campaign against "slosh" and its use
      of the technique of painting onto a "wet white" ground.
      The later chapter follows the second generation, again
      led by Rossetti but this time dominated not by a tech-
      nique but by an image (the Woman).

829. Fleming, G.H. *Rossetti and the Pre-Raphaelite Brother-
      hood*. London: Rupert Hart-Davis, 1967. 233 pp.

      Traces the P.R.B. from its founding in 1848 to its
      dissolution in 1854, which for the author is signalled
      by the election of Millais to the Royal Academy. Con-
      tributes little in the way of new knowledge about the
      Brotherhood, but offers an easy, readable survey of an
      important part of Rossetti's life. Rossetti is pre-
      sented as the chief figure and "the most personally
      fascinating" Pre-Raphaelite; the treatment is less
      sensational than some earlier ones. For a companion
      volume, see item 836.

830. Ormond, Leonée. "Mid-Victorian Parody: George Du
      Maurier's 'A Legend of Camelot.'" *Apollo* 85 (1967):
      54-58.

      Shows that the 1866 parody in *Punch* with its accom-
      panying illustrations was an attack on the romantic cult
      which had grown up around Rossetti. The pseudo-medie-
      valism, the complex imagery, and the love symbolism all
      show this intent, as does the clear borrowing from *Rosa
      Triplex*.

831. Hardie, Martin. "The Pre-Raphaelites and Some Contemp-
      oraries." *Watercolour Painting in Britain*. Vol. 3:
      The Victorian Period. New York: Barnes and Noble,
      1968, pp. 115-132.

      Pronounces Rossetti the best watercolourist among the
      Pre-Raphaelites and the watercolours of the 1850s the
      best of his own work. The colors were chosen methodi-
      cally, with a preference for blue, carmine, and viridian
      green; yellow is the favorite tonal color.

832. Ormond, Richard. "Victorian Paintings and Patronage in
      Birmingham." *Apollo* 87 (1968): 240-251.

      Traces the changing attitudes in Birmingham toward the
      Pre-Raphaelites, from the philistine ignorance of the
      1850s to the lively connoisseurship of the modern era.
      The art gallery's determination to buy Pre-Raphaelite
      work led to the purchase of Rossetti's *Beata Beatrix*
      and the sketches of the Charles Fairfax Murray collection.

833. Maas, Jeremy. "The Pre-Raphaelites." *Victorian Painters*.
      London: Barrie and Rockliff, 1969, pp. 123-146.

      Rossetti, represented by five plates, is seen as a
      conspiratorial Italian interested only in the social
      side of Pre-Raphaelitism. Only during his later asso-
      ciation with Burne-Jones did he found a school, in
      this case of "mythographers."

834. Hilton, Timothy. *The Pre-Raphaelites*. New York: Abrams,
      1970.   216 pp.

      Concentrates on the painting only, mixing narrative
      and criticism. The movement is interpreted as a res-
      ponse to social conditions, i.e. it is "the art of the
      Industrial Revolution." Rossetti is the symbolist of
      the group, and he is represented by twenty-nine plates,
      mostly in black and white.

835. Stanford, Derek. "The Pre-Raphaelite Cult of Women:
      From Damozel to Demon." *Contemporary Review* 217
      (1970): 26-33.

      Contends that the success of Pre-Raphaelitism lay in
      its encouragement of feminism. The "new woman"--sensi-
      tive, cultivated, mysterious--responded to Rossetti's
      evocation of a similar kind of elusive woman. His women

combined beauty and spirituality, and their cult allowed
the Victorians to be both sensual and refined, at least
until Rossetti became absorbed with the "darkling Venuses"
of his late years.

836.   Fleming, G.H. *That Ne'er Shall Meet Again: Rossetti,*
       Millais, Hunt. London: Michael Joseph, 1971. 468 pp.

       Takes up the narrative which item 829 had closed in
       1854. The concentration is on the three main figures
       of the now-dissolved Brotherhood. Once again Rossetti
       dominates the story, so much so that the author ends
       the book with Rossetti's death in 1882, even though
       Millais lived for another fourteen years and Hunt for
       another twenty-eight. The author tries to pursue his
       narrative from a vantage point midway between what he
       views as the unnecessary asperity of Oswald Doughty
       (see item 281) and the uncritical eulogism of Rosalie
       Grylls (see item 286). Rossetti is a great but flawed
       artist.

837.   Neve, Christopher. "The Great Pre-Raphaelite Muddle."
       Country Life 150 (1971): 280-281.

       Decries Rossetti as a sad case--impulsive and inspired
       as a young artist, but a drugged, melancholy cripple in
       his later years. There was no clear Pre-Raphaelite
       aesthetic, only a confused muddle.

838.   Davis, Douglas. "Pre-Raphaelites: Odd Brothers."
       Newsweek, 27 March 1972, pp. 78-81.

       Reviews the Lowe Art Museum exhibition (see item 108)
       and finds that the P.R.B. did not connect: Rossetti was
       an island to himself, leaving nothing that will endure,
       only a languid flatness and a radical pose.

839.   Galerie du Luxembourg. *Burne-Jones et l'influence des*
       PreRaphaelites. Paris: Galerie du Luxembourg, 1972.
       77 pp.

       In the introduction to this exhibition catalogue Julian
       Hartnoll sees Burne-Jones as profoundly influenced by
       Rossetti in technique, subject-matter, and style. This
       contention is supported both in the text and in the exhi-
       bition itself by illustrations from Rossetti's own work.

840. Gállego, Julián. "Las dos fases del Pre-Rafaelismo."
     Goya 109 (1972): 10-17.

     Explains, for an audience presumed to be unfamiliar
     with it, the Pre-Raphaelite Brotherhood: its origin,
     growth, and principles. Its two principal sources are
     said to be the Gothic revival and the Victorian preoc-
     cupation with social issues. Rossetti is considered in
     relation to three of his models: Lizzie Siddal, Janey
     Morris, and Fanny Cornforth.

841. Gaunt, William. "The Pre-Raphaelite Revolt and Its
     Sequels." *The Restless Century: Painting in Britain
     1800-1900*. London: Phaidon, 1972, pp. 24-27.

     Gives a brief chronicle of the P.R.B. Among the 191
     plates are several by Rossetti and his colleagues.

842. Hilton, Tim[othy]. "Pre-Raphaelite Problems." *Studio*
     183 (1972): 218-221.

     Finds the Pre-Raphaelites to be failures as painters,
     but still important because of their historical role in
     bridging the gap between late academic baroque and Art
     Nouveau. Rossetti's venery affected his art. He and
     his followers "only seemed to be ogling their own bourgeois
     hangups."

843. Mayoux, Jean-Jacques. "Approaches to Pre-Raphaelitism."
     English Painting: From Hogarth to the Pre-Raphaelites.
     Translated by J. Emmons. New York: St. Martin's
     Press, 1972, pp. 223-258.

     Sees Rossetti as emotionally sincere but mentally con-
     fused. Technically incompetent, Rossetti nevertheless
     is important historically because of his "Pre-Symbolistic
     vision." Included are descriptive interpretations of a
     number of Rossetti's best-known paintings.

844. Anthony, Evan. "Delayed Homage." *The Spectator* 230
     (1973): 82.

     Gives favorable notice to the delayed tribute offered
     by the Royal Academy in the form of its 1973 Rossetti
     exhibition (see item 109).

845. Bell, Quentin. "Tunnel of Love." *New Statesman* n.s. 85
     (1973): 97-98.

Finds the Royal Academy exhibition (see item 109) both
delightful and instructive. Rossetti had skill and
flair, although he could not combine pattern and aerial
space. His bent was away from atmosphere and perspective.

846. Davis, Frank. "The Tragic Genius of Rossetti." *Country
      Life* 154 (1973): 1691-1692.

      Finds the recent Royal Academy exhibition (see item 109)
      an apt summation of Rossetti's achievements and failures
      (both unspecified).

847. Feaver, William. "Primrose Path." *The Listener*, 25 Jan-
      uary 1973, pp. 129-131.

      Likens Rossetti as a painter to Elvis Presley as a
      singer: both do essentially the same thing to a series
      of interchangeable women. *Found* demonstrates Rossetti's
      high hopes and his failure to live up to them.

848. Grieve, Alastair. "Dante Gabriel Rossetti at the Royal
      Academy." *Connoisseur* 182 (1973): 50-55.

      Surveys the Royal Academy exhibition (see item 109),
      emphasizing the principal works in each of the sections.
      Seven black-and-white illustrations and a full-color
      plate of *The Blue Closet*.

849. Lightbown-W., M. "Royal Academy Exhibition: Dante
      Gabriel Rossetti, Patron and Poet." *Pantheon* 31
      (1973): 319-320.

      Believes that Rossetti at his best had a compelling
      sense of design and was a key figure in the rise of
      decadence and symbolism. Yet his oils show clammy color.

850. Melville, Robert. "The Art of Making Concessions."
      Architectural Review 153 (1973): 197-200.

      Dismisses Rossetti as a lesser artist than even the
      minor Pre-Raphaelites. He set for himself programs he
      could not carry out. His best works are the life draw-
      ings. His worst are the late autopsychological portraits
      with their "wanton spirituality, as if he were dreaming
      of having carnal knowledge of an angel."

851. Neve, Christopher. "How Rossetti Met Himself." *Country
      Life* 153 (1973): 330-331.

Sees Rossetti as a forerunner of our modern tendency
to make a religion out of sensuality and drugs. The
Royal Academy exhibition (see item 109) shows him to be
an extraordinarily imaginative painter, one who could
compress dramatic moments and freeze them by his intensity. He was obsessed with women, and his obsessions
fascinate.

852. Roberts, Keith. "Rossetti in London and Birmingham."
     Burlington Magazine 115 (1973): 136-139.

     Praises the two exhibitions (see item 109). Rossetti
     is an artist of enclosed vision--"airless, intense,
     heraldic, symbolic, dreamy"--and he has been presented
     that way. Luckily, quality is divorced from virtuosity,
     just as it is in Blake.

853. Russell, John. "Tribute to Rossetti." *Times* [London],
     21 January 1973, p. 29.

     Judges Rossetti's exhibition (see item 109) as showing
     an artist who fascinates but who fails to bring off the
     difficult conceptions he undertakes.

854. Staley, Allen. *The Pre-Raphaelite Landscape.* Oxford:
     Clarendon Press, 1973. 193 pp.

     Omits any detailed discussion of Rossetti on the grounds
     that such would have been the attitude of the general
     British public when the P.R.B. first appeared in 1850.
     But there are numerous allusions to Rossetti's unfami-
     liarity with naturalism and to his works as they relate
     to the works of other Brotherhood members.

855. Sussman, Herbert. "The Language of Criticism and the
     Language of Art: The Response of Victorian Periodicals
     to the Pre-Raphaelite Brotherhood." *Victorian
     Periodicals Newsletter* 19 (1973): 21-29.

     Traces the reaction of Victorian art critics to the
     P.R.B., from early praise of Rossetti's *Girlhood of
     Mary Virgin* through the 1850 attacks (when the Brother-
     hood was perceived as a dangerous *avant-garde*) to the
     grudging acceptance of 1852 and beyond. The *avant-garde*
     was able to remold public opinion, as this adaptation
     to them shows.

856. [Sutton, Denys?]. "The Prisoner." *Apollo* 97 (1973):
        120-126.

        Describes the renewed appeal of introverted and
        intimate art like Rossetti's. The prisoner of Tudor
        House was a man of paradox, one who combined sexual
        obsession with "do-goodism," who was both *poet maudite*
        and John Bull. Despite his originality and intensity,
        however, he was not a major artist.

857. Trickett, Rachel. "Rossetti: Justification for the
        Legend." *Studio* 185 (1973): 19-22.

        Emphasizes the way in which Rossetti epitomized the
        aesthetic dilemmas of his age: realism vs. imagination,
        immediacy vs. implication. His drawings show that he
        was not technically incompetent; quite simply, his
        talent was too varied for his obsessive vision. He is
        the painter of encounters, and his vitality justifies
        our interest in him.

858. Berry, Ralph. "Rossetti as Painter." *Mosaic* 7 (1974):
        151-155.

        Reviews Surtees' catalogue (see item 76) and concludes
        that as a painter "Rossetti was not quite good enough
        and perhaps he knew it."

859. Christian, John. *The Pre-Raphaelites in Oxford*. Oxford:
        Ashmolean Museum, 1974. 44 pp.

        Discusses the items of Pre-Raphaelite interest as-
        sociated with the city and includes eighteen illustra-
        tive plates. One short section recounts Rossetti's
        involvement with the "Jovial Campaign."

860. Roberts, Helene E. "The Dream World of Dante Gabriel
        Rossetti." *Victorian Studies* 17 (1974): 371-393.

        Categorizes Rossetti's paintings according to whether
        they partake of the "daydream" or the "unconscious dream,"
        with the latter being more passive and mystical. Ex-
        plains the techniques by which the artist attempted to
        blend his dream world and the viewer's dream world.

861. Larkin, David, ed. *The English Dreamers*. New York:
        Peacock Press, 1975. 88 pp.

        Sees the Pre-Raphaelites as portrayers of dreamscapes,

which always will be characterized by super-clarity and irrationality. Rossetti is represented by full-color reproductions (and discussions) of *Ecce Ancilla Domini!*, *Proserpine*, *La Bello Mano*, and *La Pia de' Tolomei*.

862. Nicoll, John. *Dante Gabriel Rossetti*. New York: Macmillan, 1976. 175 pp.

Views Rossetti paintings from a Marxist perspective, finding in the artist an increasing tendency to turn away from social criticism to an "escapist and complacent" endorsement of life as it is. Uses twenty-seven color plates and 100 black-and-white illustrations to substantiate the thesis.

863. Sherrill, Sarah B. "Dante Gabriel Rossetti." *Antiques* 110 (1976): 670-688.

Summarizes what Rossetti and his P.R.B. colleagues were hoping to achieve.

864. Young, Mahonri Sharp. "Pre-Raphaelites at Wilmington." *Apollo* 104 (1976): 306-307.

Notes the highlights of the exhibition at the Delaware Art Museum (see item 114). Rossetti's troubles with the completion of *Found* and other paintings are given special focus.

865. Bier, Eugene A. "Dante Gabriel Rossetti: New Light through Flat Surfaces." *Pre-Raphaelite Review* 1, no. 1 (November 1977): 80-88.

Sees Rossetti's painting as the deliberate application of medieval techniques, including two-dimensional--i.e. "flat"--representation. The judgement that Rossetti lacked technical skill is wrong. He was simply trying to use space differently, in a manner which looked back to the manuscript illustrators and forward to the Symbolists and Seurat. By this standard he was quite successful.

866. [Anonymous]. "The Pursuit of Beauty." *Apollo* 200 (1978): 446-451.

Chronicles the rising interest in the Pre-Raphaelites on the part of American collectors. Samuel Bancroft Jr. and Grenville Winthrop were the chief early buyers, W.J.

Stillman, Charles Eliot Norton, and Charles Fairfax
Murray the chief proponents. Four black-and-white illustrations of Rossetti's work, seven of work by others.

867.   Bayley, John B. "The Pre-Raphaelite Brotherhood, 1848-
1855." *Nineteenth Century* 5, no. 2 (Summer 1979):
70-75.

Discusses the aims of the original brotherhood and
relates them to the growing financial power of the middle class. By "sheer visual exorbitancy" the Pre-
Raphaelites achieved a moving intensity. The social
realism of Rossetti's *Found* makes it the most typically
Pre-Raphaelite of his paintings. As social realists
the Pre-Raphaelites were failures: they should have
adapted their analytical method to the world around them.

See also items 62, 63, 67, 70, 74, 81, 96, 97, 114, 151, 162,
203, 226, 241, 249, 252, 263, 264, 282, 306, 307, 312, 313,
315, 360, 566, 594, 912, 918, 980-1099.

SECTION B: CRITICISM OF INDIVIDUAL ARTISTIC WORKS

Because these criticisms are spread widely over many works, it
would not be fruitful to group them, as was done in the case
of the individual literary works. The arrangement is again
chronological.

868.   [Anonymous]. "Study of a Female Head." *Portfolio* 14
(1883): 167.

Reproduces and comments on a drawing of Rossetti's in
which the model does *not* have "full lips, or large eyes,
of heavy masses of hair."

869.   Monkhouse, William Cosmo. *"Rosa Triplex."* *Magazine of
Art* 6 (1883): 271-272.

Describes the drawing, explains its significance (i.e.
the arrangement of three different faces which yet suggest one chord of beauty), and praises it for its charm
and its mystical music.

870.   [Stephens, Frederic G.]. *"Ecce Ancilla Domini!* by Dante
Gabriel Charles Rossetti." *Portfolio* 19 (1888): 125-
127.

Praises the painting as the one perfectly Pre-Raphaelite work Rossetti ever did. The work is spiritually akin to Fra Angelico; it owes nothing to the German Nazarenes. Details of the picture itself and of its composition, including Stephens' own role as a model for the Angel Gabriel, are also provided.

871. Stephens, Fredric G. "*Beata Beatrix* by Dante G. Rossetti." *Portfolio* 22 (1891): 45-47.

Calls the painting quintessential Rossetti and a wonderfully subtle expression of the border-realm between life and death. The situation, the details, the symbolism, and the motive of the painting are all explained; everything is subsumed under the light of mystery.

872. Stephens, Frederic G. "*Rosa Triplex* by Dante G. Rossetti." *Portfolio* 23 (1892): 197-199.

Notes how the painting typifies Rossetti's passionate love of feminine beauty. It has no special spiritual significance, but instead contents itself with giving three views of one of his choicest models, Alexa Wilding. Five versions of the work are all described, including dates and provenance.

873. Baldwin, Elbert F. "The Nativity as Interpreted by the English Pre-Raphaelites." *Outlook* 50 (1894): 1042-1045.

Interprets the flower symbolism of *The Girlhood of Mary Virgin* and praises its realism, austerity, and originality.

874. Monkhouse, William Cosmo. "A Sketch of Tennyson by Rossetti." *Scribner's Magazine* 21 (1897): 125-126.

Discusses and reproduces a version of the sketch--then in the author's possession--of Tennyson reading *Maud*. See item 893.

875. White, Gleeson. "'A Sea Spell.' An Appreciation." *The Dome* 2 (1898): 91-94.

Sees the picture as an example of Rossetti's genius, namely the power to portray certain passionate moods. Although technically weak, it has been unfairly ignored.

876.   Marillier, Henry C. "The Salutation of Beatrice: As
       Treated Pictorially by D.G. Rossetti." *Art Journal*
       61 (1899): 353-357.

       Reproduces, distinguishes, and analyzes nine paintings
       and drawings in which Rossetti depicted the three dif-
       ferent salutations of Beatrice described by Dante in the
       Vita Nuova.

877.   Sawvel, Franklin B. "*Dante's Dream* and *Captive Andro-
       mache*." *Education, A Monthly Magazine* 21 (1900):
       32-36.

       Analyzes two paintings, one by Rossetti and one by
       Leighton, which illustrate literary works. Rossetti's
       painting captures the spirit of Dante, i.e. love-lorn
       yet heaven-exalted sorrow. Its symbols, such as poppies,
       doves, and attendant ladies, contribute to this spiri-
       tual but not literal rendering.

878.   Cary, Elisabeth Luther. "A Rossetti Model." *Scrip.
       Notes on Art* 1 (1906): 286-288.

       Identifies the model for one of the angel children in
       the Graham version of *The Blessed Damozel* as Wilfred
       Hawtrey, son of the Rev. H.C. Hawtrey.

879.   Stephens, Frederic G. "Picture of a Lady in Red."
       Notes & Queries, 10th series, 7 (1907): 129, 193.

       Describes the history and provenance of *A Vision of
       Fiammetta*, painted by Rossetti in 1877-1879. The in-
       formation is given in response to an inquiry from "I.R."

880.   Stevens, W. Bertrand. "*Ecce Ancilla Domini!* (Behold
       the Handmaiden of the Lord)." *Chautauquan* 46 (1907):
       103-104.

       Relates the history of the picture, describes it, and
       characterizes it as a combination of the simple and the
       spiritual.

881.   Burns, J[abez?]. "*Mary Magdalene at the House of Simon
       by D.G. Rossetti*." *Sermons in Art by the Great Mas-
       ters*. London: Duckworth, 1908.

       Not examined.

882.   Cary, Elisabeth L[uther]. "The New Rossetti Water Colour
          in the Metropolitan Museum." *International Studio* 35
          (1908): cxxv-cxxx.

          Describes the 1867 watercolor version of *Lady Lilith*
          done for Coltart of Liverpool. The principal difference
          from the oil version is in tone of color--there is less
          dusky brilliance, more garishness. Rossetti's later
          conception of Lady Lilith is not a degeneration; it
          simply gives greater emphasis to her serpentine quality.

883.   Binyon, Laurence. "Zeichnungen Dante Gabriel Rossettis."
          Die graphische Künste 35 (1912): 15-20.

          Studies *Hamlet and Ophelia* and *Found* as examples of
          Rossetti's imaginative skill. Although he lacks Dürer's
          mastery of line, others could profitably imitate his
          "fundamental brainwork."

884.   Robertson, W. Graham. "The Spell of Rossetti." *Time
          Was: Reminiscences.* London: Hamish Hamilton, 1931,
          pp. 86-97.

          Describes seeing the "lilac and purple horror" *Astarte
          Syriaca*. Yet the painting had exerted a powerful spell
          on the young Robertson. Vignettes of other members of
          Rossetti's circle, including Burne-Jones and the Morrises,
          are also included. American title: *Life Was Worth Living*.

885.   Williamson, G.C. "The Cases of an Art Expert. II. The
          Rossetti Miniature." *Country Life* 80 (1936): 35-36.

          Describes a photograph of Lizzie Siddal colored by
          Rossetti during her post-partum illness and later un-
          covered in an East End garret (after passing through
          the hands of Charles Augustus Howell).

886.   Murray, E. Croft. "An Early Drawing by Rossetti."
          British Museum Quarterly 11 (1937): 95-96.

          Describes a drawing by Rossetti illustrating Poe's
          poem "The Sleeper."

887.   [Anonymous]. "D.G. Rossetti (1828-1882)." *Russell-Cotes
          Bulletin* 18 (1939): 45-48.

          Offers appreciations of two paintings on loan to the
          gallery: *Arthur's Tomb*, which shows great drama and real

intensity, and *How They Met Themselves*, which gives a
vivid rendition of the lover's horror. Technically, an
interesting aspect of these two works is Rossetti's use
of gum in his watercolors.

888.   [Preston, Kerrison?]. "D.G. Rossetti's *King Rene's
       Honeymoon.*" *Apollo* 34 (1941): 153.

       Describes Rossetti's oil replica of the panel he had
       done for John Seddon's cabinet (see item 951). The
       painting shows delicacy, emotion, and imagination.

889.   Gaunt, William. "Two Portrait Drawings by Dante Gabriel
       Rossetti." *Connoisseur* 110 (1942): 140-141, 158.

       Describes two black chalk and sanguine portraits by
       Rossetti, one of Dr. Thomas Gordon Hake, the other of
       his son George Gordon Hake. Both drawings were done in
       1872, while Rossetti was at Trowan, recovering from his
       nervous breakdown.

890.   [Anonymous]. "*Venus Verticordia.*" *Russell-Cotes Bul-
       letin*, September 1946, pp. 1-3.

       Describes the painting recently purchased by the Gal-
       lery and speculates inconclusively on whether Rossetti
       was harmed by the restraint he showed to avoid the
       dangers of "Ettyism."

891.   Paden, William D. "*La Pia de' Tolomei* by Dante Gabriel
       Rossetti." *Register of the Museum of Art* [University
       of Kansas] 2, no. 1 (November 1958): 3-48.

       Recounts in great detail the relationships which lie
       behind Rossetti's famous painting. Rossetti's physical
       decline can be attributed to arterial hypertension ag-
       gravated by his love for Janey Morris and his guilt over
       his double betrayal (of Morris and of Lizzie). The pri-
       mary emphasis in explaining the painting should be on
       Rossetti's life; the author's assumption is that the
       painting, with its scene of a wife imprisoned by a cruel
       husband, can only be understood by knowing about Ros-
       setti's own *ménage à trois*. An appendix shows the sources
       chronology, and variants of *La Pia*. See also item 903.

892.   Adrian, Arthur. "The Genesis of Rossetti's 'Found.'"
       Texas Studies in Language and Literature 5 (1963):
       79-82.

Rebuts William Michael Rossetti's contention that the
painting was wholly Rossetti's own invention. The source
was a conversation between Rossetti and William Bell
Scott during which they discussed the possible meeting
of two characters portrayed in Scott's poem "Rosabell."
See also item 916.

893. Fredeman, William E. "Rossetti's Impromptu Portraits
      of Tennyson Reading 'Maud.'" *Burlington Magazine* 105
      (1963): 117-118, 413.

      Distinguishes the three different sketches which Ros-
      setti made on or near the evening of September 27, 1855.
      Only one is still extant. The author gives dimensions,
      probable order of composition, and provenance.

894. Rogers, Mildred F. "The Salutation of Beatrice: by
      Dante Gabriel Rossetti." *Connoisseur* 153 (1963):
      180-181.

      Describes the painting as a harmonious blending of the
      narrative and the visual and as a summation of Rossetti's
      yearning for ideal beauty. The history of its composi-
      tion, its subject matter, and its provenance are also
      discussed.

895. Gore, St. John. "Buscot Park: The English Pictures."
      Connoisseur 161 (1966): 4-6.

      Discusses, among other pictures on display at Buscot
      Park, Rossetti's *Venus Verticordia*, purchased by the
      first Lord Farringdon.

896. Peterson, Carl A. "*The Iliad*, George Merdith's 'Cas-
      sandra,' and D.G. Rossetti's 'Cassandra Drawing.'"
      Texas Studies in Language and Literature 7 (1966):
      329-337.

      Rossetti's surprising choice of a classical subject,
      Cassandra, for his 1861 drawing stems from his commit-
      ment to illustrate Meredith's new poem. But Rossetti
      also incorporated elements from the *Iliad*, so that the
      composite scene becomes an example of the artist's use
      of allegory and of "fundamental brainwork."

897. Peterson, Carl A. "Rossetti and the Sphinx." *Apollo*
      85 (1967): 48-53.

      Reproduces and compares Rossetti's two drawings of

the Sphinx legend, both entitled *The Question*.   They
show that the artist borrowed heavily from Ingres'
Oedipe et le Sphinx at the Louvre, a fact which he was
at pains to conceal because of inveterate pride in his
own "originality."

898.   Davis, Frank.   "Porcelein from East and West." *Country
       Life* 144 (1968): 152-153.

       Notes recent sales at Christie's, including an 1873
       drawing of Janey Morris by Rossetti, which sold for
       sixteen guineas in 1882 and now fetched 1,600 guineas.

899.   Reynolds, Graham.   "The Pre-Raphaelites and Their Circle."
       Apollo 93 (1971): 494-501.

       Describes an exhibition at the Fermoy Art Gallery, one
       which testifies once again to the pre-eminent influence
       of Rossetti.   His oil painting *A Vision of Fiammetta*
       began as an illustration of Browning's "Pippa Passes."

900.   Davis, Frank.   "A Twice-Gifted Visionary." *Country Life*
       152 (1972): 1210-1211.

       Notes the recent sale of Rossetti's small 1861 *Hanging
       the Mistletoe* for £13,500.

901.   Grieve, Alastair Ian.   *The Art of Dante Gabriel Rossetti:
       The Pre-Raphaelite Period, 1848-1850*.   Hingham: Real
       World Publications, 1973.   31 pp.

       Describes the genesis and achievement of two paintings,
       The Girlhood of Mary Virgin and *Ecce Ancilla Domini!*
       Twenty-nine black-and-white illustrations augment the
       text.

902.   Tyzack, Charles R.   "*King Arthur's Tomb*: The Versions of
       D.G. Rossetti and William Morris Compared." *Trivium*
       8 (1973): 127-132.

       Compares Rossetti's painting and Morris' poem, finding
       that the external conflict of the former (passion vs.
       repentance) has been interiorized by Morris.   Thus
       Guinevere embodies Victorian dilemmas about sexual guilt.

903.   Agosta, Lucien.   "La Pia de' Tolomei." *Library Chronicle
       of the University of Texas* n.s. 8 (1974): 39-40.

       Reproduces and describes a chalk drawing of *La Pia*

now owned by the University of Texas and not catalogued
by W.D. Paden (see item 891). The history of its
ownership is traced.

904. Johnson, Ronald W. "Dante Rossetti's *Beata Beatrix* and
the *New Life*." *Art Bulletin* 57 (1975): 548-558.

Offers a thorough discussion of Rossetti's painting
from its inception in the mid-1850s until its completion in 1870. Separate sections are devoted to:
related works (*Delia, St. Cecilia*); source material in
the *Vita Nuova*; the transfiguration theme and its associated red color symbolism; the use of the city of
Florence to represent blessedness; numerical and as-
tronomical symbolism; and the salvation of the lover
coming from his spiritual marriage.

905. Grieve, Alastair Ian. *The Art of Dante Gabriel Rossetti*.
Norwich: Real World Publications, 1976. 58 pp.

Offers--despite its title--a lengthy treatment of only
one Rossetti painting, *Found*. The remainder of the book
discusses the use of "modern-life subjects" by eleven
other Pre-Raphaelite artists, including Whistler [!].
See also item 906.

906. Oberhausen, Judy. "Rossetti's *Found*." *Delaware Art
Museum Occasional Papers No. 1*. Wilmington: Delaware
Art Museum, 1976. 55 pp.

Includes twenty-seven black-and-white reproductions of
designs and versions of Rossetti's painting, which is
in the Delaware Art Museum. The monograph investigates
Rossetti's literary and artistic sources, and gives a
chronology of the artist's work on the painting from
its initial sketch and iconography in 1853 to its (un-
finished) state at Rossetti's death in 1882. Rossetti
could not finish it, concludes the author, because the
work was an exercise and thus a burden rather than a
challenge.

907. Lourie, Margaret A. "The Embodiment of Dreams: William
Morris' 'Blue Closet' Group." *Victorian Poetry* 15
(1977): 193-206.

Concentrates on Morris' poems but also offers a close
analysis of the Rossetti watercolor by the same name; it
serves as a commentary on the poems.

908. Surtees, Virginia. "Portrait Head of Jane Morris."
      Philadelphia Museum Bulletin 73 (1977): 12-17.

      Describes an 1865 chalk drawing given to the museum
      in 1873 by an anonymous benefactor. Its background and
      provenance, as well as Rossetti's relation to the sub-
      ject, are also noted. Four black-and-white illustrations.

909. Nochlin, Linda. "Lost and *Found*: Once More the Fallen
      Woman." *Art Bulletin* 60 (1978): 139-153.

      Examines Rossetti's social-realist painting in the
      light of a whole range of nineteenth-century attempts
      to portray the fallen woman. Especially important is
      Hunt's *The Awakening Conscience*, which grows out of a
      similar experience but contradicts Rossetti's emphasis
      on damnation and despair. The author contends that
      Rossetti's works, unlike those by Blake or Paul Klee,
      do not show structural analogies between verse and
      painting. He is not a "poetic painter" but rather a
      literary illustrator like his contemporaries. *Found* is
      "a palimpsest of motifs and motivations," including
      Rossetti's own sense of being fallen.

910. O'Malley, Celia. "The Victorian Ideal." *Connoisseur*
      198 (1978): 256.

      Describes an exhibition at the Roy Miles Gallery in
      which Rossetti's *Penelope* "steals the show." The
      luxuriance, sensuality, and intense focus of this paint-
      ing give it its appeal.

911. Smith, Sarah Phelps. "Dante Gabriel Rossetti's 'Lady
      Lilith' and the Language of Flowers." *Arts Magazine*
      53, no. 6 (February 1979): 142-145.

      Sees Rossetti's flowers as symbolic objects that com-
      ment on the paintings themselves. In *Lady Lilith* the
      poppy suggests sleep and death; the roses suggest pas-
      sion (white because of the legend that roses only turned
      red after Eve kissed them); the foxglove suggests insin-
      cerity; and the daisies suggest innocence (Lilith's dis-
      guise). The painting is also compared to other works
      by Rossetti, such as *Sibylla Palmifera*, and to paintings
      by other artists, such as Whistler's *Little White Girl*.

See also items 73, 76, 78, 84-117, 151, 232, 235, 295, 530,
658, 663, 665, 669, 673, 683, 684, 707, 720, 727, 730, 737,

741, 742, 755, 764, 767, 768, 783, 786, 794, 802, 804, 827, 830, 832, 847, 848, 861, 864, 867, 915, 923, 924, 936, 943, 944, 946, 984, 1002, 1010, 1018, 1056, 1071, 1079, 1083, 1091, and 1099.

SECTION C: STUDIES OF ROSSETTI'S SOURCES AND INFLUENCES--ART

Source and influence studies restricted to a single painting or drawing will be found in Section B. This section includes studies of influences on Rossetti and also studies of his influence on others.

912. Swinburne, Louis J. *Rossetti and the Pre-Raphaelites*. New Haven: [privately printed], 1885. 42 pp.

Sees the P.R.B. as influenced by *quattrocentisti* art and by the Oxford Movement. Rossetti rejected eighteenth-century dogmatism and materialism. His art is a Romantic revolt on behalf of his own "wisdom of beauty," and his place in the history of art will be high. Reprinted from *New Englander and Yale Review* (1885).

913. Michel, André. "Le Préraphaélisme." *Histoire de l'art*. Vol. 8 Paris: Colin, [1890], pp. 376-391.

Sees Fuseli and Blake as precursors of the P.R.B. and the Oxford Movement as its religious counterpart. Rossetti's enigmatic women have a very modern air about them despite their medieval settings.

914. La Sizeranne, Robert de. "The Origins of Pre-Raphaelism." *English Contemporary Art*. Translated by H. Poynter. London: Constable, 1898, pp. 17-83.

Explains the state of English art in the 1840s and the rejuvenation given to it by the Pre-Raphaelites, who could be defined by their devotion to uncompromising truth and by Rossetti's archaicism and symbolism. Offers brief thumbnail sketches of the P.R.B.'s predecessors.

915. Parkes, Kineton. "Ruskin and Pre-Raphaelitism." *New Century Review* 7 (1900): 133-143.

Claims that *Modern Painters* created the climate of opinion which gave rise to Pre-Raphaelitism and that

Ruskin's defense saved it--"without Mr. Ruskin there
would not have been a Pre-Raphaelite movement." The
Pre-Raphaelites repaid the critic by exemplifying his
principles. Rossetti's *Dante's Dream* fulfills Ruskin's
requirements that a work be truthful, imaginative, and
beautiful.

916. Sturgis, Russell. "The Pre-Raphaelites and Their In-
      fluence." *Independent* 52 (1900): 181-183, 246-249.

      Finds in the Pre-Raphaelites a twofold interest:
      their magnetic personalities, and their influence on
      British art. They separated British art from continental
      developments by emphasizing vivid and explicit detail.
      In these respects Rossetti is the least Pre-Raphaelite
      of the original Brothers.

917. Mauclair, Camille. "The Influence of the Pre-Raphaelites
      in France." *Artist* 32 (1901): 169-180.

      Traces the influence of the P.R.B. and especially
      Rossetti on a host of French painters such as Moreau,
      Chassériau, Chenavard, and others. By means of this
      influence French and English idealistic art came into
      closer contact.

918. Muther, Richard. "Rossetti, Burne-Jones, und Watts."
      Neue Deutsche Rundschau 13 (1902): 859-881.

      The influence of Poe and Dante is said to be parti-
      cularly important in appreciating the beauty of the
      women in Rossetti's later paintings. His career is
      summarized with special reference to the Catholic ele-
      ments in his origins and his subjects. Rossetti's
      treatment of pairs of lovers (e.g. Launcelot-Guinevere,
      Paolo-Francesca) shows his recognition of the erotic
      dimension in human experience.

919. Whiting, Mary B. *"Beata Beatrix."* *Temple Bar* 126
      (1902): 270-282.

      Despite the limited concern implied by its title,
      this article lists all pictures in which Rossetti treat-
      ed Dantean materials. Dante's influence is also des-
      cribed, both in terms of Rossetti's life (the relation-
      ship with Lizzie Siddal) and in terms of the subject
      matter for Rossetti's art.

920. Zueblin, Rho Fisk. "Pre-Raphaelites: The Beginnings of
      the Arts and Crafts Movement." *Chautauquan* 36 (1902):
      57-61.

      Ties aestheticism to Ruskinian social idealism and
      finds the origin of both in the Pre-Raphaelites. True
      Pre-Raphaelitism means color, detail, and originality,
      and Rossetti was able to graft this creed to the Roman-
      tic temper.

921. Shaw, Wilfred B. "Rossetti and Botticelli: A Comparison
      of Ideals and Art." *Craftsman* 9 (1905): 341-356.

      Sees a resemblance between the two artists in terms of
      their mysticism, their technique, their devotion to
      feminine beauty, and their love of "odd, gay trappings."
      Both were expressionists, and their work is pervaded by
      a quiet melancholy. Both led revolutions in the art of
      their time and both were supplanted by artists of greater
      brilliance.

922. Muther, Richard. "The New Realism in England." *The
      History of Modern Painting*. Revised Edition. Vol. 3.
      New York: Dutton, 1907, pp. 151-209.

      Sees the original P.R.B. as aligned by sympathy in aim
      with Courbet and Millet in France--but Rossetti is aligned
      with neither group. Rather he was a precursor of the
      Impressionists, a lyricist of color whose best works
      were the late oils damned by others as lurid and overly
      remote. [Note: this article contains several errors of
      fact.]

923. Galimberti, Alice. *Il Medioevo Italiano nell'arte pre-
      raffaelita*. Rome: Direzione della Nuova Antologica,
      1922. 16 pp.

      Discusses the treatment by the P.R.B. of medieval
      Italian subjects. Rossetti's absorption in Dantean
      materials can be seen in *Dante's Dream*, *Beata Beatrix*,
      La Donna della Finestra and other works. *Mnemosyne*,
      Venus Verticordia, *La Ghirlandata* and others show how
      steeped he was in the style and expression of the early
      masters. Rossetti *is* Italianate--but this is a strength,
      not a weakness. Reprinted from *Nuova Antologica* (1922).

924. Wethered, Newton. "Pre-Raphaelitism and the Renaissance."
      From Giotto to John: The Development of Painting.
      London: Methuen, 1926, pp. 38-54.

Describes the Pre-Raphaelites as attracted to medieval
art by its simplicity, its methods, and its instinct for
color. Two Renaissance developments--the preference for
oil and the adaptation of paganism--were also incorporated

925. Waldmann, Emil. "Die Schule der Prärafaeliten." *Englisch*
      Malerei. Breslau: Hirt, 1927, pp. 86-98.

      Sees Rossetti as a painter whose work was inspired by
      Dantean subjects. He was also the last flowering of
      Romanticism.

926. Laver, James. "Rossetti and the Influence of Japan."
      Whistler. London: Faber and Faber, 1930, pp. 91-116.

      Believes Rossetti was quite similar to his contempo-
      raries like Whistler: he saw art as a vessel for poetic
      emotions. Denies that Whistler was much influenced by
      their friendship, since the two artists differed so
      profoundly on the merits of French Impressionism.

927. Neumeyer, Alfred. "Die Präraffaelitische Malerei im
      Rahmen der Kunstgeschichte des 19. Jahrhunderts."
      Deutsche Vierteljahrschrift für Literaturwissenschaft
      und Geistesgeschichte 11 (1933): 67-77.

      Claims for the P.R.B. an important place in art history
      as leaders of the reaction against realism and of the
      "cult of sensations"--a cult which was to produce artists
      like Beardsley. Rossetti's reaction to French clas-
      sicism, for example, illustrates the intentions of the
      young artists.

928. Gray, Nicolette. *Rossetti, Dante, and Ourselves*. London:
      Faber, 1947. 55 pp.

      Attempts to show how Rossetti's interpretation of Dante
      colors our own. Rossetti used literary figures pre-
      cisely because he did *not* want to tell a story. Instead
      he wanted to pictorialize inner landscapes, but to do so
      in as objective a way as possible. Dante idealizes
      Beatrice on the way to a higher reality, but for Rossetti
      the present moment is all we know and all we need to know.
      Reprinted 1974.

929. Steegman, John. "The Pre-Raphaelite Brotherhood." *Con-*
      sort of Taste 1830-1870. London: Sidgwick and Jackson,
      1950, pp. 154-179.

Sees the P.R.B., not as a successful revolution, but
rather as the natural outgrowth of earlier trends and
at the same time a temporary diversion from those trends.
Rossetti was responsible for its medievalism, which was
really a protest against the banality of the Academy.

930. Schmutzler, Robert. "The English Origins of Art
      Nouveau." *Architectural Review* 117 (1955): 109-116.

Lists Rossetti as among the three principal sources,
along with Blake and Japanese art. Rossetti's importance
is owing both to his own design work and to his propa-
gation of Blake.

931. Gállego, Julián. "P.R.B. (Los PreRafaelistas)." *Revista
      de ideas esteticos* 17 (1959): 309-327.

Traces the origin of the P.R.B. to its roots in English
painting, especially visionaries like Blake, Fuseli, and
John Martin. The German Nazarenes also played a role.
Rossetti was the most passionate, the most expansive
painter of the group. He contributed to the inward tendencies of British art, a counterbalance to Hunt's ra-
tionalistic naturalism.

932. Lethève, Jacques. "La Connaissance des peintres pré-
      raphaélites anglais en France (1855-1900)." *Gazette
      des Beaux-Arts*, période 6, 53 (1959): 315-327.

Summarizes the knowledge and reputation of the Pre-
Raphaelites in France during the last half of the nineteenth century. For most French critics the movement
was an imitation of Botticelli and the early Italians,
i.e. a deliberate primitivism. Rossetti, Millais, and
Burne-Jones attracted the most attention.

933. Gere, J[ohn] A. "Alexander Munro's 'Paolo and Fran-
      cesca.'" *Burlington Magazine* 105 (1963): 508-510.

Shows how the subject for this sculpture was probably
suggested to Munro by Rossetti, whose sketches may
even have provided the direct stimulus for Munro's work.

934. Hoffman, Edith. "Some Sources for Munch's Symbolism."
      Apollo 81 (1965): 87-93.

Shows that Edvard Munch's *Madonna*, *Eva Mudocci*, and
The Dance of Life owe much to Rossetti's *Beata Beatrix*,

Monna Vanna, and *The Bower Meadow*, respectively. It is not clear how Munch knew Rossetti's work.

935. Grieve, Alastair. "The Pre-Raphaelite Brotherhood and the Anglican High Church." *Burlington Magazine* 111 (1969): 294-295.

Demonstrates that the P.R.B. was actively interested in the Tractarian controversy. Rossetti's biblical scenes and his dramatization of a section from Keble's *The Christian Year* are examples.

936. Dorment, Richard. "Venice, the Night, and the Haunted Woman." *Arts Magazine* 45, no. 5 (March 1971): 42-45.

Shows how Whistler and Rossetti shared a fascination --almost a fetish--for abundant red hair. Courbet's *Portrait of Jo* (Whistler's mistress) is remarkably like Rossetti's *Lady Lilith*.

937. Grieve, Alastair. "Whistler and the Pre-Raphaelites." *Art Quarterly* 34 (1971): 220-223.

Traces the influence of Rossetti and Millais on Whistler. Both Rossetti and Whistler were aesthetes and both placed formal qualities over subject matter. The friendship between the two was long and deep, and they shared interests in Far Eastern art and the use of color (Rossetti being the first in either case).

938. Lucie-Smith, Edward. "Symbolist Currents in England." *Symbolist Art*. New York: Praeger, 1972, pp. 33-50.

Corrects the view of the Pre-Raphaelites as insular. Rather they were part of the idealistic spirit of the age. Rossetti is a radical painter (as shown by five plates) and his later, more symbolist works should be revaluated.

939. Christian, J[ohn]. "Early German Sources for Pre-Raphaelite Designs." *Art Quarterly* 36 (1973): 56-83.

Explains the Pre-Raphaelite use of German sources. Rossetti, for example, borrowed from Albrecht Dürer several times during the 1850s, largely at the instigation of Ruskin and William Bell Scott. His favorite was Dürer's series of woodcuts entitled *The Birth of the Virgin*.

940.   Christian, J[ohn]. "Sources for Burne-Jones's Von Bork
       Designs." *Burlington Magazine* 115 (1973): 103-109.

       Traces the paintings to Wilhelm Meinhold's *Sidonia von
       Bork, die Klosterhexe* (1847), about which Rossetti was
       very enthusiastic. This book gave a dark, menacing di-
       mension to feminine beauty. Parallel themes in Rossetti's
       work and Burne-Jones's are traced also. Rossetti and
       his enthusiasms created the climate within which the
       younger artist worked.

941.   Grieve, Alastair. "Rossetti's Illustrations to Poe."
       Apollo 97 (1973): 142-145.

       Notes and reproduces the five drawings which Rossetti
       made in the late 1840s to illustrate poems by Poe. Poe's
       themes--lovers parted by death, lost hope, ghostly echoes
       from the past--appealed to Rossetti, as did his weird and
       macabre imagery.

942.   Pittman, Philip M. "Blake, Rossetti, and the Genesis of
       the Pre-Raphaelite Idea." *Bulletin of the West Vir-
       ginia Association of College English Teachers* 2
       (1975): 1-17.

       Focuses on the Blake notebook which Rossetti bought in
       1847, contending that in it Rossetti found material
       which served as the prolegomenon for the P.R.B. The
       notebook contained more than just epigrams and jeers
       at Reynolds and the Royal Academy. Rossetti also found
       in it praise for the early Florentine painters, who were
       devotional and who sought to idealize rather than to be
       popular. Blake encouraged Rossetti's deepest instinct:
       to look within.

943.   Bentley, D.M.R. "The Pre-Raphaelites and the Oxford
       Movement." *Dalhousie Review* 57 (1977): 525-539.

       Argues for a deep interest in and close connection to
       the Oxford Movement on the part of the young Pre-
       Raphaelites, including Rossetti. There are many "Anglo-
       Catholic" details in works like *The Girlhood of Mary
       Virgin*.

944.   Bentley, D.M.R. "Rossetti and the *Hypnerotomachia
       Poliphili*." *English Language Notes* 14 (1977): 279-283.

       Demonstrates how a fifteenth-century incunabulum was

a source for Rossetti's watercolor *Arthur's Tomb* and
perhaps for other paintings and poems as well.

945. Browne, Max. "A Source for Rossetti: A Painting by Von
     Holst." *Burlington Magazine* 120 (1978): 88-92.

     Traces the influence on Rossetti's works of the painter
     Theodore Von Holst, whose *The Fortune Teller* (1840) was
     a special favorite.

946. Edelstein, T.J. "The Yellow-Haired Fiend." *Library
     Chronicle* [University of Pennsylvania] 43 (1979):
     180-193.

     Finds similarities between Rossetti's conception of
     women and the seductive, immoral heroines of Victorian
     sensation novels. Temptresses like *Lady Lilith* strongly
     resemble such golden-haired beauties as Helen Talboys
     in M.E. Braddon's *Lady Audley's Secret*.

947. Lindquist-Cock, Elizabeth. "Stillman, Rossetti, and
     Ruskin: The Struggle Between Nature and Art." *History
     of Photography* 3 (1979): 1-14.

     Focuses on W.J. Stillman as a photographer, relating
     his early photographs to his familiarity with and ac-
     ceptance of Pre-Raphaelite truth-to-nature principles.
     In the 1870s, after he had married Rossetti's model
     Marie Spartali, Stillman was influenced by Rossetti's
     darkly prophetic vision and freed himself from material-
     ism.

See also items 82, 87, 145, 202, 303, 304, 418, 658, 664, 673,
677, 678, 692, 717, 727, 729, 733, 818, 840, 870, 877, 892,
896, 897, 899, 904, 909, 967, 995, 996, 1003, 1005, 1009,
1022, 1023, 1046, 1054, 1055, 1060, 1061, 1065, 1068, 1072,
1079, 1084, 1097, and 1098.

SECTION D: ROSSETTI AS DESIGNER

This section includes discussions of Rossetti's activities as
book illustrator, mural painter, and designer of furniture,
book bindings, picture frames, and stained glass windows.
While his productivity in these areas was small, it was in
many cases influential.

948. Layard, George S. "Rossetti." *Tennyson and His Pre-Raphaelite Illustrators: A Book about a Book*. London: Stock, 1894, pp. 49-66.

Discusses Rossetti's contributions to the 1857 Moxon edition of Tennyson. The publisher had many difficulties owing to Rossetti's fastidious and dilatory habits, while Rossetti was troubled by incompetent wood engravers. The artist "Rossetti-ized" Tennyson, emphasizing sensuality and subordinating idealism. Rossetti consciously ignored the text, but produced fine work nonetheless. Reprinted 1969; see also item 181.

949. Pennell, Joseph. "A Golden Decade in English Art." *Savoy* 1 (1896): 112-124.

Sees the late 1850s and early 1860s as the golden decade of English book illustration. Rossetti's contributions to the Moxon Tennyson highlight his skill, although he was wrong to prefer Linton to the Dalziel brothers as engravers. See also item 181.

950. White, Gleeson. *English Illustration: "The Sixties," 1855-1870*. Westminster: Constable, 1897. 204 pp.

Speaks at various points about Rossetti's illustrations for his sister and for the Moxon Tennyson, about his techniques, and about his influences on subsequent illustrators (which the author judges to be enormous). Reprinted 1970.

951. Seddon, John P. *King Rene's Honeymoon Cabinet*. London: Batsford, 1898. 16 pp.

The Seddon-designed cabinet was decorated by various P.R.B. members. Two panels--"Music" and "Gardening"-- were contributed by Rossetti and are reproduced here.

952. Cary, Elisabeth L[uther]. "Rossetti as Illustrator." *Lamp* [*Bookbuyer*] n.s. 27 (1903): 321-328.

Denies that Rossetti tried to overpower any text he chose to illustrate (see item 948). Rather he tried to capture the spirit of his author while granting himself interpretive freedom, a method similar to the one he used for translations. Eight black-and-white illustrations.

953. Hunt, William Holman. *The Oxford Union Society*. London:
      Oxford University Press, 1906. 15 pp.

      A collection of photographs of the murals done by the
      Pre-Raphaelites during the "Jovial Campaign" of 1857.
      The author's introduction describes how Rossetti was
      engaged to do the frescoes and how he then attracted
      Morris and Burne-Jones. Rossetti's work, *Sir Launcelot's
      Vision of the Sangrael*, is photographed.

954. Hardie, Martin. "The Moxon Tennyson: 1857." *Book Lover*
      7 (1907): 45-51.

      Notes the fiftieth anniversary of the publication of
      this volume, a herald of the books of the 1860s. Ros-
      setti is notable for giving us the spirit of the text
      rather than illustrating it. Tennyson was puzzled.

955. Smyser, William E. "Romanticism in Tennyson and His
      Pre-Raphaelite Illustrators." *North American Review*
      192 (1910): 504-515.

      Sees Rossetti as the creator of illustrations both
      "original" and "occult," yet locates him in the natural-
      istic tradition. The illustrations "interpret, and
      imaginatively enrich" Tennyson's poetry.

956. Cary, Elisabeth L[uther]. "Dante Gabriel Rossetti,
      Illustrator." *Print Collector's Quarterly* 5 (1915):
      317-339.

      Reproduces and discusses Rossetti's illustrations of
      scenes from literature, which ranged from Dante and
      Shakespeare through Coleridge and Poe to contemporaries
      like Tennyson and Browning. As an illustrator Rossetti
      was imaginative and painstaking, but his ignorance of
      engraving technique led to differences with his engravers
      and thus to hindrances in his work. See item 181.

957. Wroot, Herbert E. "Pre-Raphaelite Windows at Bradford."
      Studio 72 (1917): 69-73.

      Describes the thirteen panels for his music room which
      Walter Dunlop commissioned from Morris and Company. The
      fourth, *Sir Tristram Drinks a Love-Philtre with Isoude*,
      was by Rossetti and is pictured. The design is praise-
      worthy.

958. Sparke, Archibald. "Pre-Raphaelite Stained Glass."
     Notes & Queries, 12th series, 4 (1918): 337.

     Offers a preliminary list of stained glass done by
     the P.R.B., including Rossetti. This list is augmented
     in later issues of the same journal (March and April
     1919). The most complete list is item 966.

959. Hardie, Martin. "Rossetti, Gabriel Charles Dante."
     Catalogue of Modern Wood Engravings. London: H.M.S.O.,
     1919, pp. 322-323, 409.

     Catalogues and describes wood engravings by Rossetti
     in the Victoria and Albert Museum. Eight illustrations
     for three books and two magazine articles are included.

960. Reid, Forrest. "The Moxon Tennyson" and "The Pre-
     Raphaelite Group." *Illustrators of the Sixties*.
     London: Faber and Gwyer, 1928, pp. 30-107.

     Judges Rossetti as a great designer, despite his
     meager output. Summarizes the difficulties Rossetti
     experienced with his engravers (see item 181).

961. [Anonymous]. "Eighty Years After." *Architectural
     Review* 79 (1936): 247-250.

     Describes the relighting of the newly refurbished
     Oxford Union murals and their completion eighty years
     before by the Pre-Raphaelites. Uses quotations from
     Derek Patmore and J.W. Mackail.

962. Patmore, Derek. "Pre-Raphaelites Restored: The Wall
     Paintings in the Oxford Union Library." *Studio* 111
     (1936): 324-325.

     Recounts the successful effort led by Sir William
     Rothenstein to restore the Oxford Union murals, of
     which Rossetti's *Launcelot's Vision of the Sangrael*
     is the best.

963. James, Philip B. *English Book Illustration, 1800-1900*.
     London: Penguin, 1947. 72 pp.

     Describes both the history and the artistic achieve-
     ment of Victorian book illustrators. Rossetti is re-
     presented by two drawings. He withdrew from book
     illustration because he would not or could not conform

to its technical requirements, despite his early success-
es in the field.

964. Friedman, Albert B. "English Illustrators of the 1860s."
      More Books 23 (1948): 372-380.

      Shows how every British artist of the period drew on
      wood at one time or another. But the separation of
      artist and engraver--e.g. Rossetti and the Dalziel
      brothers on the Moxon Tennyson--meant that the former
      almost always worked in ignorance of the requirements
      of the latter. Rossetti was especially influential on
      Arthur Hughes.

965. Friedman, Albert B. "The Tennyson of 1857." *More Books*
      23 (1948): 15-22.

      Chronicles Moxon's effort to put out his illustrated
      Tennyson. Rossetti was both the highest-paid and the
      most troublesome contributor. The artist was slow and
      complained bitterly about the Dalziel brothers (see
      item 181). But his own techniques for drawing and his
      love of minutiae were more responsible than he ever
      cared to admit. Rossetti's illustrations, however in-
      fluential, were poorly done.

966. Sewter, A.C. "D.G. Rossetti's Designs for Stained Glass."
      Journal of the British Society of Master Glass-Painters
      13 (1960-61): 419-424.

      Gives a table with a chronological history of all of
      Rossetti's stained-glass work in the years 1861-1864.
      Includes title, description, and place and date of
      execution.

967. Grieve, Alastair. "A Notice on Illustrations to Charles
      Kingsley's 'The Saint's Tragedy' by Three Pre-
      Raphaelite Artists." *Burlington Magazine* 111 (1969):
      290-293.

      The illustrations done for this volume include three
      hitherto-unidentified sketches by Rossetti, each of
      which depicts a scene from the life of St. Elizabeth of
      Hungary.

968. Barber, Giles. "Rossetti, Ricketts, and Some English
      Publishers' Bookbindings of the Nineties." *The
      Library*, 5th series, 25 (1970): 314-330.

Studies Art Nouveau bookbinding, which has its forerunner in Rossetti, who designed the bindings for his
own books and for Swinburne, Hake, Forman, his brother,
and his sisters. Rossetti's bindings are discussed in
the light of his intentions as revealed by his letters.
Seven full-page photographs illustrate the text. A
follow-up letter on p. 173 of the same volume is also
relevant.

969. Watkinson, Raymond. *Pre-Raphaelite Art and Design*.
Greenwich, Conn.: New York Graphic Society, 1970.
208 pp.

Begins with separate chapters on Rossetti, Brown,
Hunt, and Millais, then offers a chronological survey
of the Brotherhood's activities. Considers Rossetti
as an artist and as a graphic designer, judging that
Rossetti exercised enormous influence on the latter
field, especially through the Moxon Tennyson. Summarizes
Rossetti's relationship with Morris and Burne-Jones,
distinguishing between Rossetti's aestheticism and
Morris's social commitment.

970. Verey, David. "Two Early Churches by Bodley." *Country
Life* 149 (1971): 1246-1249.

Describes George Bodley's All Saints Church, Selsey,
which contained two angel medallions and two stained-
glass windows by Rossetti. The windows, illustrating
the Visitation and the Sermon on the Mount, have a
"decidedly secular air."

971. Jervis, Simon. "Gothic at No. 95 Piccadilly: New Light
on the Taste of John Jones." *Apollo* 95 (1972): 206-
211.

Attributes to Rossetti two portraits, entitled *Flos*
and *Fructus*, on the end roundels of a bookcase designed
by Charles Foster Hayward, who was probably introduced
to Rossetti by John Seddon.

972. Ovenden, Graham. *Pre-Raphaelite Photography*. New York:
St. Martin's Press, 1972. 111 pp.

Includes, among others, twenty-four plates of Rossetti's
treatments and studies of Janey Morris.

973. Surtees, Virginia. *"The Early Italian Poets* by D.G.
      Rossetti with His Illustrations." *Princeton Uni-
      versity Library Chronicle* 33 (1972): 230-231.

      Reproduces and describes six illustrations which Ros-
      setti drew in one of his copies of his *Early Italian
      Poets,* plus his rejected design for the title page.

974. Allentuck, Marcia. "New Light on Rossetti and the
      Moxon Tennyson." *Apollo* 97 (1973): 176.

      Reproduces the proof of Rossetti's *Sir Galahad* design
      for the Moxon Tennyson. A comparison of the proof with
      the finished product will enable the viewer to decide if
      his design was as simple as Rossetti claimed or as
      elaborate as his engravers charged (see item 181).

975. Grieve, Alastair. "The Applied Art of D.G. Rossetti--
      1. His Picture Frames." *Burlington Magazine* 115
      (1973): 16-24.

      Demonstrates the care Rossetti gave to the design of
      his picture frames. He emphasized decorative effect,
      flatness, and the use of inscription and symbol. Spe-
      cific types of frames are described and related to the
      pictures they accompany. Rossetti meant his works to
      be seen as aesthetic wholes: the alleged "gloom" of
      the later works, for example, comes from seeing them
      without their balancing frames.

976. Grieve, Alastair. "Rossetti's Applied Art Designs--
      2. Book Bindings." *Burlington Magazine* 115 (1973):
      79-83.

      Denies the attribution of two designs to Rossetti made
      by Barber (item 968). Rossetti can be praised for his
      skill in uniting front and back spine, for his sensi-
      tive use of color, and for his artistic restraint.

977. Whitworth, F. "A Guinevere from the Barn." *Country
      Life* 156 (1974): 999.

      Assigns to Rossetti a stained-glass roundel of Queen
      Guinevere recently found in Surrey.

978. Cromey-Hawke, N. "William Morris and Victorian Painted
      Furniture." *Connoisseur* 191 (1976): 32-43.

      Discusses, among other topics, Rossetti's contributions

to Victorian painted furniture, including his door panels
for the settle at Red Lion Square, his chairs and table
for William Morris, and his bookcase panel for Colonel
Cock's mansion.

979. [Anonymous]. *Pre-Raphaelite Illustrations from Moxon's
      Tennyson by Dante Gabriel Rossetti, John Everett
      Millais, William Holman Hunt.* London: Academy Editions,
      1978. [28 pp.]

      Consists of the thirty black-and-white illustrations
      by the Pre-Raphaelites which appeared among the fifty-
      five illustrations in the Moxon Tennyson. Rossetti is
      represented by five.

See also items 88, 116, 181, 229, 733, 767, 930, 1004, and
1063.

Studies of Rossetti
as a Poet-Painter

This section includes studies which consider both aspects of Rossetti's work--he is viewed not just as poet and not just as painter but as poet-painter.

980.　Gosse, Edmund. "Dante Gabriel Rossetti." *Century Magazine* 24 (1882): 718-725.

　　　Pays tribute to Rossetti as a magnetic "point of fire" who stirred the imagination and stimulated creativity in others. He was characterized by a genuine fleshly mysticism, although at times his preference for the medieval and the spiritual led to the quality Rossetti abhorred most: quaintness. His important place in English intellectual history is assured.

981.　Placci, Carlo. "Dante Gabriele Rossetti." *La Rassegna Nazionale* 9 (1882): 427-446.

　　　Written by a native Italian to acquaint an Italian audience with the life and artistic significance of Rossetti, both in painting and in poetry. Special emphasis is placed on Rossetti's skills as an interpreter of Italian literature and culture--his translations, for example, can be highly praised.

982.　Tirebuck, William Edwards. *Dante Gabriel Rossetti, His Work and Influence.* London: Stock, 1882. 63 pp.

　　　Begins the tradition of judging Rossetti as foremost a transplanted Italian, the living contradiction to British common sense. As an artist in either medium he is colorful, compact, subtle, unified. On the negative side, he is also foreign, eccentric, and mannered.

983.　Myers, Frederick W.H. "Rossetti and the Religion of Beauty." *Essays: Modern.* London: Macmillan, 1883, pp. 312-334.

　　　Tries to reconcile Rossetti's worship of beauty with traditional religious attitudes. Rossetti's Love can be transmuted into an exaltation of the mystic element in men, i.e. a quietistic devotion to Platonic ideals. His fame signals the beginning of the democratic ideal in art--the dominance of the man of culture. Reprinted from *Cornhill Magazine* (1883).

984.　Quilter, Harry. "The Art of Rossetti." *Contemporary Review* 43 (1883): 190-203.

Explains the gloom of Rossetti's art by the circumstances of his upbringing and by his "alien" spirit. All of his work is colored by the dominant theme, "Love baffled by Death." He is at his best when he dramatizes that theme in a simple story, at his worst when he intellectualizes or spiritualizes it. A picture like *Beata Beatrix* or a poem like "Jenny" allows us to see his grasp of the beautiful and his willingness to confront painful themes.

985. Ward, Julius H. "Rossetti in Poetry and Art." *Church Review* 41 (1883): 371-379.

Reviews seven recent books and articles on Rossetti and finds that his new fame is quite justified. Rossetti illustrates what should be the modern sphere of Christian art, i.e. the treatment of sacred objects as if they were real life. He is fertile, chaste, imaginative, and inspirational--a "transcendent genius."

986. Sharp, William. "The Rossettis." *Fortnightly Review* 45 (1886): 414-429.

Surveys the life and work of Gabriele Rossetti and each of his four children. Dante Gabriel as a poet is too literary, too rarified, for the average taste, but his strengths are power, imagination, and insight. As a painter he is a weak draughtsman but a splendid colorist.

987. Shields, Frederic. "Some Notes on Dante Gabriel Rossetti." *Century Guild Hobby Horse* 1 (1886): 140-154.

Comments on the 1883 Royal Academy exhibition, describes the general tendencies of Rossetti's work, and reprints a draft of Rossetti's sonnet on Blake which the poet had given to the author.

988. Nicholson, Peter Walker. *Dante Gabriel Rossetti, Poet and Painter*. The Round Table Series, vol. 6. Edited by H. Baildon. Edinburgh: Brown, 1887. 36 pp.

Offers a portrait of Rossetti as a man alienated from his age and dedicated to a single vision, so that his poetry has the color, force, and detail of painting and his painting has the subtlety, expression, and symbolism of poetry. His work has a tragic depth despite its narrow focus. His introspection and pity give him an ethical dimension that is often overlooked.

989. Rossetti, William Michael. *Dante Gabriel Rossetti as Designer and Writer*. London: Cassell, 1889. 302 pp.

Offers an extensive year-by-year chronology of Rossetti's work as a painter-poet. Also includes a prose paraphrase of "The House of Life" by the editor, one which reveals William Michael's tact and his reluctance to reveal intimate biographical details. Based on *Art Journal* articles (1884); reprinted 1979.

990. La Sizeranne, Robert de. "Rose +Croix, Préraphaélites et esthètes--la reconnaissance esthétique des deux côtés de la manche." *Le Correspondent* 166 (1892): 1127-1140.

Finds connections between Rosicrucian principles and the P.R.B., extending from resemblances in doctrine to resemblances in initials (R + C vs. P R B). Watts and Burne-Jones exhibit the greatest similarities, but Rossetti has some in both poetry and painting.

991. Quilter, Harry. "Dante Gabriel Rossetti as Student and Friend" and "The Painting and the Poetry of Dante Gabriel Rossetti." *Preferences in Art, Life, and Literature*. London: Swan Sonnenschein, 1892, pp. 15-22, 80-95.

Portrays Rossetti as weak, self-indulgent, querulous, and insensitive, as a corrective to the portraits offered by Caine, Knight, and others (see items 148 and 157). Contains several anecdotes, most of them claiming Ford Madox Brown as the source. As for the work, Rossetti is obsessed both in painting and in poetry with only one theme: "love baffled by death." He shows a conflict between passionate egoism and a sense of dramatic fitness. But Buchanan's strictures against his sensualism are unjustified. Second chapter modified from *Contemporary Review* (1883) and *Eclectic Review* (1883); see item 984.

992. Weigand, Wilhelm. "Die Präraphaeliten." *Essans*. Munich: Merhoff, 1892, pp. 242-252.

Asks whether true Romanticism can co-exist with bourgeois comfort; Rossetti and the P.R.B. seem to show that it can. As a poet Rossetti is atavistic, but he also expresses a distinctly modern pain, so that his work is not irrelevant.

993. Destrée, Olivier G. *Les Préraphaélites: Notes sur l'art
      decoratif et la peinture en Angleterre*. Brussels:
      Dietrich, 1894. 111 pp.

      Contains a chronological catalog of Rossetti's paint-
      ings compiled by John Anderson and a selection of Ros-
      setti's poems translated into French. Rossetti is viewed
      as the culmination of England's artistic absorption in
      Italy and in the Arthurian legend.

994. Wood, Esther. *Dante Gabriel Rossetti and the Pre-
      Raphaelite Movement*. London: Sampson, Low, Marston,
      1894. 323 pp.

      Studies Rossetti as the leader of an "ethical revolu-
      tion," one who stresses in both poetry and painting the
      problematic, obscure, even tragic aspects of life. He
      is a genius who unites all forms of knowledge and who
      reconciles the physical and the spiritual world. Other
      topics include the growth of the P.R.B., the influences
      on it, its goals, and its effects on contemporary art.
      Special emphasis is given to the religious dimension in
      Pre-Raphaelite works. Reprinted 1972.

995. Nordau, Max. "The Pre-Raphaelites." *Degeneration*.
      New York: Appleton, 1895, pp. 67-99.

      Attacks the mysticism of the P.R.B. as a sign of
      their unhealthy minds. Pre-Raphaelitism can be traced
      to German and French Romanticism and to "the religious
      enthusiasm of degenerate and hysterical Englishmen."
      As for Rossetti, he is a parasite on Dante, an imbecile,
      and a weak-minded mystic. A critical analysis of "The
      Blessed Damozel" and of the ballad refrains is used to
      buttress the author's case. Translated from the German
      Entartung (1893).

996. Plowman, Thomas F. "The Aesthetes, the Story of a
      Nineteenth Century Cult." *Pall Mall Magazine* 5
      (1895): 27-44.

      Wishes to correct misapprehensions about the aesthe-
      ticism of the 1870s. It had its origin in the Gothic
      revival and especially in the two phases of Pre-
      Raphaelitism. Rossetti was the dominant figure: he
      tried to break down barriers, both in painting through
      his medievalism and in poetry through his "pessimistic
      amativeness" coupled with an aversion to cherished ideals.

997. [Anonymous]. "The Rossettis." *London Quarterly Review* 87 (1896): 1-16.

Reviews recent publications on the Rossettis and concludes that Dante Gabriel was wilful and defective in his moral aim, so that--like Poe--he fell victim, both in poetry and painting, to the seductive power of physical beauty.

998. Harper, Janet. "Dante Gabriel Rossetti: Artist and Poet." *Westminster Review* 146 (1896): 312-321.

Judges Rossetti favorably. As a painter he is a great colorist "embodying the purest classical spirit." As a poet he combines realism and reverence; he is also a master of condensation, of diction, of dramatic interest.

999. Ortensi, Ulisse. "Artisti contemporanei: Dante Gabriele Rossetti." *Emporium* 4 (1896): 83-95.

Surveys Rossetti's career as both poet and painter. Includes twenty-five illustrations, with special emphasis given to those works which illustrate Italian subjects. His works show vividness, intensity, and spirituality--a spirituality which is successfully reconciled to the physical world.

1000. [Warre, F. Cornish]. "Dante Gabriel Rossetti." *Quarterly Review* 184 (1896): 185-214.

Reviews seven books on Rossetti. Finds him the chief exponent of aestheticism and of a new and more elevated sincerity. But in painting he fails to relate his ideas properly and sometimes sacrifices beauty to truth--he is too wilful, too didactic. As a poet he lacks gaiety and variety, but he is original, romantic, a master of moods.

1001. Bristol, Frank M. "The Poet-Painter." *The Ministry of Art*. Cincinnati: Curts and Jennings, 1897, pp. 153-177.

Sees Rossetti as romantic and idealistic, absorbed in the love between man and woman. His gift is to make us feel. He is inventive and richly colorful, albeit serious and melancholy.

1002.   Radford, Ernest. "The Life and Death of *The Germ*."
        Idler 13 (1898): 227-233.

        Summarizes the contents of each of the four numbers
        of *The Germ* and speaks reverentially of Rossetti's
        contributions. Includes also six black-and-white il-
        lustrations of paintings by Rossetti, including the
        Salutation of Beatrice, the most "beseechingly beau-
        tiful" picture in all of art.

1003.   Agresti, Antonio. *Poesie di Dante Gabriele Rossetti
        tradotte con uno studio su la pittura inglese e su
        l'opera pittorica e la vita dell' autore*. Florence:
        Barbera, 1899.

        Translates fourteen poems by Rossetti into Italian
        and, in the introduction, provides a survey of the
        history of English painting and relates Rossetti's
        artistic work to that history.

1004.   Bourget, Paul. "Études anglaises." *Études et portraits*.
        Paris: Lemerre, 1899, pp. 114-119.

        Discusses Rossetti's Oxford murals and his poem
        "Jenny," which continues the tradition of offering a
        sympathetic treatment to the fallen woman. Reprinted
        from *Le Journal de Debats* (1884).

1005.   Wilmersdoerffer, A. "Dante Gabriel Rossetti und sein
        Einfluss." *Westermanns Illustrierte Deutsche Monats-
        hefte* 85 (1899): 592-610.

        Intends to popularize Rossetti for the German public
        by recounting his achievements in both art and poetry
        and his influence on artists like Burne-Jones. Offers
        a retrospective of Rossetti's career, illustrating it
        with nine black-and-white reproductions of his paintings.

1006.   Cary, Elisabeth L[uther]. *The Rossettis: Dante Gabriel
        and Christina*. New York: Putnam, 1900. 310 pp.

        The chief emphasis is on Dante Gabriel. The family
        background and the origin of the P.R.B. are chronicled,
        then Rossetti's adult years, with separate chapters on
        his poetry and his temperament. The portrait of the
        painter-poet is a sympathetic one, and emphasizes his
        use of imagery, his passion for details, his narrow
        range, his intensity, and his visionary power. He

does come off as morally weaker than Christina, however. Thirty-one black-and-white illustrations; reprinted 1979; see also item 696.

1007. Kassner, Rudolf. "Dante Gabriel Rossetti." *Die Mystik, die Künstler, und das Leben: über englische Dichter und Maler im 19. Jahrhunderts.* Leipzig: Diederichs, 1900, pp. 132-158.

Adapts Nietzsche's contention that "life is a woman" to a description of Rossetti's work. Rossetti creates his own myth, with himself and Lizzie Siddal as the chief mythological figures. He is the greatest poet-painter in world literature, one who combines Poe and Dante in literature, the Renaissance and the modern world in painting.

1008. [Taylor, Una]. "William Morris and Dante Gabriel Rossetti." *Edinburgh Review* 19 (1900): 356-379.

Judges Rossetti's art to be "the climax of personality," combining poetic motives and naturalistic methods. He is the painter of sensuous mysticism, the poet of foregone opportunities. Rossetti's spirituality is unfortunately tinged with coldness, utilitarianism, yet his sympathetic temperament will be an enduring artistic legacy.

1009. Agresti, Antonio. "La Vita Nuova di Dante e i quadri di D.G. Rossetti." *La Vita Nuova di Dante con le illustrazioni di D.G. Rossetti.* Rome: Roux e Viarengo, 1902, pp. xi-xxix.

Sees Rossetti as the painter of the soul, yet one whose poetical works show the influence of his father and thus have significance for the Italian *risorgimento*. His translation of the *Vita Nuova* is the finest yet done in English. His illustrations of Dante [ten of which are included] give evidence of sensitive and careful workmanship. See also item 733.

1010. Aronstein, Philipp. "Dante Gabriel Rossetti und der Praeraphaelismus." *Verhandlungen des zehnten allgemeinen deutschen Neuphilologentages vom 20. bis 23. Mai 1902 zu Breslau.* Hannover: Meyer, 1903, pp. 114-122.

Places Rossetti at the confluence of the political-

social, ethical-religious, and aesthetic-artistic currents of his time. He was the greatest artist of his
group, principally because of the intensity of his
feeling, yet his choice of subjects clearly shows the
influence of these currents. Several examples, such
as "Jenny" and *Found*, illustrate such a claim.

1011.   Wiley, Edwin. "Dante Gabriel Rossetti and the Pre-
        Raphaelites." *The Old and the New Renaissance:*
        A Group of Studies in Art and Letters. Nashville:
        M. E. Church, 1903, pp. 117-168.

        Sees the 1850s as producing "the greatest painters
        England has ever known," with the Pre-Raphaelites lead-
        ing the way. They were aesthetic revolutionaries, led
        by a "rare and precious genius," Rossetti. His paint-
        ing and poetry both show deep sorrow without morbidity.
        His work is magnetic because it has unity, just as his
        life did.

1012.   Dalby, W. Burkitt. "Rossetti and His Circle." *London*
        Quarterly Review 104 (1905): 21-39.

        Contends that the minute workmanship of the Pre-
        Raphaelites was related to the scientific movement
        which they despised. Rossetti was the central figure,
        an absorbing personality whose mystical works form
        "a *resumé* of the dream life of the race."

1013.   Waldschmidt, Wolfram. *Dante Gabriel Rossetti, der*
        Maler und der Dichter: Die Anfänge der präraphael-
        itische Bewegnung in England. Leipzig: Diederichs,
        1905. 163 pp.

        Includes studies of gothicism in Rossetti and of
        his use of the trance. Use of the trance associates
        Rossetti with Dante, Chaucer, Blake, Coleridge, and
        Poe; trance-like creation is a revolt against material-
        ism. Feminine beauty is the outer garment clothing the
        beauty of the soul. "The House of Life" is objective,
        not subjective.

1014.   Earle, Anne M. "Pre-Raphaelite Ideals." *Book News*
        24 (1906): 681-686.

        Sees the ideals as: the complexity of art; the impor-
        tance of emotional truth; the greatest possible reali-
        zation of one's material. Rossetti was part of Roman-

ticism, "the second Renaissance in England." His work, both in poetry and in painting, fulfilled those high ideals.

1015. Galletti, Alfredo. "Un Poeta-pittore dell' amore e della morte: Dante Gabriele Rossetti." *La Lettura* 6 (1906): 322-329.

Not examined.

1016. Jiriczek, Otto L. "Dante Gabriel Rossetti." *Hochland* 4 (1906): 183-195.

Recounts with satisfaction Rossetti's career and the rise of his popularity in Germany. He is a miraculous flower blooming in the soil of two cultures, the English and the Italian, although his later years were shadowed, personally and artistically, by a deep melancholy.

1017. Krapp, Lorenz. "Dante Gabriel Rossetti." *Kultur* 8 (1907): 89-98.

Chronicles Rossetti's career, drawing mostly on Singer [item 716]. Notes how the poetry is dominated by rose (love) and blood (death) imagery and how the painting shows a strange fusion of realism and transcendentalism. Rossetti is the greatest poet-painter since the Renaissance.

1018. Ranftl, Johann. "Dante Gabriel Rossetti." *Historisch-politische Blätter für das Katholische Deutschland* 139 (1907): 477-500, 575-597.

Summarizes Rossetti's life in considerable detail, then evaluates him as a painter and poet. His painting evolves from medievalism to an obsession with the sitting woman more characteristic of the Renaissance; *The Beloved* is the high point of his career. The poems penetrate the heart more deeply than the paintings, and they are dominated by the tragic figure of Miss Siddal.

1019. Graf, Arturo. "Preraffaelliti, simbolisti ed esteti." *Foscolo, Manzoini e Leopardi*. Turin: Loescher, 1908, pp. 303-345.

Defines Pre-Raphaelitism in painting as a naturalism gone awry, so that it ends up in an absorption with the bizarre, the florid, the arcane. In poetry Pre-

Raphaelitism means fulfilling Zola's request: the poets
will supply the music while the rest of us work. Rossetti is both the best painter and the best poet of the
movement. Reprinted from *Nuova Antologica* (1897).

1020.   Ashbee, Charles Robert. "The Pre-Raphaelites and Their
        Influence upon Life." *House Beautiful* 27 (1910):
        75-77, 101-104, 112.

        Considers such topics as the origin of Pre-Raphaelitism
        its anti-materialism, and its emphasis on sincerity,
        beauty, and subjectivity. Rossetti was responsible for
        the cult of Keats, whose works provided subjects, tech-
        niques, and a dominant tone (joy). Rossetti also add-
        ed a kind of spiritual earnestness.

1021.   Laurent, Raymond. "Le Préraphaélisme en Angleterre."
        Études anglaises. Paris: Grasset, 1910, pp. 37-73.

        Sees the death of Lizzie Siddal as the turning point
        in Rossetti's career: he abandons idealism in favor of
        the tormented and damned women who will dominate his
        work for the two decades which remain. Through his
        symbolism he wants his poems and paintings to evoke,
        not just intellectualize. Reprinted from *Nouvelle
        Revue* (1906).

1022.   Bassalik-de Vries, Johanna C.E. *William Blake in His
        Relation to Dante Gabriel Rossetti*. Basel: Brin,
        1911. 58 pp.

        Discusses Rossetti's role in the revival of interest
        in Blake and their many similarities as poet-painters,
        as decorators, and as mystics.

1023.   Butterworth, Walter. *Dante Gabriel Rossetti in Relation
        to Dante Alighieri*. London: Sheratt and Hughes, 1912.

        Observes that Rossetti drew most of his Dantean themes,
        both in poetry and in painting, from the *Vita Nuova* and
        its treatment of idealized love. Both Dante and Ros-
        setti were great intellects with imagination and a
        genuine sense for beauty. But the stern and sublime
        aspects of Dante's art were hidden from Rossetti, who
        was too much misdirected by sensuousness and morbidity.
        Rossetti's treatment of Dantean subjects in his paint-
        ings is given a chronlogical listing. Reprinted from
        the *Manchester Quarterly* (1912).

1024. Grasé, J.C.G. "Dante Gabriel Rossetti." *Onze Eeuw* 14
(1914): 75-112.

In Dutch.

1025. Symons, Arthur. " A Note on Rossetti." *North American
Review* 204 (1916): 128-134.

Calls Rossetti the most gifted painter since Michael-
angelo and Blake, and the most perceptive poet-critic
of the modern age. But he lacked control over his
imagination.

1026. Venkatesan, N.K. *Dante Gabriel Rossetti: The Pre-
Raphaelite Painter-Poet.* Madras: Srinivasa Vara-
dachari, 1918. 28 pp.

Reprinted from the [Madras] *Educational Review* (1918);
not examined.

1027. Lynd, Robert. "Rossetti and Ritual." *Old and New
Masters.* London: Unwin, 1919, pp. 132-145.

Sees Rossetti's work as "rites of words and colours,"
i.e. rituals by which the artist might find spiritual
peace. This ritualism paved the way for later poets
like Yeats.

1028. Mather, Frank Jewett. "The Rossettis." *Bookman* [New
York] 49 (1919): 139-147.

Opens with a novelistic view of a typical evening at
the Charlotte Street house in 1848. Even at such an
early date Rossetti--"dominating, genial, merciless
toward ... pretense"--is the center of everybody's
attention. In later years his painting will show
"an exquisite soul-sickness"; but his poetry, especially the ballads, will be among the greatest the
century will produce.

1029. Dupré, Henri. *Un Italien d' Angleterre, le Poète-
peintre, Dante Gabriel Rossetti.* Paris: Dent, 1921.
148 pp.

Emphasizes the Italian strain in Rossetti's work--
his idealism, romanticism, Marianism--which is the
source of his originality. His realism, on the other
hand, has its roots in German as well as Italian literature.

1030. Fehr, Bernhard. "Dante Gabriel Rossetti." *Die Englische
       Literatur des 19. und 20. Jahrhunderts*. Vol. 1.
       Berlin: Akademische Verlags-gesellschaft, 1923, pp.
       216-223.

       Connects Rossetti's poetry to his mystical painting,
       since the two must be seen as inseparable. Offers a
       brief retrospective of Rossetti's career as painter-
       poet.

1031. Block, Lotte. "Dante Gabriel Rossetti, der Malerdichter,
       eine Untersuchung seines künstlerischen Schaffens."
       *Giessener Beiträge zur Erforschung der Sprache und
       Kultur Englands und Nordamerikas* 2 (1925): 249-295.

       Sees Rossetti's Italian origins as a great influence
       on his personality and work. English literature and a
       curiously old-fashioned taste in art also have an effect.
       As a poet Rossetti is death-obsessed, as a painter he
       dwells in fantasy. In his best work, such as the poem
       "Silent Noon," both poet and painter converge.

1032. Davies, Charles. *Dante Gabriel Rossetti*. London:
       Merton Press, 1925. 157 pp.

       Studies Rossetti's poetry and painting in relation
       to his age, particularly his alteration of the "emo-
       tional stress of poetic thought" in the Victorian
       period by emphasizing the union of beauty and passion
       and by offering a more profound psychological method.
       After reviewing the dominant trends in Victorian
       poetry and Rossetti's apprenticeship as a P.R.B.
       painter, the author discusses Rossetti's correlation
       of the two arts, where his medievalism warped his
       achievement in either and where his pursuit of an
       impossible goal limited his success. Chapters on
       Rossetti's artistic qualities and on his influence
       on later poets--e.g. the Decadents--conclude the
       study.

1033. Tietz, Eva. "Das Malerische in Rossettis Dichtung."
       Anglia 51 (1927): 278-306.

       Argues that Rossetti's poetry is colored by his
       "painter's eye" and that his diction appeals to the
       visualizing faculty of the reader. Separate sections
       deal with Rossetti's choice of materials and his
       means of representation. His use of color, of light

and shade, of types, of portrait techniques, and of composition methods all reveal his devotion to a mode of painting which was essentially impressionistic and decorative.

1034. B., F. "Dante Gabriel Rossetti, 1828-1882." *Boek-enschouw* 22 (1928): 65-70.

In Dutch.

1035. De Bruyn, Jeanne. "Dante Gabriel Rossetti Herdacht, 12 Mei 1828-9 April 1882." *Dietsche Warande* 28 (1928): 957-971.

In Dutch.

1036. Hodgson, Geraldine. "Dante Gabriel Rossetti." *Church Quarterly Review* 106 (1928): 353-362.

Relates Rossetti to the platonic tradition of "divinely mad" poets, and sees the worship of beauty which characterizes his painting and poetry as an integral part of his personality, not an affectation.

1037. Mégroz, R[odolphe] L. "Dante Gabriel Rossetti (1828-1928)." *Dublin Magazine* n.s. 3 (1928): 270-277.

A centenary tribute--for a fuller appreciation by the author see item 1038 (below).

1038. Mégroz, R[odolphe] L[ouis]. *Dante Gabriel Rossetti, Painter-Poet of Heaven in Earth.* London: Faber, 1928. 339 pp.

Proceeds from the assumption that life and work reflect each other and that Rossetti's poetry and painting relate "like a series of spiral curves." The first section is mainly biographical and covers Rossetti's parents, his education, and his relationship with women, particularly Lizzie Siddal and his sister Christina. The second section, mainly critical, covers such topics as "Dante and the Divine Woman," fleshliness, imagery, archaicisms, and Rossetti's "dreamworld." The emphasis is on psychological interpretations. Reprinted 1971.

1039. Proix, Jean. *Un Mysticisme Esthetique ... pour le Centenaire de la Naissance de Dante Gabriel Rossetti.*

Paris: L'Artisan du Livre, 1928. 52 pp.

Not examined.

1040. Smith, Garnet. "Dante Gabriel Rossetti." *Contemporary
       Review* 133 (1928): 624-631.

A centenary essay. As a painter Rossetti is most
valued for the influence he exerted on others. As a
poet Rossetti's chosen metier is the ballad, where he
centers on the theme of tragic betrayal, and the
sonnet, where he centers on love. Antithesis is the
guiding principle for all of his work.

1041. West, Geoffrey. "Revaluations: Dante Gabriel Rossetti."
       Outlook [London] 61 (1928): 596-597.

Denies Rossetti a place among the leaders of painting or poetry, even historically. But he does deserve
some study for his own sake. Rossetti is "good, indeed,
but scarcely great" because of his mercenary nature and
his lack of self-discipline. All his life he frittered,
and thus remained "a congenital amateur."

1042. Brocklehurst, J.H. "Dante Gabriel Rossetti." *Manchester
       Literary Club Papers* 55 (1929): 94-115.

Describes Rossetti's charming but irresolute character, his decisive role in the history of English art,
and his intense, visionary painting. Unfortunately
Rossetti as a poet seemed to prefer "amorous dalliance"
rather than "the strenuous pursuit of knowledge and
business success."

1043. Formichi, Carlo. "Dante Gabriele [sic] Rossetti." *Uni-
       versity of California Chronicle* 31 (1929): 267-280.

Offered in the mistaken belief that 1929 marks the
centenary of Rossetti's birth. Summarizes Rossetti's
personality--he was generous, affectionate, wilful, in-
consistent, restless. In his work he sought to represent Dante and Dantean ideals: the love of beauty
is but an anticipation of the beauty of the soul;
sonorous rhythm must be used to express the deepest
inner feelings. Rossetti is the best artist for self-
expression since Shakespeare.

1044. Symons, Arthur. "Dante Gabriel Rossetti." *Studies in Strange Souls*. London: Sawyer, 1929, pp. 7-49.

Sees Rossetti's imagination as compounded of "lust of the eyes," intensity of conception, enchantment, and an air of "voluptuousness brooding over destiny." Accords to Rossetti both intellectual sanity and an exquisite sensibility. But his tragic love of beauty betrays him. Reprinted 1979.

1045. Welby, T[homas] E[arle]. *The Victorian Romantics, 1850-1870*. London: Howe, 1929. 161 pp.

Surveys the fortunes of Rossetti, Morris, Burne-Jones, Swinburne, and Simeon Solomon. Rossetti's poetry is "oppressive" and "often grotesquely anthropocentric." But his paintings are judged to be "exceptional achievements," the product of a mind at once energetic, intense, and compassionate. Reprinted 1966.

1046. Whiting, Mary Bradford. "Dante and Rossetti." *Congregational Quarterly* 7 (1929): 207-214.

Sees Dante's influence on Rossetti as greatest in the latter's attitude toward Love and Death. The theme of intercommunion of spirits is another link between the two poets--it gives Rossetti his mystical quality. Thirty-one paintings inspired by Dantean subjects are listed.

1047. Borchardt, Rudolf. "Dante Gabriel Rossetti." *Die Horen* 6 (1930): 53-62, 133-152.

Protests against the "Italian blood" theories of Rossetti's art--after all, we do not write about Browning's "Germanic" nature merely because his maternal grandfather was named Wiedermann. Both Rossetti's strengths and weaknesses are thoroughly English. His genius is to see the world anew, to promote a rebirth of wonder in the midst of an arid century. He is a genuine hero and his fame will increase.

1048. Cammell, Charles Richard. *Dante Gabriel Rossetti and the Philosophy of Love*. Edinburgh: Poseidon Press, 1933. 21 pp.

Claims for Rossetti a high place in English painting and poetry. He is not only the philosopher of love,

he is its priest, prophet, and cultist. Traces Rossetti's love philosophy to Christian and pagan roots
and to the love poetry of medieval Provence and Italy.
He is a strange, even tragic, metaphysician. Reprinted
1972; originally from *The Scotsman* (1933).

1049. Housman, Laurence. "Pre-Raphaelitism in Art and
       Poetry." *Essays by Divers Hands* n.s. 12 (1933):
       1-30.

       Views the Pre-Raphaelites, both in their poetry and
       in their painting, as English Lutherans: more important
       now for their revolutionary impact than for their doc-
       trines. They were Romantic individualists, flaunting
       their opposition to the Grand Style, their credo best
       summarized by a close examination of their "List of
       Immortals." Wonder and romance flower in their work,
       and their freshness is best seen in the thrusting chin
       of Rossetti's heroines.

1050. Hueffer, Ford Madox. "Pre-Raphaelite Epitaph." *Saturday
       Review of Literature* 10 (1934): 417-419.

       Believes that recent books on the Pre-Raphaelites in
       general and Rossetti in particular establish the fact
       that they are dead aesthetically but live as fascinat-
       ing personalities.

1051. Moore, Dom Thomas V. "Dante Gabriel Rossetti." *Dublin
       Review* 200 (1937): 345-360.

       Interprets Rossetti's career as a conflict between
       good and evil, with the latter eventually triumphant.
       The soul, as portrayed by beautiful women, is the image
       of God. But Rossetti's poetic and pictorial art--and
       his life--are failures, because self-expression alone
       cannot suffice. Replied to by item 259.

1052. Bowman, Estella. "Rossetti and His Circle." *Northwest
       Missouri State Teachers College Studies* 2 (1938):
       43-66.

       Draws on published materials to present a short
       survey of Rossetti's career, with glimpses of his P.R.B.
       associates. Finds in all of them a paradox between
       their artistic goal of fidelity to nature and their
       mystical, exotic accomplishments. Their poetry and
       painting stirred the mind, although their movement
       proved to be ephemeral.

1053. Child, Ruth C. "Introduction." *The Aesthetic of Walter
       Pater*. New York: Macmillan, 1940, pp. 1-12.

       Relates Pater's aestheticism to the principles of con-
       temporaries like Rossetti. Pater and Rossetti shared
       interests in sensuousness, the intermingling of the
       arts, exoticism, and a melancholy tone.

1054. Preston, Kerrison. *Blake and Rossetti*. London: Moring,
       1944. 111 pp.

       Calls Rossetti the "greatest imaginative genius born
       in England in the nineteenth century." Offers short
       hagiographical biographies of the two poet-painters,
       essays on their art, and black-and-white reproductions
       of several of their paintings. Reprinted 1971.

1055. Eulenberg, Herbert. *Die Prä-Raphaeliten*. Düsseldorf:
       Die Faehre, 1946. 48 pp.

       Sketches the background of the P.R.B., including the
       German Nazarean painters, and then gives quasi-fictional
       accounts of four main figures in English aestheticism:
       Rossetti, Burne-Jones, Ruskin, and Swinburne. Rossetti
       is presented as a poet and painter born out of his due
       time, a *trecento* Italian living on in a world hostile
       to his talents.

1056. Christoffel, Ulrich. "Rossetti und Burne-Jones."
       *Malerei und Poesie: die symbolische Kunst des 19.
       Jahrhunderts*. Vienna: Gallus-Verlag, 1948, pp. 59-84.

       Describes Rossetti's difficulties in reconciling art
       and poetry during the 1850s. The best mixture of the
       two occurs in the painting *Dante's Dream*, which com-
       bines poetic insight and artistic symbolism. In his
       later years narcotics dulled his talent, but Rossetti's
       works stand out against the grey background of the
       nineteenth century. Includes black-and-white plates.

1057. Tinker, Chauncey B. "The Amusing Pre-Raphaelites."
       *Essays in Retrospect: Collected Articles and
       Addresses*. New Haven: Yale University Press, 1948,
       pp. 75-82.

       Points out the amusing, even ridiculous aspects of
       the Pre-Raphaelites and their work: Rossetti's exag-
       gerated necks and lips, for example. Yet in view of

their poems and their paintings our laughter must be
like Beerbohm's (item 227)--affectionate and respect-
ful. Reprinted from *Literary Review* (1923).

1058.   Hough, Graham. "Rossetti and the P.R.B." *The Last
         Romantics*. London: Duckworth, 1949, pp. 40-82.

Finds in the members of the P.R.B. a tension between
naturalism and archaic romance. Rossetti is a late
flowering of the Romantic movement, and a study of
"Hand and Soul" reveals the importance to him of fidel-
ity to one's inner experience. Although he fails in
his attempt to grasp the love mythology of Dante, Rossetti's significance as a poet and a painter lies in
his exposure of "the central neuroses of our culture."

1059.   Buckley, Jerome H. "The Fear of Art." *The Victorian
         Temper: A Study in Literary Culture*. Cambridge,
         Mass.: Harvard University Press, 1951, pp. 161-184.

Recapitulates the "Fleshly School" controversy as an
example of the attitudes of some Victorians toward
sexuality and art. Rossetti emerges as an artist concerned with universal values, a poet-painter who had
no quarrel with contemporary doctrines about the
morality of art. Buchanan's attack is symptomatic of
a diseased mind.

1060.   Dickason, David H. *The Daring Young Men: The Story of
         the American Pre-Raphaelites*. Bloomington: Indiana
         University Press, 1953. 304 pp.

Demonstrates the influence of the P.R.B. on some
nineteenth-century American poets, painters, and archi-
tects and on journals like *Crayon* and *The Craftsman*.
Rossetti's influence on the painters John LaFarge and
T.C. Farrar and on the poet Ezra Pound is described.
The chief conduits for Rossetti's influence were the
painter William J. Stillman and the poets Joaquin
Miller and Buchanan Read; their relationships to
"the Master" are treated in detail.

1061.   Doughty, Oswald. "Rossetti's Conception of the 'Poetic'
         in Poetry and Painting." *Essays by Divers Hands* n.s.
         26 (1953): 89-102.

Describes Rossetti as "morbid, emotional, exotic,
and sensuous," a drugged and demoralized man who exer-

cised his fascination by combining a devotion to the
pictorial with a tendency towards idealizing. The
origins of this aestheticism go back at least to the
"picturesque" school of Claude Lorraine and ultimately
to Plato. The energy for both poetry and painting comes
from devotion to a "love-ideal, the search for a soul
partner."

1062. LeRoy, Gaylord C. "Dante Gabriel Rossetti." *Perplexed
Prophets: Six Nineteenth Century British Authors*.
Philadelphia: University of Pennsylvania Press, 1953,
pp. 121-147.

Tries to explain the decline of Rossetti's joviality
in terms of his reaction to a drab and dishonest civili-
zation. The poet-painter retreats into art, and the
result is tragedy: tragedy in the form of great personal
suffering, and tragedy in the form of artistic failure,
despite his immense talents.

1063. Wellend, D.S.R. *The Pre-Raphaelites in Literature and
Art*. New York: Barnes and Noble, [1953]. 216 pp.

A Pre-Raphaelite sampler. Includes a sampling of
Rossetti's work as a poet, prose writer, painter, and
designer. In his lengthy introduction the author sees
transferences between Rossetti's poetry and painting,
but they are accidental, unconscious. Rossetti is a
moralist, symptomatic of an age gone forever after
World War I.

1064. DePilato, Sergio. *Dante Gabriele Rossetti, poeta e
pittore*. Rome: Edizioni Conchiglia, 1954.

Not examined.

1065. Kühnelt, H.H. "Die Bedeutung der italienischen Malerei
für den Dichter Dante Gabriel Rossetti." *Anglia* 72
(1955): 438-454.

Argues that the influence on Rossetti's poetry of such
Italian painters as Botticelli, Fra Angelico, Giorgione,
and Veronese has been overlooked. They influenced theme,
color, and composition not only in his painting but also
in his ballads and "The Blessed Damozel." They also
gave him models for the welding of music and painting.

1066. D'Agostino, Nemi. "I Preraffaeliti." *Belfagor* 14
       (1959): 404-414.

       Sees the primary motive of the P.R.B. as moral pro-
       test against a bourgeois and materialistic epoch. Ros-
       setti is a strange compound of platonism, hedonism,
       and skepticism, both in his poetry and in his painting.
       Also surveys briefly the history of critical estimates
       of the Pre-Raphaelites.

1067. Sypher, Wylie. "Nazarenes, Lyonnais, and Pre-Raphael-
       ites." *Rococo to Cubism in Art and Literature*.
       New York: Random House, 1960, pp. 197-215.

       Disparages Pre-Raphaelite art as mannered, esoteric,
       cold, ornamental, and moralistic. But eventually its
       stylization freed the artist from the tyranny of nar-
       ration. Rossetti's painting and poetry succeed in
       arresting time, but his vision is often hampered by
       his design and by his anxious symbolism.

1068. Savarit, Jacques. *Tendances mystiques et ésotériques
       chez Dante-Gabriel Rossetti*. Paris: Didier, 1961.
       421 pp.

       Puts Rossetti's poetry and painting within the frame-
       work of European mysticism from 1830 until the end of
       the century, and particularly within the framework of
       English Romanticism which forms an important part of
       that mystical tradition. The author's aesthetic prin-
       ciples are basically Crocean. He analyzes such topics
       as Rossetti's "mystical eroticism" and such archetypes
       as the "platonic mediatrix," identified here with Janey
       Morris. M. Savarit concludes that the special tone of
       Rossetti's work comes from "l' influx massif des spécu-
       lations mystico-ésotériques."

1069. Johnson, Wendell Stacy. "D.G. Rossetti as Painter and
       Poet." *Victorian Poetry* 3 (1965): 9-18.

       Catalogs the similarities between Rossetti's paintings
       and his poems: subjects (extraordinary women), images
       (flowers, hair, stars), technique (human figures as
       the visual center). An analysis of paired works shows
       how color and line on the one hand and diction and
       tense on the other can produce parallel effects, thus
       justifying Rossetti's own claim that he was a poet
       who painted.

1070. Talon, Henri. "Dante Gabriel Rossetti, peintre-poète dans *La Maison de Vie*." *Études anglaises* 19 (1966): 1-14.

   Sees Rossetti as attempting to make his two arts complementary in order to tap more fully what Conrad was to call "the springs of responsive emotion." Music does for poetry what color does for painting. The complementary nature of the two arts, especially the "painterly" dimension of the poet, is best seen in his treatment of feminine beauty and in his use of light and water images. See also item 569.

1071. Praz, Mario. "Time Unveils Truth." *Mnemosyne: The Parallel between Literature and the Visual Arts*. Princeton University Press, 1967, pp. 29-54.

   Compares Rossetti's works like the poem and picture *Lady Lilith* to other works such as Courbet's *The Woman with the Mirror*. This is to Rossetti's disadvantage because--as is typical of him--he produces one side of a two-faced morbid image.

1072. Hunt, John Dixon. *The Pre-Raphaelite Imagination 1848-1900*. Lincoln: University of Nebraska Press, 1968. 262 pp.

   Focuses on the art of the 1890s as the culmination of a movement which began with the P.R.B. in 1848. Examines the writers and painters under five topics: medievalism, auto-psychology, symbolism, modern science, and the image of woman. Rossetti emerges as a poet with a sonorous ear and a good eye for detail. The women who haunt his canvases are embodiments of his idealism; the author traces this obsession to the Ottley designs which the P.R.B. studied in the 1840s. Rossetti is interested more in sensuality than in ethics.

1073. Nakamura, Giichi. *Hogetsu Shimamura and Pre-Raphaelism*. Tokyo: [no publisher listed], 1970. 19 pp.

   Shows how Shimamura, an art critic and novelist who studied at Oxford from 1902 to 1905, returned to Japan afire with enthusiasm for the blend of naturalism and mysticism which he found in Rossetti. His highest praise was reserved for Rossetti's idealism of women in his painting and poetry.

1074. Nakamura, Giichi. *The Shirakaba and Pre-Raphaelism.*
       Tokyo: [no publisher listed], 1970. 29 pp.

       Traces the introduction of Pre-Raphaelitism to Japan
       through the pages of the journal *Shirakaba* in the years
       1910-1923. Rossetti was very popular with young poets
       and painters.

1075. Sonstroem, David. *Rossetti and the Fair Lady.* Middle-
       town, Conn.: Wesleyan University Press, 1970. 252 pp.

       Claims that 95% of Rossetti's poems and 98% of his
       paintings treat love and/or feminine beauty. Groups
       these works into four types: the blessed damozel, the
       femme fatale, the sinner, and the victim. Each type
       is then analyzed in considerable detail. The author
       sees in these works the "biography of a fantasy," since
       these types and motifs appear in Rossetti's life as
       well as his art. Special attention is given to Janey
       Morris, who is the embodiment of many of these fantasies.
       See also item 472.

1076. Stein, Richard L. "Dante Gabriel Rossetti: Painting
       and the Problem of Poetic Form." *Studies in English
       Literature* 10 (1970): 775-792.

       Claims that some obscurities in Rossetti's verse can
       be explained by understanding the formal assumptions
       governing painting, in particular the assumption that
       narrative and decorative material can be sharply juxta-
       posed and also the assumption that physical and sym-
       bolic descriptions can be mixed.

1077. Fraser, Ross. "Jenny's Clock." *Landfall* 25 (1971):
       160-171.

       Mentions Rossetti's connections with Burne-Jones and
       describes two Rossetti drawings in the Auckland [New
       Zealand] City Art Gallery. Judges Rossetti to be a
       poet of somber but insightful images, one who had
       "marvelous moments of illumination."

1078. Hönnighausen, Lothar. *Präraphaeliten und fin de siècle:
       symbolistische Tendenzen in der englischen Spät-
       romantik.* Munich: Fink, 1971. 489 pp.

       Studies the evolution of English art in the last half
       of the nineteenth century, from the Romantic symbolism

of Keble and Ruskin to the "new symbolism" of Wilde
and Yeats. There are references to Rossetti throughout. His poems figure in such movements or events as
Pre-Raphaelite realism, archaicism, pictorialism, the
revival of allegory, and the renewed emphasis on the
effects of sound devices like alliteration. "The
Blessed Damozel" and the Willowwood sonnets receive
special attention. His paintings are used to illustrate such topics as symbolic facial traits and the
doppelgänger motif.

1079. Bequette, M.K. "Dante Gabriel Rossetti: The Synthesis
       of Picture and Poem." *Hartford Studies in Literature*
       4 (1972): 216-227.

       Finds, through a study of the sonnets Rossetti wrote
       to accompany Titian's *Venetian Pastoral* and his own
       Proserpine, that the poet creates a spatial bond between
       canvas and viewer. This bond either draws the viewer
       into the painting or else reminds him of his distance
       from the subject.

1080. Fraser, Robert S., ed. *Essays on the Rossettis*.
       Princeton: University Library, 1972. [117 pp.]

       A special edition of the *Princeton University Library
       Chronicle*, used as the catalog for a Rossetti exhibit.
       Includes items 54-56, 430, 474, 659, and 993.

1081. Warner, Janet. "D.G. Rossetti: Love, Death, and Art."
       Hartford Studies in Literature 4 (1972): 228-240.

       Sees Rossetti as a great synthesizer: of love and
       death, of the sinister and the spiritual, of poetry
       and painting. The sonnets for pictures are the best
       places to witness this synthesizing process at work.

1082. Heath, Jeffrey M. "Waugh and Rossetti." *Evelyn Waugh
       Newsletter* 7 (1973): 5-6.

       Identifies a copy of Waugh's Rossetti biography (item
       241) as belonging to T. Sturge Moore, the *TLS* reviewer
       who thought Evelyn must be "a dainty Miss." Waugh's
       testy public quarrel with Moore stemmed from his pride
       in the book, a pride which grew out of Waugh's deep
       interest in Pre-Raphaelitism. Nevertheless Waugh did
       think that Rossetti's morals were shabby and that his
       medievalism was perverse and self-indulgent.

1083.   Leggett, Bernie. "A Picture and Its Poem by Dante
        Gabriel Rossetti." *Victorian Poetry* 11 (1973):
        241-246.

        Shows how Rossetti transformed his *Mary Magdalene at
        the Door of Simon the Pharisee* into the sonnet "Mary
        Magdalene" by finding verbal equivalents, such as pauses
        and a stair-like typography, for the dialectical struc-
        ture and upward (toward the spiritual) motion which
        characterize the painting.

1084.   Parry, Graham. "An Englishman Italianate: Dante
        Gabriel Rossetti's Double Life." *Caliban* 10
        (1973): 35-41.

        Begins with a view of "Hand and Soul" as a parable
        illustrating Rossetti's distinctive sensibility and his
        variance from his Pre-Raphaelite colleagues. Rossetti
        was imbued with Dantean material, but he chose from it
        only those aspects with which he had a personal associa-
        tion. His paintings--like his life--dramatized his
        absorption in an earlier period; in his poetry he sought
        a modern equivalent for the *dolce stil nuovo*.

1085.   Gelpi, Barbara C. "The Image of the Anima in the Work
        of Dante Gabriel Rossetti." *Victorian Newsletter*,
        no. 45 (Spring 1974): 1-7.

        Shows how a female figure, similar to the *anima* figure
        popularized by C.G. Jung, recurs in both Rossetti's
        poetry and his painting. This figure holds out the
        illusory hope that the self can be fully integrated.
        She is a guide for an explanation of the unconscious,
        especially in "The House of Life"; but she becomes too
        powerful, too absorbing, and therefore too dangerous.

1086.   Sambrook, James, ed. *Pre-Raphaelitism: A Collection of
        Critical Essays*. Chicago: University of Chicago
        Press, 1974.   277 pp.

        Contains seventeen essays by and about the Pre-
        Raphaelites, revaluating both poetry and painting.
        Only one of the seventeen, John Dixon Hunt's essay
        "A Moment's Monument: Reflections on Pre-Raphaelite
        Vision in Poetry and Painting," is published here for
        the first time. In it Hunt traces Rossetti's devotion
        to the concept of capturing in poetry and art a single
        significant moment, an "iconic present" which sums up

both past and future. Other Rossetti-related material
includes items 194, 440, 446, 465, 793, 1058, 1059,
1061, and 1069.

1087. Geraths, Armin. "Dante Gabriel Rossetti." *Epigonale*
Romantik: Untersuchungen zu Keats, Rossetti, Mrs.
Browning und Rupert Brooke. Frankfurt: Akademik
Verlag, 1975, pp. 73-108.

Analyzes Rossetti's use of poetry as a means of in-
terpreting art, finding in Rossetti's review of Hake's
poetry the key to his own practice: "the productive
and the receptive poetic mind are members of one con-
stellation." These two minds come into spiritual con-
tact through the work of art. A lengthy explication
of the sonnet "The Day Dream" shows this process at
work.

1088. Mukoyama, Yasuko. *Raphael Zenpa Undo to D.G. Rossetti*
to. Tokyo: Aoyama Gakuin Joshi Tandai Gakugei Konwakai,
1975.

In Japanese.

1089. Stein, Richard L. *The Ritual of Interpretation: The*
Fine Arts as Literature in Ruskin, Rossetti, and
Pater. Cambridge, Mass.: Harvard University Press,
1975. 314 pp.

Offers detailed analyses of those sonnets which Rossetti wrote to accompany paintings. Relates all of
the poetry to what the author views as Rossetti's crea-
tion of an emotionally intense response to art objects.
Rossetti is elliptical in his forms and art-obsessed
in his themes. Therefore his distinctive traits as a
painter can be shown to correlate with his distinctive
traits as a poet. See also item 1076.

1090. Ainsworth, Maryan W. *Dante Gabriel Rossetti and the*
Double Work of Art. New Haven: Yale University Art
Gallery, 1976. 116 pp.

Contains two papers, the title essay and "The Prince's
Progress," by the author, plus "The Double Vision in
Portraiture" by Susan Casteras, "Allegorizing on One's
Own Hook" by Susan Bandelin, and "Lustral Rites and
Dire Portents" by Jane Bayard. Together these five
essays and the sixty-four black-and-white illustrations

offer a chronological summary of Rossetti's achievement
as a poet-painter. The contributors view Rossetti as
an artist who sought correlatives for himself, i.e. icons
"energized by his dreams and experience." His interest
was in psychological states and in moments anticipating
or severing a union. These essays also constitute the
catalog for a Rossetti exhibit staged at the Yale University Art Gallery in the fall of 1976. The focus of
the exhibit was on artistic works which illustrated
literary works by Rossetti or others, hence the "double
work" described by the title.

1091. Bentley, D.M.R. "Light, Architecture, and Awe in
        Rossetti's Early Annunciations." *Ariel: a Review of
        International English Literature* 7 (1976): 22-30.

        Sees light, architecture, and awe as three elements
        which together form a *gestalt* of the Incarnation in
        Rossetti's early poems and paintings, especially *Ecce
        Ancilla Domini!*

1092. Amaya, Mario. "Dante Gabriel Rossetti and the Double
        Work of Art." *Art in America* 65 (1977): 90-93.

        Reviews the Yale exhibit (see item 1090), finding it
        stimulating, thought-provoking, and beautiful. As an
        artist Rossetti can be stiff or makeshift, but he is
        at his best when he illustrates poetry, perhaps because
        his achievement as a poet exceeds his achievement as
        a painter.

1093. Bentley, D.M.R. "Rossetti's 'Ave' and Related Pictures."
        Victorian Poetry 15 (1977): 21-35.

        Treats Rossetti's use of Marian themes in the early
        paintings and in the poem "Ave," which the author claims
        should be located within the Catholic tradition and
        which he sees as transcending all Victorian Marian poems
        except Hopkins'.

1094. Bentley, D.M.R. "Dante Gabriel Rossetti's Last Years:
        'Hope, with Eyes Upcast.'" *Mosaic* 12 (1978): 1-22.

        Contradicts the view that Rossetti's last years were
        characterized by unleavened despair. Basing his con-
        clusion on analyses of both poetry and painting, the
        author argues instead that Rossetti came to view life
        as a purgatorial experience linked to a non-doctrinal
        religious eschatology.

1095.   Landow, George P.   "'Life touching lips with immortal-
            ity': Rossetti's Typological Structures." *Studies in
            Romanticism* 17 (1978): 247-265.

        Argues that Rossetti used Christian typology in two
ways: first, in the orthodox way, where one event is
used to prefigure another and later event; second, in
a more Rossettian manner, where one event can connect
with eternity, i.e. time and eternity interpenetrate.
Sees typology as a major device for linking Rossetti's
painting and poetry.   Includes a detailed analysis of
Rossetti's triptych for Llandaff Cathedral.   [Note:
portions of this article are revised and developed in
Chapter 3, "Typological Symbolism in the Works of
Other Members of the Pre-Raphaelite Circle," of the
author's *William Holman Hunt and Typological Symbolism*
(1979).]

1096.   Lottes, Wolfgang.   "'Take Out the Picture and Frame the
            Sonnet': Rossetti's Sonnets and Verses for His Own
            Works of Art." *Anglia* 96 (1978): 108-135.

        Analyzes seventeen paired pictures and sonnets, and
concludes that the sonnets add to--in fact are necessary
for--our interpretations of the pictorial work.   Also,
the sonnets give to the paintings the fourth dimension
of time.

1097.   Waters, Gregory L.   "Blake and Rossetti." *English
            Record* 29 (1978): 23-27.

        Sees both men as concerned with the shaping power of
the imagination, but Blake was a more successful com-
municator.   Rossetti's fascination with Blake is summarized; but Rossetti misunderstood Blake's ideas
about love and womanhood, as a comparison of their
physical-symbolic paintings and poems will show.

1098.   Ireland, Kenneth R.   "A Kind of Pastoral: Rossetti's
            Versions of Giorgione." *Victorian Poetry* 17 (1979):
            303-315.

        Compares two versions of the poem "A Venetian Pas-
toral," showing how the later version gives evidence
of a greater maturity in accent and organization.
Rossetti's response to Giorgione prefigures his own
use, both in poems and in paintings, of dreamlike
spells, of sensuousness, and of enshrined moments.

1099. Sussman, Herbert L. *Fact into Figure: Typology in
       Carlyle, Ruskin, and the Pre-Raphaelite Brotherhood*.
       Columbus: Ohio State University Press, 1979. 158 pp.

       Explains the artistic beliefs and stylistic practices
       of the P.R.B. and reconstructs their literary paradigm
       for art. They were attempting to revive a sacramental
       view of nature and hence produced a "symbolic realism"
       in which the outer world was both fact and sign. There
       are references to Rossetti throughout, fourteen il-
       lustrations from his works, and extended treatments of
       Ecce Ancilla Domini!, *The Blessed Damozel*, *Beata
       Beatrix*, and *The Salutation of Beatrice* among his
       paintings and "My Sister's Sleep" and "The Blessed
       Damozel" among the poems. Rossetti's revisions are
       seen as the removal of the religious and/or transcen-
       dental contexts for eroticism and as the replacement
       of historicism by symbolism.

See also items 5, 61, 594, 602, 684, and 734.

Dissertations

This section includes doctoral dissertations about or related to Rossetti. Wherever possible the author and title are followed by the citation from *Dissertation Abstracts* (later *Dissertation Abstracts International*), abbreviated here as *DA*. For the earlier years, where such a citation is impossible, the title is followed by the degree-granting institution. Some dissertations were published separately and are therefore listed in other sections as well.

1100. Watkin, Ralph G. "Robert Browning and the English Pre-Raphaelites." Breslau, 1905.

1101. Horn, Kurt. "Zur Entstehungsgeschichte von Dante Gabriel Rossettis Dichtung." Königsberg, 1909.

1102. Bassalik-de Vries, Johanna C.E. "William Blake in His Relation to Dante Gabriel Rossetti." Zurich, 1910.

1103. Ulmer, Hermann. "Dante Gabriel Rossettis Versetechnik." Munich, 1911.

1104. Kitchen, Paul C. "The Influence of Dante on Rossetti." University of Pennsylvania, 1913.

1105. Schoepe, Max. "Der Vergleich bei Dante Gabriel Rossetti." Kiel, 1913.

1106. Villard, Léonie. "The Influence of Keats on Tennyson and Rossetti." Paris, 1914.

1107. Urech-Daysh, C. "Dante Gabriel Rossetti." Lausanne, 1915.

1108. Pundt, Herbert. "Dante Gabriel Rossettis Einfluss auf die Gedichte des jungen William Morris." Breslau, 1922.

1109. Zakrzewska, Maja. "Untersuchungen zur Konstruktion und Komposition von Dante Gabriel Rossettis *The House of Life*." Freiburg, 1922.

1110. Broers, Bernarda C. "Mysticism in the Neo-Romantics." Amsterdam, 1923.

1111. Geisler, Friedrich. "Dante Gabriel Rossetti: das Roman-

tische in Persönlichkeit und Dichtung." Marburg,
1923.

1112. MacIntyre, Carlyle F. "Der Gebrauch der Farbe in Ros-
       settis Dichtung." Marburg, 1923.

1113. Block, Lotte. "Dante Gabriel Rossetti, der Malerdichter.
       Giessen, 1925.

1114. Schäfer, Josy. "Rossettis Ansichten über Kunst und
       Künstler." Erlangen, 1925.

1115. Tietz, Eva. "Das Malerische in Rossettis Dichtung."
       Königsberg, 1925.

1116. Zenker, Augustin. "Dante Gabriel Rossetti: sein Stil
       im weitesten Sinne." Vienna, 1925.

1117. Ghose, S.N. "Dante Gabriel Rossetti and Contemporary
       Criticism (1849-1882)." Strasbourg, 1929.

1118. Axmann, M. "Die Präraffaelitische Dichtung im Urteile
       Ihrer Zeit." Breslau, 1930.

1119. Bachschmidt, Friedrich W. "Das Italienische Element
       in Dante Gabriel Rossetti." Münster, 1930.

1120. Farmer, Albert J. "Le Mouvement esthétique et 'decadent'
       en Angleterre 1873-1900." Paris, 1931.

1121. Gregory, John B. "A Bibliographical and Reference
       Guide to the Life and Works of Dante Gabriel Ros-
       setti with a Study of the Pre-Raphaelite Movement."
       London, 1931.

1122. Klenk, Hans. "Nachwirkungen Dante Gabriel Rossettis:
       Untersuchungen an Werken von Christina Rossetti,
       Coventry Patmore, Philip Bourke Marston, Theodore
       Watts-Dunton, Arthur E.W. O'Shaughnessy, Ernest
       Dowson, John Davidson." Erlangen, 1932.

1123. Klinnert, Adelheid. "Dante Gabriel Rossetti und Stefan
       George." Bonn, 1933.

1124. Nothwang, Irene. "Die Frau, die Liebe, und der Tod
       bei Dante Gabriel Rossetti." Tübingen, 1933.

1125. Seiler, Magdalene. "Dante Gabriel Rossettis künstlerisch
       Entwicklung." Greifswald, 1936.

1126. Sanford, John A. "Dante: Rossetti: Pre-Raphaelitism: A Study in the Early Poetry of Dante Gabriel Rossetti." Cornell, 1937.

1127. Culler, Helen S. "Studies in Rossetti's Reading." Yale, 1944. See also *DA* 27 (1967): 4244A-4245A.

1128. Cooper, Robert M. "Dante Gabriel Rossetti: Lost on Both Sides." *DA* 15 (1947): 415.

1129. Kühnelt, Harro. "Edgar Allan Poe und Dante Gabriel Rossetti." Innsbruck, 1948.

1130. Lang, Cecil Y. "Studies in Pre-Raphaelitism." Harvard, 1949.

1131. Boyd, Evelyn M. "Dante Gabriel Rossetti's *The House of Life*: A Study of Its Italian Background." *DA* 14 (1954): 1217-1218.

1132. Flemming, Hans T. "Die stilistische Entwicklung der Malerei von Dante Gabriel Rossetti." Berlin Freie Universität, 1954.

1133. Wahl, John R. "Two Pre-Raphaelite Poets: Studies in the Poetry and Poetic Theory of William Morris and D.G. Rossetti." Oxford, 1954.

1134. Fredeman, William E. "The Pre-Raphaelites and Their Critics: A Tentative Approach toward the Aesthetic of Pre-Raphaelitism." *DA* 16 (1956): 1441.

1135. Ryals, Clyde de L. "Decadence in British Literature before the *Fin de Siècle*." *DA* 17 (1957): 3004.

1136. Cervo, N.A. "The Pre-Raphaelites: A Perspective." Toronto, 1958.

1137. Holberg, Stanley M. "Image and Symbol in the Poetry and Prose of Dante Gabriel Rossetti." *DA* 20 (1958): 1016.

1138. Henderson, Stephen E. "A Study of Visualized Detail in the Poetry of Tennyson, Rossetti, and Morris." *DA* 20 (1959): 1015.

1139. Johnston, Robert D. "Imagery in Rossetti's *House of Life*." *DA* 20 (1960): 2783-2784.

1140. Savarit, Jacques. "Tendances mystiques et ésotériques
       chez Dante-Gabriel Rossetti." Geneva, 1960.

1141. Peterson, Carl A. "The Poetry and Painting of Dante
       Gabriel Rossetti." *DA* 21 (1961): 3460.

1142. Keane, Robert N. "The Pre-Raphaelite Brotherhood: 1848-
       1853." *DA* 26 (1965): 2726-2727.

1143. Laurent, Martha L. "Tennyson and the Poetry of *The
       Germ*: A Study of the Early Pre-Raphaelite Poets'
       Relation to Tennyson." *DA* 26 (1965): 2186.

1144. Sonstroem, David A. "Four Fair Ladies of Heaven and
       Hell: The Fantasy and Morality of Dante Gabriel Ros-
       setti." *DA* 26 (1965): 154.

1145. Parry, Graham. "The Purpose and Tendency of Early
       Pre-Raphaelite Art, 1848-1857." *DA* 27 (1966): 1417A.

1146. Staley, Allen. "Pre-Raphaelite Landscape and Outdoor
       Painting." *DA* 27 (1966): 425A-426A.

1147. Juhnke, Anna K. "Dante Gabriel and Christina Rossetti:
       The Poetry of Love, Death, and Faith." *DA* 27 (1967):
       4222A.

1148. Pittman, Philip M. "Mythologos: A Study in the Poetic
       Technique of Dante Gabriel Rossetti." *DA* 28 (1967):
       4140A.

1149. Gordon, Kathryn I. "Dante Gabriel Rossetti's *House of
       Life*: A Critical Edition." *DA* 29 (1968): 2262A.

1150. Hobbs, John N. "The Poetry of Dante Gabriel Rossetti."
       DA 29 (1968): 602A.

1151. Howard, Ronnalie J.R. "The Poetic Development of
       Dante Gabriel Rossetti, 1847-1872." *DA* 29 (1968):
       3613A.

1152. Hosmon, R.S. "Adventure in Bohemia: A Study of the
       Little Magazines of the Aesthetic Movement." *DA*
       30 (1969): 3907A.

1153. Spector, Stephen J. "The Centripetal Journey: The
       Poetry of Dante Gabriel Rossetti." *DA* 31 (1969):
       1241A.

1154. Stein, Richard L. "Art and Literature: Studies in
       John Ruskin, Dante Gabriel Rossetti, and Walter
       Pater." *DA* 31 (1970): 6634A.

1155. Christ, Carol T. "The Aesthetic of Particularity in
       the Poetry of Rossetti, Browning, and Hopkins." *DA*
       31 (1971): 6596A.

1156. Gervais, Claude. "The Victorian Love-Sonnet Sequence."
       DA 32 (1971): 964A-965A.

1157. Golden, Arline H. "Victorian Renascence: The Amatory
       Sonnet Sequence in the Late Nineteenth Century." *DA*
       32 (1971): 6605A-6606A.

1158. Harris, Ronald L. "Interior Action in Rossetti's *The
       House of Life*." *DA* 31 (1971): 5363A.

1159. Hayward, Ralph M. III. "Dante Gabriel Rossetti's *The
       Early Italian Poets*: A Study in the Art of Transla-
       tion." *DA* 32 (1971): 2643A.

1160. Lewis, Roger C. "The Poetic Integrity of D.G. Rossetti's
       Sonnet Sequence, *The House of Life*." *DA* 31 (1971):
       6016A.

1161. Boos, Florence S. "Dante Gabriel Rossetti: Sex, Prosody,
       and Literary Antecedents." *DA* 33 (1972): 2922A.

1162. Fox, Steven J. "Art and Personality: Browning, Ros-
       setti, Pater, Wilde, Yeats." *DA* 33 (1972): 751A.

1163. Hammond, Lewis K. "The Treatment of Sexuality in the
       Poetry of Dante Gabriel Rossetti." *DA* 32 (1972):
       6427A.

1164. Gitter, Elisabeth G. "Rossetti and *The Early Italian
       Poets*." *DA* 33 (1972): 2325A.

1165. Jessic, Frank S., Jr. "Brave Words in Eden: A Study
       of Tactile Values as a Basis for Spiritual Insight
       in the Poetry of Dante Gabriel Rossetti." *DA* 33
       (1972): 1684A.

1166. Klein, Dewayne R. "Dante Gabriel Rossetti and the
       Emblem." *DA* 33 (1972): 6875A.

1167. Christensen, Trilby B. "Theme and Image: The Structure

of D.G. Rossetti's *House of Life*." *DA* 33 (1973):
4403A-4404A.

1168. Stirling, Edwin M. "Browning and the Rossetti Circle:
The Rise and Fall of a Relationship." *DA* 33 (1973):
5693A-5694A.

1169. McNamara, Joseph S. "Shed Flowers and the Attenuated
Dream: The Quest for Order in the Paintings and
Poetry of D.G. Rossetti." *DA* 35 (1974): 2284A-2285A.

1170. Miller, John R. "Dante Gabriel Rossetti from the Gro-
tesque to the 'Fin de Siècle': Sources, Characteristics and Influences of the 'Femme Fatale.'" *DA*
35 (1974): 5355A.

1171. Mobley, Lawrence F. "Time in the Painting and Poetry
of Dante Gabriel Rossetti." *DA* 35 (1974): 3756A.

1172. Pistorius, Alan P. "D.G. Rossetti and Early Yeats."
DA 34 (1974): 6654A.

1173. Roetzel, Priscilla A. "Pre-Raphaelite Style in Painting and Poetry." *DA* 34 (1974): 5835A.

1174. Waters, Gregory L. "III. Blake and Rossetti." *DA*
35 (1974): 3775A-3776A.

1175. Bizzaro, Patrick A. "The Aesthetic of Beauty in Nineteenth Century England: Shelley, Rossetti, and Swinburne." *DA* 36 (1975): 2212A.

1176. Fallis, Jean T. "The Sacred and the Profane: Trans-
valuation of Religious Symbol in Hopkins, Rossetti,
and Swinburne." *DA* 36 (1975): 1524A.

1177. Leggio, Gail C. "Dante Gabriel Rossetti and the Cult
of Images." *DA* 36 (1976): 5321A-5322A.

1178. McMillan, Connie Beth. "A Catalogue of the Letters of
Dante Gabriel Rossetti at the University of Texas at
Austin." *DA* 36 (1976): 6657A.

1179. Pridgen, Rufus A. "Apocalyptic Imagery in Dante
Gabriel Rossetti's *The House of Life*." *DA* 36 (1976):
8079A.

1180. Coyle, Kathleen M. "'Madhouse Cells': The Love Poem

Sequences of Clough, Tennyson, Arnold, Meredith, and Rossetti." *DA* 36 (1976): 8071A-8072A.

1181. Darling, Susan. "Psychosexual Aspects of the Poetry of Dante Gabriel Rossetti." *DA* 37 (1976): 328A-329A.

1182. Delsey, Thomas J. "Dante Gabriel Rossetti's *The House of Life*: A Variorum Text and Critical Edition." *DA* 37 (1976): 1567A.

1183. Goff, Barbara M. "Artists and Models: Rossetti's Images of Women." *DA* 37 (1976): 330A-331A.

1184. Keenum, John M. "Browning and Rossetti: The Two Voices of Victorian Poetry." *DA* 37 (1976): 333A.

1185. Rodeiro, Joseph M. "A Comparative Study of English 'Pre-Raphaelitism' and Italian 'Pre-Raphaelitisms': Influence on the 'Modernismo' Art of Don Julio Romero de Torres and the Literature of Don Ramon del Valle Inclan in Their Use of the Feminine Mystique." *DA* 37 (1976): 7120A.

1186. Agosta, Lucien L. "Dante Gabriel Rossetti and the Commentators: The Evolution of a Tradition." *DA* 38 (1977): 2800A.

1187. Goldberg, Gail L. "Diverse Visions in the Work of Dante Gabriel Rossetti." *DA* 38 (1977): 4179A.

1188. Heidemann, August W. "The Literary Ballad in the Nineteenth Century: Ballads of Wordsworth, Coleridge, Keats, and Rossetti." *DA* 37 (1977): 6476A.

1189. Lyczko, Judith E. "Dante Gabriel Rossetti: Studies in the Dantesque and Arthurian Imagery of the Paintings and Drawings." *DA* 37 (1977): 6116A-6117A.

1190. Strickland, Edward P.M. "Metamorphoses of the Muse: A Study of Woman as Symbol of the Romantic Imagination." *DA* 37 (1977): 5818A.

1191. Greenberg, Mark L. "Dante Gabriel Rossetti and William Blake." *DA* 39 (1978): 6141A.

1192. Hardy, Julia A. "A Reputation Study of the Pre-Raphaelites, 1848-1860." *DA* 39 (1978): 1587A.

1193. Johnston, Arthur C. "Narcissism and D.G. Rossetti's
         The House of Life." *DA* 38 (1978): 6143A.

1194. Smith, Sarah H.P. "Dante Gabriel Rossetti's Flower
         Imagery and the Meaning of His Painting." *DA* 40
         (1979): 510A.

1195. White, Curtis. "Heretical Songs [short stories]." *DA*
         40 (1979): 2703A.

Index

This index includes all authors, all names mentioned in earlier titles or citations, and all places which have special significance for a study of Rossetti (e.g. Kelmscott). At the end of the regular index is a special topical index for the annotations of Rossetti's poetry and painting. It has not been necessary to index Rossetti's works because the two sections on individual works in the bibliography proper can serve this purpose. All references in the index are to item number rather than page number.

Dante Gabriel Rossetti--Topical Index for Annotations

POETRY